The Internet
FOR
DUMMIES®
13TH EDITION

The Internet For Dummies® 13th Edition

Published by
John Wiley & Sons, Inc.
111 River Street
Hoboken, NJ 07030-5774
www.wiley.com

Copyright © 2012 by John Wiley & Sons, Inc., Hoboken, New Jersey

Published by John Wiley & Sons, Inc., Indianapolis, Indiana

Published simultaneously in Canada

For general information on our other products and services, please contact our Customer Care Department within the U.S. at 877-762-2974, outside the U.S. at 317-572-3993, or fax 317-572-4002.

For technical support, please visit www.wiley.com/techsupport.

Wiley also publishes its books in a variety of electronic formats and by print-on-demand. Not all content that is available in standard print versions of this book may appear or be packaged in all book formats. If you have purchased a version of this book that did not include media that is referenced by or accompanies a standard print version, you may request this media by visiting http://booksupport.wiley.com. For more information about Wiley products, visit us www.wiley.com.

Library of Congress Control Number: 2011941733

ISBN: 978-1-118-09614-7 (pbk); ISBN: 978-1-118-16503-4 (ebk); ISBN: 978-1-118-16504-1 (ebk); ISBN: 978-1-118-16502-7 (ebk)

Manufactured in the United States of America

10 9 8 7 6 5 4 3 2 1

WILEY

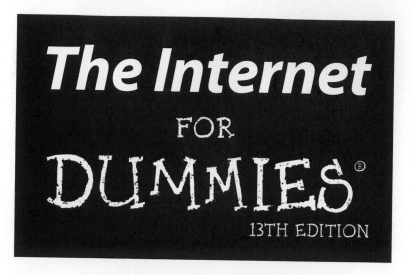

The Internet

FOR

DUMMIES®

13TH EDITION

**by John R. Levine
and Margaret Levine Young**

WILEY

John Wiley & Sons, Inc.

About the Authors

John R. Levine was a member of a computer club in high school — before high school students, or even high schools, had computers — where he met Theodor H. Nelson, the author of *Computer Lib/Dream Machines* and the inventor of hypertext, who reminded us that computers should not be taken seriously and that everyone can and should understand and use computers.

John wrote his first program in 1967 on an IBM 1130 (a computer somewhat less powerful than your typical modern digital wristwatch, only more difficult to use). He became an official system administrator of a networked computer at Yale in 1975. He began working part-time — for a computer company, of course — in 1977 and has been in and out of the computer and network biz ever since. He got his company on Usenet (the Internet's worldwide bulletin board system) early enough that it appears in a 1982 *Byte* magazine article on a map of Usenet, which then was so small that the map fit on half a page.

Although John used to spend most of his time writing software, now he mostly writes books (including *UNIX For Dummies* and technical books such as *Linkers and Loaders* and *qmail*) because it's more fun and he can do so at home in the tiny village of Trumansburg, New York, where in his spare time he was the mayor for several years and can hang around with his daughter when he's supposed to be writing. John also does a fair amount of public speaking. (Go to www.johnlevine.com to see where he'll be.) He holds a BA degree and a PhD in computer science from Yale University, but please don't hold that against him.

In high school, **Margaret Levine Young** was in the same computer club as her big brother, John. She stayed in the field throughout college against her better judgment and despite John's presence as a graduate student in the computer science department. Margy graduated from Yale and went on to become one of the first PC managers in the early 1980s at Columbia Pictures, where she rode the elevator with big stars whose names she wouldn't dream of dropping here.

Since then, Margy has co-authored more than 25 computer books about topics that include the Internet, UNIX, WordPerfect, Microsoft Access, and (stab from the past) PC-File and Javelin, including *The Internet For Dummies Quick Reference* and *UNIX For Dummies,* and *Windows Vista: The Complete Reference* and *Internet: The Complete Reference* (both from Osborne/McGraw-Hill). She met her future husband, Jordan, in the R.E.S.I.S.T.O.R.S. (the computer club we mentioned). Her other passion is her children, along with music, Unitarian Universalism, reading, knitting, gardening (you can never grow too much garlic), and anything to do with eating. She lives in Vermont (see www.gurus.org/margy for some scenery) and works as the Web Team Manager for the Unitarian Universalist Association (www.uua.org).

Please visit both authors online at net.gurus.org.

Dedication

John and Margy dedicate this book to their father, Bob Levine, who after 90 years is still working hard to make the world a better place.

Authors' Acknowledgments

We thank Shelby Meyerhoff, social networker extraordinaire, for writing the chapters about Facebook and Twitter.

Mark Enochs hustled us through the editorial process despite our attempts to drag it out while (no doubt at great personal cost) making us look like better writers than we are. Rebecca Whitney is the editor for whom we get down on our knees and beg when we begin an update to this book. Steve Hayes gets us organized, which is no easy task. Thanks also to the rest of the gang at John Wiley & Sons, especially those listed on the Publisher's Acknowledgments page.

John thanks Tonia, and Margy thanks Jordan, for holding everything together. We all thank Bill Gladstone at Waterside Productions for encouragement. The entire contents of this book were edited and submitted to the publisher by using the web — practicing what we preach. We thank our Internet providers: Finger Lakes Technologies Group (Trumansburg, New York — Hi, Paul!), Lightlink (Ithaca, New York — Hi, Homer!), and Shoreham. net (Shoreham, Vermont — Hi, Don and Jim!).

Finally, thanks to all the smarties (we wouldn't say wiseacres) who sent us comments about previous editions and helped make this one better. If you have ideas, comments, or complaints about this book, whisk them to us at internet13@gurus.org.

Visit our website at net.gurus.org for updates and more information about the topics in this book.

Publisher's Acknowledgments

We're proud of this book; please send us your comments at http://dummies.custhelp.com. For other comments, please contact our Customer Care Department within the U.S. at 877-762-2974, outside the U.S. at 317-572-3993, or fax 317-572-4002.

Some of the people who helped bring this book to market include the following:

Acquisitions and Editorial

Sr. Project Editor: Mark Enochs

Executive Editor: Steve Hayes

Copy Editor: Rebecca Whitney

Technical Editor: Lee Musick

Editorial Manager: Leah Cameron

Editorial Assistant: Amanda Graham

Sr. Editorial Assistant: Cherie Case

Cover Photo: © iStockphoto.com / Alex Slobodkin

Cartoons: Rich Tennant (www.the5thwave.com)

Composition Services

Project Coordinator: Sheree Montgomery

Layout and Graphics: Carrie A. Cesavice, Lavonne Roberts

Proofreaders: Laura Bowman, Jessica Kramer

Indexer: Potomac Indexing, LLC

Publishing and Editorial for Technology Dummies

Richard Swadley, Vice President and Executive Group Publisher

Andy Cummings, Vice President and Publisher

Mary Bednarek, Executive Acquisitions Director

Mary C. Corder, Editorial Director

Publishing for Consumer Dummies

Kathy Nebenhaus, Vice President and Executive Publisher

Composition Services

Debbie Stailey, Director of Composition Services

Contents at a Glance

Table of Contents

Introduction

Welcome to *The Internet For Dummies*, 13th Edition. The Internet has become so interwoven in today's life — work, school, politics, and play — that ignoring it is no longer an option. This book describes what you do to become an *Internaut* (someone who navigates the Internet with skill) — how to get started, what you need to know, and where to go for help. And, we describe it in plain old English.

When we first wrote *The Internet For Dummies* 18 years ago (yikes!), a typical Internet user was a student who connected from college or a technical worker who had access at the office. The World Wide Web was so new that it had only a few hundred pages. The Net has grown like crazy to include a billion (dare we say it?) normal people, connecting from computers at home or work, along with students ranging from elementary school to adult education. This lucky 13th edition focuses on the parts of the Net that are of the most interest to typical users — how to find things on the World Wide Web, download interesting things from the Net, send and receive electronic mail (e-mail), and shop, invest, chat, and play games online.

About This Book

We don't flatter ourselves to think you're interested enough in the Internet to sit down and read the entire book (although it should be a fine book for the bathroom). When you run into a problem using the Internet ("Hmm, I *thought* that I knew how to find old TV shows on the Net, but I don't seem to remember"), just dip into the book long enough to solve your problem.

Pertinent sections include

- Understanding what the Internet is
- Staying safe online
- Getting your computer (or phone or whatever) connected to the Internet
- Climbing around the World Wide Web
- Finding people, places, and things
- Communicating by e-mail
- Hanging out with friends using Facebook, instant messaging, and other methods

- ✔ Watching movies, listening to radio shows, shopping, and other fun online activities
- ✔ Putting your own stuff online with websites and social networks

How to Use This Book

To begin, please read the first two chapters. They give you an overview of the Internet and some important safety tips. If you have children or grandchildren, read Chapter 3, too. When you're ready to get yourself on the Internet, turn to Part II and read Chapter 4. Chapter 6 describes how to use the web — you aren't truly online until you can see a web page. Parts III through VI egg you on and provide extra support — they describe the web and e-mail and other stuff you can do on the Internet.

Because the Internet is ever-changing, we put additional information online, which we can update more often than this book can be republished. We authors have a website with updates and history and other interesting articles, at net.gurus.org.

When you have to follow a complicated procedure, we spell it out step by step wherever possible. When you have to type something, it appears in the book in **boldface.** Type it just as it appears. Use the same capitalization we do — a few systems care deeply about CAPITAL and lowercase (small) letters. Then press the Enter key. The book tells you what should happen when you give each command and what your options are.

When you have to choose commands from menus, we use the ⇨ symbol. For example, we write File⇨Exit when we want you to choose the File command from the menu bar and then choose the Exit command from the menu that appears.

Who Are You?

In writing this book, we made a few assumptions about you:

- ✔ You have or would like to have access to the Internet.
- ✔ You want to get some work done online. (We consider the term *work* to include the concept *play*.)
- ✔ You aren't interested in becoming the world's next great Internet expert, at least not this week.

How This Book Is Organized

This book has six parts, and the parts stand on their own. Although you can begin reading wherever you like, you should at least skim Parts I and II first to become acquainted with some unavoidable Internet jargon and find out how to get your computer on the Net.

Here are the parts of the book:

In Part I, "Welcome to the Internet," you find out what the Internet is and why it's interesting (at least why we think it's interesting). Also, this part gives you vital Internet terminology and explains concepts that help you as you read the later parts of the book. Part I discusses security and privacy issues and gives some thoughts about children's use of the Net.

For the nuts and bolts of getting on the Net, read Part II, "Internet, Here I Come!" For most users, by far the most difficult part of using the Net is getting to that first connection, with software loaded, configuration configured, and modem modeming or broadband banding broadly. After that, it's (relatively) smooth sailing. We also tell you how to use the World Wide Web, the Net's most popular application. You also get a briefing on avoiding and blocking online hazards, such as viruses and spam.

Part III, "Hanging Out with Friends Online," looks at the important Net communication services: sending and receiving e-mail, swapping instant messages, and chatting. You find out how to exchange e-mail with people down the hall or on other continents, how to make the most of Internet-based phone and video conferencing programs, how to use instant messaging programs to chat with your online pals, how to get going with Facebook and Twitter (the ultimate answers to free time), and how to use e-mail mailing lists to keep in touch with people of similar interests.

Part IV, "The Web Is Full of Cool Stuff," dives into the web in more detail. We discuss how to get around on the web, how to find stuff (which isn't as easy as it should be), and how to shop online. We also include chapters on listening to music, watching videos, shopping, and managing your finances on the Internet.

Part V, "Putting Your Own Stuff on the Net," talks about how to post all kinds of material on the Internet. Putting your writing, photos, and videos online is easier than ever because of the range of free web services you can use, including blogs, which let anyone be an online journalist.

Part VI, "The Part of Tens," is a compendium of ready references and useful facts (which, we suppose, suggests that the rest of the book is full of useless facts).

This book's Cheat Sheet, which summarizes how to use the most important web browsers and e-mail programs in the book, is online at `www.dummies.com/cheatsheet/internet`.

Icons Used in This Book

Lets you know that some particularly nerdy, technoid information is coming up so that you can skip it, if you want. (On the other hand, you may want to read it.)

Indicates that a nifty little shortcut or timesaver is explained.

Gaack! We found out about this information the hard way! Don't let it happen to you!

Indicates something to file away in your memory archives.

What Now?

That's all you need to know to get started. Whenever you hit a snag using the Internet, just look up the problem in the table of contents or index in this book. You'll either have the problem solved in a flash or know where you need to go to find expert help.

Because the Internet has been evolving for more than 30 years, largely under the influence of extremely nerdy people, it wasn't designed to be particularly easy for normal people to use. Don't feel bad if you have to look up a number of topics before you feel comfortable using the Internet. Until recently, most computer users never had to face anything as complex as the Internet.

Feedback, Please

We love to hear from our readers. If you want to contact us, please feel free to do so, in care of

Dummies Press

10475 Crosspoint Blvd.

Indianapolis, IN 46256

Better yet, send us Internet e-mail at `mailto:internet13@gurus.org` (our friendly robot usually answers immediately; the human authors read all the e-mail and answer as much as they can) or visit this book's web page at `net.gurus.org`. These e-mail addresses put you in contact with the authors of this book; to contact the publisher or authors of other *For Dummies* books, visit the publisher's website at `www.dummies.com` or send paper mail to the address just listed.

Part I

Welcome to the Internet

The 5th Wave

By Rich Tennant

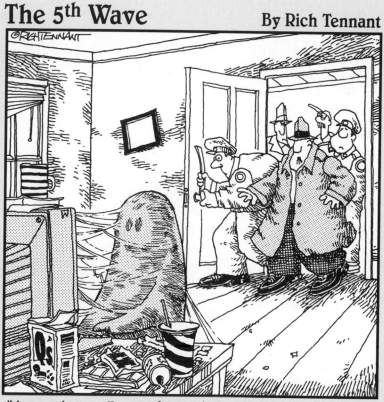

"Awww jeez — I was afraid of this. Some poor kid, bored with the usual chat lines, starts looking for bigger kicks. Pretty soon they're surfin' the seedy back alleys of cyberspace, and before you know it they're into a file they can't 'undo.' I guess that's why they call it the web. Somebody open a window!"

In this part . . .

The Internet is an amazing place. But because it's full of computers, everything is more complicated than it should be. We start with a look at what the Internet is and how it got that way. We tell you what's happening, what people are doing, and why you should care. We pay special attention to security problems, privacy issues, and family concerns — particularly the knotty issue of determining the best way for kids to work with the Internet.

Chapter 1

What's So Great about the Internet?

In This Chapter

▶ What, really, is the Internet?

▶ For that matter, what is a network?

▶ What is the Internet good for?

*I*t's huge, it's sprawling, it's globe spanning, and it has become part of our lives. It must be . . . the Internet. We all know something about it, and most of us have tried to use it, with more or less success. (If you've had less, you've come to the right place.) In this chapter, we look at what the Internet is and can do, before we dive into details in the rest of this book.

If you're new to the Internet, and especially if you don't have much computer experience, *be patient with yourself.* Many of the ideas here are completely new. Allow yourself some time to read and reread. The Internet is a different world with its own language, and it takes some getting used to.

Even experienced computer users can find using the Internet more complex than other tasks they've tackled. The Internet isn't a single software package and doesn't easily lend itself to the kind of step-by-step instructions we'd provide for a single, fixed program. This book is as step-by-step as we can make it, but the Internet resembles a living organism mutating at an astonishing rate more than it resembles Microsoft Word and Excel, which sit quietly on your computer. After you get set up and practice a little, using the Internet seems like second nature; in the beginning, however, it can be daunting.

So What Is the Internet?

The Internet — also known as the *Net* — is the world's largest computer network. "What is a network?" you may ask. Even if you already know, you may want to read the next couple of paragraphs to make sure that we're speaking the same language.

A computer *network* is a bunch of computers that communicate with each other, sort of like a radio or TV network connects a bunch of radio or TV stations so that they can share the latest episode of *American Idol*.

Don't take the analogy too far. In *broadcast* networking, TV networks send the same information to all stations at the same time; in computer networking, each particular message is routed to a particular computer, so different computers can display different things. Unlike TV networks, computer networks are two-way: When computer A sends a message to computer B, B can send a reply back to A.

Some computer networks consist of a central computer and a bunch of remote stations that report to it (for example, a central airline-reservation computer with thousands of screens and keyboards in airports and travel agencies). Other networks, including the Internet, are more egalitarian and permit any computer on the network to communicate with any other computer. Many wireless devices — the cellphone, Palm handheld, BlackBerry, iPhone, and their ilk — expand the reach of the Internet right into our pockets. (Hands off our wallets!)

The Internet isn't simply one network — it's a network of networks, all freely exchanging information. The networks range from the big, corporate networks to tiny ones (such as the one John built in his back bedroom, made from a couple of old PCs he bought at an electronics parts store) and everything in between. College and university networks have long been part of the Internet, and now high schools and elementary schools are joining in. Lately, the Internet has become so popular that many households have more than one computer and are creating their own little networks that they connect to the Internet.

What's All the Hoopla?

Everywhere you turn, you can find traces of the Internet. Household products, business cards, radio shows, and movie credits list their website addresses (usually starting with *www* and ending with "dot com") and their e-mail addresses. New people you meet would rather give you an e-mail address than a phone number. Everyone seems to be "going online" and "googling it."

The Internet affects our lives on a scale as significant as the telephone and television. When it comes to spreading information, the Internet is the most significant invention since the printing press. If you use a telephone, write letters, read a newspaper or magazine, or do business or any kind of research, the Internet can radically alter your worldview.

On networks, size counts a great deal: The larger a network is, the more stuff it has to offer. Because the Internet is the world's largest interconnected group of computer networks, it has an amazing array of information to offer.

When people talk about the Internet, they usually talk about what they can do, what they have found, and whom they have met. The number of available services is too huge to list in this chapter, but here are the Big Three:

- ✔ **Electronic mail (e-mail):** This service is certainly the most widely used — you can exchange e-mail with millions of people all over the world. People use e-mail for anything for which they might use paper (mail, faxes, special delivery of documents) or the telephone (gossip, recipes, love letters) to communicate — you name it. We hear that some people even use it for stuff related to work. Electronic *mailing lists* enable you to join group discussions with people who have similar interests and to meet people over the Net. Part IV of this book has all the details.

- ✔ **The World Wide Web:** When people talk these days about surfing the Net, they often mean checking out sites on this (buzzword alert) global multimedia hyperlinked database. In fact, people are talking more about the web and less about the Net. Are they the same thing? Technically, the answer is "No." But practically speaking, the answer for many people is "Pretty close." We tell you the truth, the whole truth, and nothing but the truth in Part III of this book.

  Websites can provide you with information ranging from travel information to how to raise chickens. You can also look at videos, listen to music, buy stuff, sell stuff, and play video games.

  The software used to navigate the web is a *browser*. The most popular browsers now are Firefox, Google Chrome, and Internet Explorer. We tell you all about them in Chapter 6.

- ✔ **Instant messaging (IM'ing):** Programs such as Windows Live Messenger, Yahoo! Messenger, and AOL Instant Messenger let you send messages that "pop up" on the recipient's screen. We hear tales of nimble-fingered youth carrying on upward of 13 IM sessions simultaneously. Some websites also provide messaging services. We tell you about IM programs in Chapter 12.

The Internet is unlike any other communications media we've ever encountered. People of all ages, colors, creeds, and countries freely share ideas, stories, data, opinions, and products.

Does the Internet truly reach every continent?

Some skeptical readers, after reading the claim that the Internet spans every continent, may point out that Antarctica is a continent, even though its population consists largely of penguins, who (as far as we know) aren't interested in computer networks. Does the Internet go there? It does. A few machines at the Scott Base on McMurdo Sound in Antarctica are on the Internet, connected by radio link to New Zealand. The base at the South Pole has a link to the United States. See the polar webcam at www.usap.gov.

At the time we wrote this book, the largest Internet-free land mass in the world was probably an uninhabited island in the Canadian arctic — Devon Island, perhaps. (You can look it up on the Internet.) Even there, a satellite connection can provide an Internet connection, so perhaps nowhere on the surface of the earth is truly Internet-free.

Anybody can access it

One great thing about the Internet is that it's the most open network in the world. Thousands of computers provide facilities that are available to anyone who has Internet access. Although pay services exist (and more are added every day), most Internet services are free for the taking after you're online. If you don't already have access to the Internet by way of your company, your school, your library, or a friend, you can pay for access by using an Internet service provider (ISP). We talk about some ISPs in Chapter 4.

One significant change in Net use in the past few years has been the move to ever smaller, lighter, and cheaper equipment to connect to it. A *netbook* is a small, inexpensive computer, about the size and weight of this book, that's intended mainly for connecting to the Net. If a netbook is too big for you, a smartphone such as the Apple iPhone or one using Google Android puts a computer, and the Internet, in your pocket with an always-on connection.

It's politically, socially, and religiously correct

Another great thing about the Internet is that it is what one may call "socially unstratified." That is, one computer is no better than any other, and no person is any better than any other. Who you are on the Internet depends solely on how you present yourself when you're using your computer. If what you say makes you sound like an intelligent, interesting person, that's who you are. It doesn't matter how old you are or what you look like or whether you're a student, business executive, or construction worker. Physical disabilities don't matter — we correspond with deaf and blind people. If they hadn't felt like telling us, we never would have known. People become famous (and infamous) in the Internet community as a result of their own efforts.

The Net advantage

The Internet has become totally mainstream, and you're falling further behind the curve — and at a faster rate — if you haven't yet gotten started. Increasingly, news gets out on the Internet before it's available any other way, and the cyberdeprived are losing ground.

Cloudy with a chance of servers

Computers these days are very, very fast — so fast that they have far more processor power than they can use. (Your computer is drawing shimmery, semitranslucent, animated borders around the windows on your screen because it has nothing better to do between keystrokes.) Computer servers turn out to have the same problem — it takes a large website to keep a server busy, and servers are often idle for most of the day.

It also turns out that it's much more efficient to run many computer servers in one place, where they can share mounting racks, power, air conditioning, and fast network connections, so for many years the standard way to run a web server has been to rent space for it in a data center. But those servers are still idle most of the time. The advanced, cutting-edge *virtualization* technology allows one superfast server to operate as though it were many independent, reasonably fast, *virtual* servers and, more importantly, to start and stop virtual servers as needed. So now, someone who before would have owned or rented a few physical computers can now ask a data center to start up virtual servers when they're needed and stop them when they aren't. Because different virtual servers are busy at different times, this situation tends to even out the load, particularly when a company is big enough to have data centers in several parts of the world; people in Europe are using their virtual servers while Californians are asleep, and vice versa. A name such as *demand-allocated, geographically distributed virtual servers* isn't snappy enough, so they call it *cloud computing* instead.

From a user's point of view, no difference exists between a website run in cloud and one run any other way, but cloud computing enables website operators to run a substantial web operation and not have to buy server equipment or even know the exact locations of the servers they're using. Cloud providers tend to be big companies that already have big data centers — notably, Amazon and Microsoft. (John uses the Amazon cloud service and believes that his data is probably somewhere near Seattle. The website Margy manages, www.uua.org, lives in a cloud over Virginia.)

Fun historical fact: Virtualization was invented by IBM researchers in 1967, and mainframe computers have used it for four decades, so maybe it's not all that cutting-edge. But don't tell cloud enthusiasts or else you'll hurt their feelings.

Here are some of the ways people use the Internet:

- **Find information:** Many websites have information free for the taking. It ranges from IRS tax forms that you can print and use to help-wanted ads, real estate listings, and recipes. From U.S. Supreme Court decisions and library card catalogs to the text of old books, digitized pictures (many suitable for family audiences), and an enormous variety of software — from games to operating systems — you can find virtually anything on the Net. You can check the weather forecast, view movie listings, find your childhood sweetheart, browse catalogs, and see school closings for anywhere in the world, from anywhere in the world.

  Special tools known as *search engines* and *directories* help you find information (and people) on the web. See Chapter 13 to find out how to search for the information you need.

- **Stay in touch:** *Weblogs* (or *blogs*) let people and organizations distribute current information about themselves rapidly and easily. *Microblogs,* such as Twitter, combine the Net with mobile phone text messages to let people stay up to date anywhere, at any time.

- **Get an education:** Schoolteachers coordinate projects with classrooms all over the globe. College students and their families exchange e-mail to facilitate letter-writing and keep down the cost of phone calls. Students do research from their home computers. The latest encyclopedias are online.

- **Buy and sell stuff:** On the Internet, you can buy anything from books about beermaking to stock in microbreweries. And you can make some cash by cleaning out your closets and selling your old junk on eBay. Software companies sell software and provide updates on the Net. Most software distribution is migrating to the Internet, where a customer can download and install programs without waiting for a CD to arrive. We talk about the relevant issues in Chapter 15.

- **Travel:** Cities, towns, states, and countries are using the web to put up (or *post*) tourist and event information. Travelers find weather information, maps, and museum hours as well as plane, train, and bus schedules and tickets. While you're at it, you can buy your airplane tickets, rent a car, and make hotel reservations.

- **Use intranets:** Businesses have figured out that this Internet concept is truly useful, and they create their own, private networks — like mini-Internets. On these *intranets,* companies use web pages for posting company information such as benefits, filing expense reports and time sheets, and ordering supplies. An intranet helps an organization provide information that employees can see from inside the company that folks on the outside can't see, including manuals, forms, videos of boring meetings, and, of course, endless memos. In some organizations, e-mail and intranets reduce the amount of paper wasted on this stuff.

- **Play games:** Internet-based multiuser games can easily absorb all your waking hours and an alarming number of what would otherwise be your sleeping hours. You can challenge other players who can be anywhere in the world. Many kinds of games are available on the web, including such traditionally addictive games as bridge, hearts, chess, checkers, and go. In Chapter 20, we tell you where to find these games.

✔ **Find love:** People are finding romance on the Net. Singles ads and matchmaking sites vie for users. The Internet long ago grew beyond the original bunch of socially challenged, 22-year-old, nerdy guys and now has turned into the world's biggest matchmaker, for people of all ages, genders, preferences, and life situations.

✔ **Heal:** Patients and doctors keep up to date with the latest medical findings, share treatment experience, and support one another around medical problems. We even know of some practitioners who exchange e-mail directly with their patients.

✔ **Invest:** People research financial information, buy stock, and invest money online, as we tell you about in Chapter 16. Some online companies trade their own shares. Investors are finding new ventures, and new ventures are finding capital.

✔ **Participate in nonprofits:** Churches, synagogues, mosques, schools, clubs, teen centers, and other community organizations post pages telling web users about themselves and inviting new people. The online church newsletter *always* arrives before Sunday.

Where did the Internet come from?

The ancestor of the Internet is the *ARPANET,* a project funded by the Department of Defense (DoD) in 1969, as an experiment in reliable networking and to link DoD and military research contractors, including many universities doing military-funded research. (ARPA stands for Advanced Research Projects Administration, the branch of the DoD in charge of handing out grant money. For enhanced confusion, the agency is now known as *DARPA* — the added *D* is for *Defense,* in case anyone wondered where the money came from.) Although the ARPANET started small — connecting three computers in California with one in Utah — it quickly grew to span the continent and, via radio link, Europe.

In the early 1980s, the ARPANET grew into the early Internet, a group of interlinked networks connecting many educational and research sites funded by the National Science Foundation (NSF), along with the original military sites. By 1990, it was clear that the Internet was here to stay, and DARPA and the NSF bowed out in favor of the commercially run networks that make up today's Internet. (And, yes, although Al Gore didn't invent the Internet, he was instrumental in keeping it funded so that it could turn into the Internet we know now.) Familiar companies such as AT&T, Comcast, Sprint, and Verizon run some networks; others belong to specialty companies, such as Level3 and Cogent. No matter which one you're attached to, they all interconnect, so it's all one giant Internet. For more information, read our web page at http://net.gurus.org/history.

Okay, What Next?

If you're ready to jump on the Internet, first read Chapter 2 for some safety tips. If you have children (or grandchildren), read Chapter 3 about what kids should (and shouldn't) do online.

Done? Chapter 4 tells you how to get connected!

Turn off the computer now and then

We can tell you from experience that when you're on the Net, the hands on the clock slow down and stop and you can spend more time online than you can imagine. For some people, it's impossible to go ten minutes without checking e-mail, dirty dishes are ignored while visiting "just one more" web page, and they reach the point of possibly having an Internet addiction. Remember that the Net is a fine adjunct to real life — not a substitute.

As our friend and longtime Net user Jean Polly regularly says: The Internet is closing! Go outside and play!

Chapter 2

Is the Internet Safe? Viruses, Spyware, Spam, and Other Yucky Stuff

....

....

*W*e like the Internet. It has been part of our lives — and livelihoods — for years. We'd love to tell you that all the stuff you may have read about the dangers of connecting a computer to the Internet is hype. We can't. The success of the Internet has attracted unsavory people who view you as a money tree ready to be plucked. (Nothing personal — they see everybody that way.) In a few countries, perpetrating Internet fraud is now a major part of the national economy.

Even if no one steals your money, people can collect information about your online activities, which results in a real loss of privacy. And, some people are trying to take over your computer so that they can use it for nefarious purposes. When a new computer is hooked up to the Internet, it isn't a question of *whether* it will come under cyberattack, but *when*. And not in months or days — but in hours or minutes.

When you combine the Internet with cellphones and global positioning systems (GPSs), privacy issues become even scarier. Cellphone providers can tell where you are whenever you have your phone with you. Phones or other online devices with a GPS can help you find your way around, but they can also report on your whereabouts.

Now that we've given you the bad news, relax: The Internet doesn't have to be a dangerous place. Using the Internet is like walking around a big city — yes, you need to be careful, use some protection, and stay out of dangerous areas, but you can also safely take advantage of the wonders that the Net has to offer.

This chapter describes the types of issues that abound on the Internet:

- **Privacy issues** involve how much people can find out about you over the Internet.
- **Security issues** have to do with keeping control over which programs are running on your computer.
- Just plain **annoyance issues** include ending up with a mailbox full of *spam* (junk e-mail) or web browser windows popping up with advertisements.

Throughout the rest of this book, we include instructions for staying safe by using a firewall, a virus checker, a spyware scanner, and some common sense. Chapter 3 talks about rules for letting kids use the Internet, and most of the suggestions make sense for grown-ups, too.

Privacy: Who's Who and What They Can Tell about You

Advances in technology are eroding the privacy that most of us take for granted. Technology we use every day — credit cards, cellphones, electronic key cards, and automobile toll transponders — allow our every purchase and movement to be tracked. The Internet is an extension of this trend. Many of your online activities can be watched and recorded — sometimes for innocent reasons and sometimes not.

All this is further compounded by the amount of publicly available information that is now conveniently available to a far greater public over the Internet. When paper records were maintained by government officials and people had to visit the office and dig through files for the specific information they wanted, a lot less information abuse was possible. Now the potential exists for anyone anywhere to access information about people hitherto unknown, and to gather information from various sources, including online directories. No longer is a geographical or time deterrent enough.

Some people worry that snoops on the Net will intercept their private e-mail or web pages. That's quite unlikely, actually, other than the specific case of public Wi-Fi networks; see the sidebar "The perils of free Wi-Fi," later in this chapter. The more serious problem is that advertisers build profiles of the sites you visit and the stuff you buy. Most web ads are provided by a handful of companies, such as Google's DoubleClick, AOL's Advertising.com, and Microsoft's Razorfish, which can use their ads to determine that the same person (you) is visiting a lot of different websites. Using this information, these companies can create a profile. They say they don't create these personal profiles, but they don't say they won't in the future.

Several techniques for gathering information about you as you use the Internet, or tricking you into providing information, are described in the next few sections.

Who is the party to whom I am speaking?

Although the Internet seems completely anonymous, it isn't. People used to have Internet usernames that bore some resemblance to their true identities — their names or initials or some such combination in conjunction with their university or corporation names gave fairly traceable routes to real people. Creating a new e-mail address now takes just a few minutes, so revealing your identity is definitely optional.

Depending on who you are and what you want to do on the Net, you may, in fact, want different names and different accounts. Here are some legitimate reasons for wanting them:

- ✔ You're a professional — a physician, for example — and you want to participate in a mailing list or newsgroup without being asked for your professional opinion.

- ✔ You want help with an area of concern that you feel is private and you don't want your problem known to people close to you who may find out if your name is associated with it.

- ✔ You do business on the Internet, and you socialize on the Net. You may want to keep these activities separate.

Most Net activities can be traced. If you start to abuse the anonymous nature of the Net, you'll find that you aren't so anonymous after all.

Safety first

The anonymous, faceless nature of the Internet has its downside, too. To protect you and your family, take these simple precautions:

- ✔ Before posting information on a social networking site like Facebook or Google Plus, carefully review your privacy settings. See Chapter 10 for details. These sites give the impression that the information you provide will be visible only to your close, personal friends, but it ain't necessarily so.

- ✔ When posting information that appears on a public website (other than your own, or your social networking sites) or in any discussion venue, don't use your full name. This advice doesn't apply if you're working in a business context, such as posting information on your company's website.

- ✔ Never provide your name, address, or phone number to someone you don't know.

- ✔ Never believe anyone who says that he's from "Facebook tech support," "eBay fraud prevention," "PayPal administration," or a similar-sounding authority and asks you for your password. No legitimate entity will ever ask you for your password.

- ✔ Be especially careful about disclosing information about kids. Don't fill out profiles that ask for a kid's name, hometown, school, age, address, or phone number, because they're invariably used for "targeted marketing" (also known as junk mail).

Although relatively rare, horrible things have happened to a few people who have taken their Internet encounters into real life. Many wonderful things have happened, too. We've met some of our best friends over the Net, and some people have met and subsequently married. We just want to encourage you to use common sense whenever you set up a meeting with a Net friend. A person you e-mail or swap instant messages with is still largely a stranger, and if you want to meet in person, take the same precautions you would take on a first date with someone you don't know: Meet in a public place, perhaps with a friend along, and be sure that your family knows where you are and when you're planning to be back.

The Net is a wonderful place, and meeting new people and making new friends is one of the big attractions. We just want to make sure that you're as careful as you would be in the rest of your life.

Phishing for inphormation

Phishing is the fastest-growing Internet crime, and you're the target. The good news is that protecting yourself is easy when you and your family know how to spot the phish-hook.

Learn what phishing looks like. After you start using the Internet and receiving e-mail (as described in Chapter 8), there's an excellent chance that you'll receive a message like this one:

```
Subject: Ebay Important Warning

From: eBay Billing Department! <Service@eBay.com>

eBay Fraud Mediation Request

You have recieved this email because you or someone
had used your account to make fake bids at eBay.


THE FRAUD ALERT ID CODE CONTAINED IN THIS MESSAGE
WILL BE ATTACHED IN OUR FRAUD MEDIATION REQUEST FORM,
IN ORDER TO VERIFY YOUR EBAY ACCOUNT REGISTRATION
INFORMATIONS.

Fraud Alert ID CODE: 00937614

Please access the following form to complete the
verification of your eBay account registration
informations:

http://www.eBay.com/cgi bin/secure/Fraud Alert ID CODE:
     00937614

If we do not receive the appropriate verification within
48 hours, then we will assume this eBay account is
fraudulent and will be suspended.

Regards, Safeharbor Department (Trust and Safety
Department), eBay Inc.
```

Sounds authentic and scary, doesn't it? Think you had better deal with this message right away? Better think again. You are the phish, and this message is the bait. The underlined text in the middle is the hook. Click it and soon an official-looking page appears that looks just like an eBay sign-in page. After you enter your username and password, another official-looking page asks for your credit card number, PIN, billing address, checking account details (complete with a helpful graphic so that you can find the right numbers on your personal checks), Social Security number, date of birth, mother's maiden name, and driver's license number. The page is smart enough to reject an invalid credit card number. If you fill in all the information and press Continue, you see a valid eBay page that says you've logged out. Then, who knows? The bad guys know enough about you to do anything from making a small purchase paid for by your credit card to full-scale identity theft that can take months or years to straighten out.

This message *did not* come from eBay. Millions of these types of messages are sent over the Internet every day.

Certain clues might alert you. The misspelled words *recieved* and *informations* suggest that the author is someone whose English skills are limited. And, if you take the trouble to save the e-mail to a file and then print it, the underlined link in the middle of the message looks like this:

```
<http://192.168.45.67/cgi_bin>http://www.eBay.com/cgi_bin/
              secure/Fraud Alert ID CODE: 00937614
```

The text between the angle brackets (< and >) is where the link goes in reality, to a website with a numeric address. (When we tried clicking the link two days after we got the mail, the website had already been shut down. Those eBay security folks are on the ball.)

Don't take the bait

Phishers have gotten a lot more skillful since the earliest phishes a decade ago, and now often have good editors and use a spell checker, so you can't rely on spelling and grammar mistakes, although they're dead giveaways when you spot them. Here are a few additional tips:

- ✔ Assume that every e-mail that leads you to a page seeking passwords or credit card numbers or other personal information is a phishing expedition.

- ✔ If the e-mail purports to be from a company you've never heard of, ignore it.

- ✔ If the message says that it's from a company with whom you have an account, go to the company's website by typing the company's URL into your browser (see Chapter 7), *not* by clicking a link in the e-mail. When you get to the company's website, look for the My Account link. If there's a problem, when you log in, you should see a notice. If there's no way to log in and you're still concerned, forward a copy of the e-mail to the customer service department or pick up the phone and call the number on your card or monthly statement.

One trick phishers use to fool Internet users is *website spoofing* — tricking your browser into displaying one address when you're actually at another site. Some browsers allow a website to show only its main address so that it doesn't look so geeky. Phishers take advantage of this ability. Better web browsers offer protection against website spoofing — they always show the actual web address of the page you're on.

To summarize, make sure that your family knows this rule well: Never, *never*, **never** enter passwords, credit card numbers, or other personal information at a web page you opened by clicking a link in an e-mail.

Web bugs track the ads you read

Ever since the World Wide Web became a household word (okay, three words), companies have increasingly viewed their Internet presence as a vital way to advertise their goods and services and conduct their business. They spend millions of dollars on their websites and advertising e-mail (the legitimate kind you actually asked for) — and want very much to know just how people use them. It's a small wonder that when you visit a site, companies can keep track of your actions as you move from link to link within the site. But they *really* want to know what you were doing before you entered their sites — and even more they want to know whether you read their mail. To gather this intelligence, they insert tiny images in mail messages that they call *web beacons* — everyone else calls them *web bugs* — that report your actions back to the mailer.

Most mail programs offer the option not to fetch images in mail messages from unknown or untrusted senders, which stops web bugs and also makes your mail reading faster.

Cookies can be good

When you browse the web (as described in Chapter 6), the web server needs to know who you are if you want to do things that require logging in, collecting items in a virtual shopping cart, or completing any other process that requires that the website remember information about you as you move from page to page. The most commonly used trick that allows websites to track what you're doing is setting cookies. A *cookie* is a tiny file, stored on your computer, that contains the address of the website and codes that your browser sends back to the website every time you visit a page there. Cookies don't usually contain personal or dangerous information; they're mostly innocuous and — believe it or not — useful.

Do not track, or maybe do

With the increasing awareness of online privacy issues have come proposals for do-not-track laws, analogous to telephone do-not-call laws. The idea is that whenever you visit a website, you can tell your web browser to send a do-not-track indicator that tells the website not to track you. (Many browsers, including Firefox, already have this feature.) We have mixed feelings about whether it's a good idea.

For one thing, it's not at all clear what *do not track* means. If you order from, say, Amazon, it uses cookies to remember your session and your shopping cart, and to recognize you when you return using the same browser. Most people agree that this strategy is acceptable because it's all the same company and you deliberately made the first visit to Amazon. Well, okay, lots of people have set up Google accounts to use Gmail (see Chapter 8) and other Google services. Because the DoubleClick ad network is part of Google, it's okay for DoubleClick to track you because it's all the same company, right? Uh, no. Privacy researchers have multiday conferences to deal with issues such as this one, and the questions are far from resolved.

The other, even more serious, problem is that *you can't tell whether a site is obeying do-not-track.* If a marketer ignores your do-not-call listing, you can tell because your phone rings, but if it ignores your do-not-track listing, how can you tell? Suspiciously relevant spam from companies you've never heard of?

The United States is the only advanced country without comprehensive privacy laws, and do-not-track laws are just a Band-Aid. Don't settle for less.

If you plan to shop on the web (described in Chapter 15) or use other web services, cookies make it all possible. When you're using an airline reservation site, for example, the site uses cookies to separate the flights you're reserving from the ones that other users are reserving at the same time. On the other hand, you might use your credit card to purchase an item or a service on a website, and the site uses a cookie to remember the account with your credit card number. Suppose that you provide this information from a computer at work and the next person to visit that site uses the same computer. That person could, possibly, make purchases on your credit card. Oops.

Internet users have various feelings about cookies. Some of us don't care about them, and some of us view them as an unconscionable invasion of privacy. You get to decide for yourself. Contrary to rumor, cookie files cannot get other information from your hard drive, give you a bad haircut, or otherwise mess up your life. They collect only information that the browser tells them about. Your web browser lets you control whether and when cookies are stored on your computer; see Chapter 7 for details.

Google yourself

One big attraction of the Internet is *all the data out there* that's now easy to access. Some of that data is about you. If you have your own blog or have a personal website (see Chapters 17 and 18), expect that all the information you put up there is available for everyone to see — usually, forever. (We find stuff about ourselves from more than 25 years ago.) Other people also put up information — newsletters, event listings, pictures from events, and other pictures, for example. Your online data trail may be longer than you think. If you haven't done it before, search the web for your own name. Enter your name in quotes in either the Google or Bing search box and press Enter. If you have a common name, you may need to throw in your middle initial or add the name of your town or school. (If you do this often, you're *ego surfing*.)

The web browser equivalents of web bugs are *tracking cookies*. If several websites show ads from the same advertising network, the ad network can use cookies to tell whenever you're looking at one of its ads. By piecing together the information from many websites, these tracking companies form a clear picture of where you go online — and what you look at when you get there. Many are careful to provide only statistical information to their clients, but the potential for abuse is there. It's worth noting that U.S. courts set a lower standard of protection for "business records" gathered in this way than they do for personal papers stored in our homes. Fortunately, most web browsers provide an option to reject *third-party* cookies, or cookies from anyone other than the source of the web page itself; this makes tracking cookies go away.

We know where you are

Cellphones and GPS receivers make the privacy situation even more complicated. Anyone with a cellphone can take pictures or videos of you and e-mail them to friends or post them to the web, which can be anywhere from innocent fun to citizen journalism to seriously creepy. (We've read news reports of people standing with their cellphones at the foot of stairwells and escalators and trying to take pictures up girls' skirts. Ewww.) Modern cellphones have built-in GPS receivers, primarily intended to provide your location if you call 911, but also potentially usable to track your location whenever the phone is on.

Security: How People Can Take Over Your PC

You can download and install software directly over the Internet, which is a useful feature. If you need a viewer program to display and print a tax form or when you want to install a free upgrade to a program that you purchased earlier, it just takes a few clicks. How convenient!

However, other people can also install programs on your computer without your permission. Hey, wait a minute — whose computer is it, anyway? These programs can arrive in a number of ways, mainly by e-mail or your web browser.

Viruses arrive by e-mail

Computer *viruses* are programs that jump from computer to computer, just as real viruses jump from person to person. Computer viruses can spread using any mechanism that computers use to talk to each other, such as networks, data CDs, and DVDs. Viruses have been around computers for a long time. Originally, viruses lived in program files that people downloaded using a file transfer program or their web browsers. Now most viruses are spread by opening files that are sent by e-mail, as attachments to mail messages, although instant messaging (IM; see Chapter 12) is a popular alternative.

There was a time long ago when people in the know (like we thought we were) laughed at newcomers to the Internet who worried about getting viruses by e-mail. E-mail messages back then consisted only of text files and could not contain programs. Then e-mail attachments were introduced. People could then send computer software — including those sneaky viruses — by e-mail. Isn't progress wonderful?

What viruses do

When a virus lands on your computer, it has to manage somehow to get executed. Getting *executed* in computer jargon means being brought to life; a virus is a program, and programs have to be run in order to start doing their nefarious work. After a virus is running, it does two things:

1. Looks around and tries to find your address book, which it uses to courteously send copies of itself to all your friends and acquaintances, often wrapped up in authentic-sounding messages ("Hey, enjoyed the other night, thought this file would amuse you!").

2. Executes its payload, which is the reason that virus writers go to all that trouble and assume the risk. (They do occasionally end up in jail.)

The *payload* is the illegal activity that the virus is running from your machine. A payload can record your every keystroke (including your passwords). It can launch an attack at specific or random targets over the Internet. It frequently sends spam from your computer. Whatever it's doing, you don't want it doing it. Trust us: If your computer starts to act quirky or extremely sluggish, chances are good that you've contracted a virus — or 20.

In the good old days, virus writers were content just to see their viruses spread, but like everything else about the Internet, virus writing is now a big business, in many cases controlled by organized crime syndicates.

What you can do about viruses

Don't worry *too* much about viruses — excellent virus-checking programs are available that check all incoming mail before the viruses can attack. In Chapter 4, which describes connecting to the Internet, we recommend installing a virus checker. After you install it, be sure to update it regularly so that you're always protected against the latest viruses. You can subscribe to receive updates automatically.

Worms come right over the Net

A *worm* is like a virus, except that it doesn't need to hitch a ride on an e-mail message. A worm simply jumps directly from one computer to another over the Net, entering your computer by way of security flaws in its network software. Unfortunately, the most popular type of network software on the Net, the kind in Microsoft Windows, is riddled with security holes — so many that if you attach a nice, fresh Windows machine to a broadband Net connection, the machine is overrun with worms in less than a minute.

If you rigorously apply all security updates from Microsoft, they fix most of the known security flaws, but it takes a lot longer than a minute to apply them all. Hence, we strongly encourage anyone using a broadband connection to use a hardware *firewall,* a box that sits between the Net and your computer and keeps the worms out. If you have a broadband connection, you probably should use an inexpensive *router* to hook up your computers, anyway, and all these devices include a firewall as a standard feature. See Chapter 4 for more information.

Spyware arrives via websites

Spyware (which includes *adware*) is similar to a virus, except that your computer catches it in a different way. Rather than arrive by e-mail, spyware is downloaded by your browser. Generally, you need to click something on a web page to download and install spyware, but many people have been easily misled into installing spyware that purports to be a graphics viewer or another type of program they think they might want.

Know what spyware does

Spyware got its name from being frequently used for sneaky purposes, such as spying on whatever you're typing. Sometimes, spyware gathers information about you and sends it off to another site without your knowledge or consent. A common use for spyware is finding out which sites you're visiting so that advertisers can display pop-up ads (described later in this chapter) that are targeted to your interests.

Targeted advertising isn't inherently evil. The Google AdSense program, for example, places ads on participating web pages based on the contents of those pages. Targeted ads are worth more to advertisers because you're more likely to respond to an ad about something you're already reading about.

Spyware can also send spam from your computer, capture every keystroke you type and send it to a malefactor over the Net, and do all the other Bad Things that worms and viruses do.

Don't voluntarily install spyware

Lots of cute little free programs are available for download, but don't install them unless you've checked to see that they're safe *and* useful. Most free toolbars, screen savers, news tickers, and other utilities are spyware in disguise. Besides, the more programs you run on your computer, the slower all your other programs run. Check with friends before downloading the latest program. Or, search the web for the program's name (see Chapter 13) to find positive or negative reviews. Download programs only from reputable websites. Keep your computer free from software clutter.

Protect your computer from spyware

Spyware programs are often designed to be hard to remove — which can mess up your operating system. Rather than wait until you contract a bad case of spyware and then try to uninstall it, a better idea is to inoculate your computer against spyware. To block spyware, be careful about the screen elements you click. Install a spyware-checking program that can scan your system periodically, such as the free Microsoft Windows Defender. See Chapter 4 for details.

Are Macs the solution?

We hear you Apple Macintosh users gloating as you read this chapter: "We don't have these problems. Why don't people just use Macs?" Mac users still have to put up with phishing and other forms of junk e-mail, and spyware has started to appear on Macs. But to date, almost none of the viruses or worms affect Macs, and the threat of spyware is lower than for PCs. Although this situation can change, we think that Mac users will always have an easier time on the Net. First, Macs are so scarce (compared to Windows machines) that it isn't worth a virus writer's time to attack them — partly because this scarcity also makes it hard to spread Mac viruses. Most e-mail addresses in a Mac user's address book belong to Windows users anyway, so if a Mac virus makes copies of itself, the copies it mails out don't find nice,

vulnerable homes. (Designing a virus that runs on *both* Windows and Macs is difficult, even now.) Finally, the Mac OS X is designed to be more secure than Windows and is difficult to infect.

Current Intel-based Macs can run Windows programs, or can even be set up to run native Windows, for applications that are Windows-only. We know of companies whose support staffs run *everything* on Macs — because they don't get infected. When employees need to run something on a PC, they do it in a window on the Mac screen. Cool.

But don't be silly. All our advice about not clicking on unknown links or downloading untrusted software also applies to *you,* Mac users.

Spyware can attack Macs and even phones

Mac computers aren't immune to spyware. (See the nearby sidebar, "Are Macs the solution?") The Macintosh operating system is by design more secure than Windows, so few viruses and little spyware attack it. But a Mac user is just as likely as a PC user to be fooled into clicking a link to a free porn site that downloads spyware to your computer along with that sexy video. Even smartphones (such as the iPhone or Android phones) can be infected with spyware, and although most spyware targets Windows, it also targets other kinds of computers and phones, so think before you click on any of these devices.

Pop-up browser windows pop up all over the place

One of the worst innovations in recent decades is the *pop-up* window that appears on your screen unbidden (by you) when you visit certain websites. Some pop-ups appear immediately, and others are *pop-unders,* which are hidden under your main window until you close it. The pop-ups you're most likely to see are ads for mortgages and airline tickets. (No, we don't give their names here; they have plenty of publicity already.)

Adware: Just another kind of spyware

Adware, a controversial type of software that many people consider to be spyware, is installed as part of certain programs that are distributed for free. It watches what you do on your computer and displays targeted ads — even when you run other programs. We think that no users in their right minds would knowingly install a program that peppers them with ads — and we want laws to ban the practice, pointing out that adware often behaves like a parasite, by obscuring or replacing ads from competing websites.

Before downloading a free program, make sure that you understand what the deal is. If you aren't sure, don't download it. Make sure that your kids know not to download free games, song lyrics, and the like — most are infested with adware. If you don't, before you know it, you'll have so many pop-up ads that you'll have to unplug your computer to shut it up.

Several mechanisms can make pop-ups appear on your computer:

✔ A website can open a new browser window. Sometimes this new window displays an ad or other annoying information. But sometimes the new window has useful information — some websites use pop-up windows as a sort of Help system for using the site.

✔ Spyware or other programs can display pop-up windows.

Luckily, web browsers now can prevent most websites from opening unwanted new browser windows. See Chapter 7 to find out how to tell your browser how to display fewer pop-ups.

What's the secret word, Mr. Potter?

Everywhere you go these days, someone wants you to enter a password or pass code. Even Harry Potter has to tell his password to a magic portrait just to enter the Gryffindor dormitory (although there's apparently no security between the boys' and girls' wings). Security experts are nearly unanimous in telling us how we should protect all our passwords:

✔ Pick complex passwords that are long enough that no one can guess them.

Never use as a password a word that occurs in the dictionary. Consider sticking a number or two into your password.

✔ Never use the same password for different accounts.

- Memorize your passwords and never write them down.
- Change your passwords frequently.
- Find out how hard a hacker would have to work to guess your password. Microsoft has a site that tells you, at `www.microsoft.com/protect/yourself/password/checker.mspx`.

This sound advice is intended for everyone — except ordinary human beings. Most of us have far too many passwords to keep track of and too little brain to store them in.

The perils of free Wi-Fi

Wi-Fi, the wireless way that your laptop can connect to the Internet, is available in many public places, including airports and coffee shops. As explained in Chapter 4, when you use Wi-Fi to connect your computer to the Internet, you locate the network and click Connect and then start using the Internet. One of the first things you'll probably do is use your web browser to check your e-mail or connect to your company's network, And, in the process, you type a password or two.

Can you trust the Wi-Fi network? How do you know that the Wi-Fi network isn't listening to what you type, including your passwords? Well, you don't.

Wi-Fi snooping is surprisingly easy. A thief sets up a computer in an airport lounge or a coffee shop with a computer listening to all the radio traffic on the local Wi-Fi network. She monitors what you type and uses your passwords to send spam or empty your bank account or perform other nefarious deeds.

What's a traveling Internet user to do? You can significantly decrease the likelihood of snooping by using secure `https` websites (which show a lock icon in the browser) rather than unsecured `http` websites. A secure site

encrypts the traffic between your browser and the website so that even if someone is listening in, all they see is the meaningless encrypted traffic. If you use a mail program such as Thunderbird or Outlook to check your mail (see Chapter 8), set your incoming and outgoing mail connections to use encryption (often called *SSL* or *TLS*), which offers the same benefits.

If you absolutely must use public Wi-Fi to check your e-mail while you're on the road and you don't have an `https` or SSL connection, here's what to do (advice courtesy of our friend Mark Steinwinter):

1. Before you leave on your trip, change your e-mail password (and any other password you plan to use).

2. While on your trip, limit your public Wi-Fi use to the accounts whose passwords you changed before leaving. Go ahead and use websites that don't require a password.

3. As soon as you return home, change your e-mail password again. You can change it back to the one you used before your trip, or to another password. Just assume that a Bad Guy has the password you used on your trip, and never use this password again.

One common-sense approach is to use a single password for accounts where you have little risk of loss, such as the one you need in order to read an online newspaper. Use separate, stronger passwords for the accounts that truly matter (such as your online banking account). If you feel you can't remember them all, write them down and keep them in a safe place, not on a PostIt note stuck to your monitor.

Our warning about not using a password that's in the dictionary — take that one seriously! Hackers managed to find a hole in our firewall one day, and we had stupidly left one password set to a normal English word (*weather,* if you must know). It took the hackers less than two hours to break into our computer, by simply having their computer type every English word until they found one that worked.

When making up a password, stick numbers and punctuation into words or glue two words together with some numbers, or spell things backward. Use both capital and lowercase letters, too. If your kids are Fred and Susie and your house number is 426, how about Fred426susiE? Or Susie426dreF? Using the first letters of every word in a phrase is a good method, too. If your favorite song is "I Wanna Hold Your Hand," by The Beatles, it wouldn't be that difficult to remember a password like Iwhyh1963. You get the idea!

Be careful with password hints

Website operators are tired of dealing with customers who forget their passwords, so a new computer tool has emerged in the past few years — the password hint. When you create a new account, the friendly identity manager software asks for your username and new password. It then makes you select and answer a couple of security questions, such as "What's your favorite color?" or "What's your pet's name?"

Sometime in the future, you try to log in to that account — and find that you forgot its pesky password. No problemo! You're asked the security questions you picked; if you type the right answer, you're in. The problem is that a thief pretending to be you sees the same challenge. Rather than guess your password, all he has to guess is your favorite color (blue, maybe?) and figure out your pet's name (and did your kid post captioned photos of Rover on the school website as part of his third grade computer literacy project?).

If you encounter one of these password hints when you sign up for an important account, pick questions whose answers an attacker can't glean by researching you. And, there's no rule that says you have to answer the security questions truthfully. You can pick a friend's pet, for example, or a color you detest, or you can say that your favorite color is Rover and your pet's name is Purple. You just have to remember your less-than-truthful answers to these questions.

Over the years, we've ended up with so many passwords that we started storing them in a text file — which anyone with access to our PC could read! This idea is certainly one of the world's worst. If you have a lot of passwords and no way to remember them, consider using a password manager, which is designed to store your passwords in a safe place. Of course, you have to remember one password — for your password manager. We use KeePass, a freeware, open source program that you can download from www.keepass.info for PCs and Macs. See Chapter 19.

Spam, Bacon, Spam, Eggs, and Spam

Pink tender morsel,
Glistening with salty gel.
What the hell is it?

Hawaiian lunch meat?
Someone else's old shoe heels?
We may never know.

— SPAM haikus, found on the Internet, sometimes credited to Christopher James Hume and Reber Clark

More and more often, we receive unsolicited bulk e-mail (abbreviated UBE but usually called *spam*) from organizations or people we don't know. Spam is the online version of junk mail. Offline, junk mailers have to pay postage. Unfortunately, online, the cost of sending out a bazillion pieces of junk mail is virtually zilch.

E-mail spam (not to be confused with SPAM, the meat-related product from Minnesota that's quite popular in Hawaii) means that thousands of copies of an unwanted message are sent to e-mail accounts and even to instant message programs. The message usually consists of unsavory advertising for get-rich-quick schemes or dubious drugs — something that you might not want to see and that you definitely don't want your children to see. Many spam messages tout worthless stocks that the spammers have bought and hope you'll buy at inflated prices. The message is *spam,* the practice is *spamming,* and the person sending the spam is a *spammer.* Phishing often involves spam, too.

Spam, unfortunately, is a major problem on the Internet because it's extremely cheap for sleazy advertisers to send. We receive hundreds or thousands of pieces of spam a day, and the number continues to increase. Spam doesn't have to be commercial (we've seen religious and political spam), but it has to be unsolicited; if you asked for it, it isn't spam.

Why it's called spam

The meat? SPAM might be short for *spiced ham*. Oh, you mean the unwanted e-mail? It came from the Monty Python skit in which a group of Vikings sing the word *spam* repeatedly in a march tempo, drowning out all other discourse. (Search for *Monty Python spam* at your favorite search engine and you'll find plenty of sites where you can listen to it.) Spam can drown out all other mail because some people receive so much spam that they stop using e-mail entirely.

Why it's so bad

You may think that spam, like postal junk mail, is just a nuisance we have to live with. But it's worse than junk mail, in several ways. Spam costs you money. E-mail recipients pay much more than the sender does to deliver a message. Sending e-mail is cheap: A spammer can send thousands of messages an hour from a PC. After that, it costs you time to download, read (at least the subject line), and dispose of the mail. The amount of spam is now about 20 times the amount of real e-mail, and if spam volume continues to grow at its alarming pace, pretty soon real e-mail will prove to be useless because it's buried under the junk. Another problem is that spam filters, which are supposed to discard only spam, can throw away good messages by mistake.

Not only do spam recipients have to bear a cost, but all this volume of e-mail also strains the resources of the e-mail servers and the entire Internet. ISPs have to pass along the added costs to its users. Spam volume doubled or tripled for many years, and is still growing, although not as fast. Large Internet providers we know tell us that more than 95 percent of its incoming e-mail is spam, and many ISPs have told us that as much as $2 of the monthly fee goes to handling and cleaning up after spam. Spammers send 100 *billion* spam messages *every day*. And, as ISPs try harder to filter out spam, more and more legitimate mail risks being mistaken for spam and bounced or discarded.

Many spam messages include a line that instructs you how to get off their lists, something like "Send us a message with the word REMOVE in it." Reply to messages or click links to unsubscribe *only* if the messages are from lists that you remember subscribing to or from companies you have done business with. Anyone else will either ignore you or add you to other spam lists.

What you can do about it

You don't have to put up with a lot of spam. Spam filters can weed out most of the spam you receive. See Chapter 8 to see how to use the spam filter that may already be built into your e-mail program or how to install a separate spam filtering program. Also visit www.cauce.org, the Coalition Against Unsolicited Commercial E-mail, which is the major grass roots antispam organization.

Safety: How to Keep Yourself and Your Family Safe

Viruses, spyware, phishing, pop-ups, spam — is the Internet worth all this trouble? No, you don't have to give up on the Internet in despair or disgust. You just have to put in a little extra effort to use it safely. In addition to the technological fixes we suggest (virus checkers, spyware scanners, and pop-up blockers), you need to develop some smarts about online security. Here's a quick checklist:

- **Develop healthy skepticism.** If it sounds too good to be true, it isn't true. No one in Africa has $25 million to share with you if you help them move it out of the country, nor did you win a sweepstakes you never entered. As the old saying goes, there's a fool born every minute. Today's sucker doesn't have to be you.

- **Keep your computer's software up to date.** Both Microsoft and Apple have features that make this process more or less painless. Use them. The latest software updates usually fix exploitable security flaws.

- **Use a firewall and keep it updated.** Your computer probably has firewall software built in. Make sure that your firewall is turned on. Some malware programs know how to turn off protective software, so check it every week or so. We recommend using a router — a device that lets you share Internet connections among several computers (whether wired or wireless) — because routers include built-in firewall programs that malware programs cannot disable or bypass. These units are so cheap that you should get one even if you have only one computer. (See Chapter 5 for details.)

- **Install virus-protection and spyware-protection software and keep it current.** You can get either free or paid software. Use it. Chapter 4 tells you how to install virus checkers and spyware scanners.

You must keep the virus description files in your antivirus software updated — automatically if possible, and every week at least. (New viruses are launched every day.) Your antivirus software should automatically download the updates; check your documentation.

✔ **Don't open an e-mail attachment unless it's from someone you know *and* you're expecting it.** Contact the sender if you aren't sure.

✔ **Don't click links in e-mail messages unless you're sure that you know where they lead.** If you click one and the site you end up at wants your password or credit card number or dog's name, close your browser window. Don't even think about giving out any information.

✔ **Pick passwords that are hard to guess, and never give them to anyone else.** Don't give them to the nice lady who says she's from the Help desk or to the bogus FBI special agent who claims to need it for tracking down a kidnapped child. No one.

✔ **Be consistent.** If you share your computer with several family members or housemates, make sure that every person understands these rules and agrees to follow them.

For more tips about staying safe online, the U.S. government runs the OnGuard Online site at www.onguardonline.gov.

Chapter 3

Kids and the Net

· ·

In This Chapter

▶ Recognizing good and not-so-good ways that kids use the Internet

▶ Getting wise to some concerns about the Internet

▶ Working up parental guidelines for using the Internet

▶ Looking at the Internet in schools

· ·

*F*ace it: Most kids are way more comfortable on the Internet than their parents (and grandparents) are. Schools assign kids to do research on the web and e-mail information to other students or their teachers. Online games are designed for kids of all ages. Forbidding your kids from using the Net altogether is hopeless (unless they're younger than about 6), but you want to keep your kids safe. This chapter talks about what's great — and what's scary — about children and youth using the Internet.

With millions of kids online, a discussion about family Internet use is critical. (Obviously, if this isn't your concern, just skip this chapter and go to another one.)

Really Cool Ways Kids Use the Net

The Net is amazing. It can help kids do the things they *have* to do (like homework) as well as what they *want* to do:

✔ **Research homework assignments:** The Internet is an incredible way to expand the walls of a school. The Net can connect kids to libraries, research resources, museums, other schools, and other people. Kids can visit the American Museum of Natural History for information about anthropology and other natural sciences (at http://amnh.museum) and the Sistine Chapel (as of when we wrote this chapter, although web pages can move at any time); they can watch spotted newts in their native habitat; they can hear new music and make new friends; or they can learn about the history of computing (as shown in Figure 3-1). These days, many schools assume that kids have access to the web, so parents had better be ready.

✔ **Make e-friends in other countries:** School projects such as the Global Schoolhouse (GSH) connect kids around the world by working collaboratively on all types of projects. Its annual cyberfairs have brought together more than 500,000 students from hundreds of schools in at least 37 countries! Kids can find out more at the Global SchoolNet website, `www.globalschoolnet.org`, where they can also subscribe to lots of mailing lists. (We explain in Chapter 6 how to reach these locations so that you can come back here later and help your kids follow up on them.)

✔ **Practice foreign languages:** Kids can visit online chat rooms, where they can try out their French or Spanish or Portuguese or Russian or Japanese or even Esperanto.

✔ **Pay for downloaded music:** Kids love music, and they can buy music over the Internet in several ways. (Adults can too, as it turns out.) The Apple iTunes music store, at `www.apple.com/itunes`, sells songs for about 99 cents. Other sites, such as `www.napster.com`, let you download as many songs as you like for a monthly fee. See Chapter 14 for details.

Figure 3-1:
Many
museums
have useful
information
online.

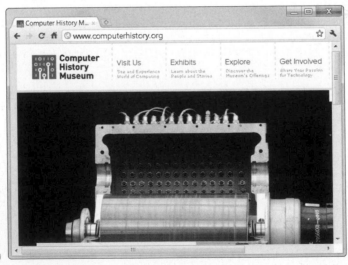

✔ **Write an encyclopedia article:** Wikipedia, at `http://en.wikipedia.org`, is a free online encyclopedia that anyone can contribute to. It's a useful research tool, but, even better, kids can add the material they found while researching those term papers to make Wikipedia even better. A worldwide team of volunteer writers and editors updates the material continually, and you — or your child! — can be one of them. (See Chapter 21 to find out what a wiki is.)

✔ **Put your own pictures, music, or other stuff on the web:** A website can be as clever or as stupid as you like. You and your kids can post your stories or artwork for family and friends to admire. We explain how to do these things in Part V.

When you or your kids search for a topic, you may see pages written by the world's greatest authority on that topic, some crackpot pushing a harebrained theory, a college kid's term paper, a guy on a bulletin board who thinks he's an expert, or, more likely, all of the above. Some websites are maintained by hate groups and push truly nasty venom. Learning how to identify all these types of information and misinformation is one of the most valuable skills that children (or anyone else) can acquire.

Games on the web

You can find almost any game on the web, from classic solitaire to video games to games that secretly teach you something. Here are a few places to look for single-player and multiplayer games:

✔ **AddictingGames:** One of the countless websites dedicated to solitary gaming is at `www.addictinggames.com`. A good search engine can help you find others, such as Miniclip (`www.miniclip.com`).

✔ **Game Show Network:** The GSN cable-television games network has a website where you can play along with the shows at `www.gsn.com`. If you win, your name may even appear on TV!

✔ **Games.com:** The site `www.games.com` (from AOL) has numerous solitaire games available to anyone willing to create a free account.

✔ **Merchandising advertising:** Many corporations advertise their products in downloadable games. If you like Legos, for example, try `www.lego.com/en-us/games/default.aspx`. The websites for certain action movies offer related games.

✔ **Minecraft:** This great site (`www.minecraft.org`) for Lego-lovers enables you to build almost anything out of digital blocks.

✔ **MSN Games:** Puzzle, card, word, trivia, and other types of games are available at the Microsoft site `http://zone.msn.com`. Yahoo! Games at `http://games.yahoo.com` is the same idea.

✔ **VirtualNES:** If you loved your old Nintendo game console, you'll love `www.virtualnes.com`, which offers classic Nintendo Entertainment System games for free. (It's legal because the games are now out of copyright.)

So-So Ways Kids Use the Net

Here are some ideas that adults might consider a waste of time, but hey, we can't be serious all the time:

- ✔ **Play games:** Many popular games (both traditional — such as chess, bridge, hearts, and go — and video) have options that let kids compete against other players on the Internet. See the earlier sidebar "Games on the web."

- ✔ **Hang out with friends:** The Facebook website (see Chapter 10) allows people to share their thoughts, photos, videos, and random comments. Many teenagers appear to live in Facebook.

- ✔ **Talk on a videophone:** Thanks to software such as Yahoo! Messenger and Skype, kids can see their friends while talking to them (not recommended on bad hair days). Chapter 12 talks about free video programs.

- ✔ **Shop:** What can we say? Internet shopping is like shopping at the mall, except that the Internet is always open and you don't have to hunt for a parking place. Kids can sell stuff too. Chapter 15 gets you started.

Not-So-Good Ways Kids Use the Net

Make sure that your kids or grandkids stay away from the following ideas, which will just get them into trouble, some of it serious:

- ✔ **Plagiarism:** That's the fancy word for passing off other people's work as your own. Plagiarizing from the Internet is just as wrong as plagiarizing from a book — and is (for that matter) a lot easier for teachers to catch because teachers can use search engines, too.

- ✔ **Cheating:** Using translating software to do language homework is also no good. Besides, automated translations still no substitute for the real thing are not being.

- ✔ **Revealing too much personal information:** When chatting on the Net with people your kids don't know, they might be tempted to give out identifying information about themselves or your family, but it's dangerous — doing so can get your kids stalked, ripped off, or worse. Even revealing their e-mail addresses can invite unwanted junk mail. Some seemingly innocent questions that strangers ask online aren't so innocent, so we go into more detail later in this chapter about what to watch for.

- ✔ **Sharing copyrighted music and videos:** Now that kids can easily buy music online, they don't have much excuse for using file sharing software to trade music or videos without permission. The music and movie industries are getting better at finding people who do that — and are taking legal action against them. It can cost you a lot of money.

✔ **Visiting porn and hate sites:** This advice is between you and your kids. Parents should make clear rules about what types of websites are acceptable, post the rules near the computer, and stick to them.

✔ **Pretending to be someone else online:** Kids should make up pseudonyms so that they don't have to use their real names. (This strategy can be one way to limit how much any stranger finds out.) But, pretending that you're a talent agent for *American Idol* or the latest reality show looking for a date is a bad idea.

✔ **Hanging out in adult chat rooms:** If kids pretend to be older than they are, they can get themselves *and* the chat room hosts into trouble.

✔ **Letting the Internet take over your life:** If the only thing your kids want to do after school is get online, it's time to set some limits. (Ditto for you and your work!)

Truly Brain-Dead Things Kids Should Never Do

Here are some ideas that kids should *never* consider because they can lead directly into major trouble:

✔ **Meet online friends in person without telling a parent:** If a child or youth meets someone online and wants to meet that person face to face, it's fine — maybe. But parents need to take precautions! First, make sure that your kid tells you about the meeting so that you can decide together how to proceed. Second, no one (child, youth, or adult) should ever meet an online friend in a private place: Always arrange to meet in a public place, such as a restaurant. Finally, go to the meeting with your child, in case they have been completely misled. (You can lurk discreetly nearby, so bring a book.)

✔ **Do anything illegal — online or off:** The Internet feels totally anonymous, but it's not. If kids or adults commit a crime, the police can get the Internet connection records from your Internet service provider (ISP) and find out who was connected over which modem on which day at what time and with which numeric Internet (IP) address, and they'll find you.

✔ **Break into other computers or create viruses:** This little escapade might have been considered a prank back in the 1980s, but the authorities have long since lost their sense of humor about it. Kids *have* gone to jail for it.

The Internet and Little Kids

We are strong advocates of allowing kids to be kids, and we believe that humans are better teachers than computers are. Now that you know our predisposition, maybe you can guess what we're going to say next: We are not in favor of sticking a young child in front of a screen. How young is too young? We believe that younger than age 5 is too young. At young ages, kids benefit more from playing with trees, balls, clay, crayons, paint, mud, monkey bars, bicycles, other kids, and especially older siblings. Computers make lousy babysitters. If your young children use computers, choose their programs and websites carefully, and limit their screen time.

We think that Internet access is more appropriate for somewhat older kids (fourth or fifth grade and older), but your mileage may vary. Even so, we think it's a good idea to limit the amount of time that anyone, especially a kid, spends online. We (despite our good looks) have been playing with computers for 35 years (each), and we know what happens to kids who are allowed to stay glued to their computers for unlimited lengths of time. Trust us: *It is not good.* Do you remember those old sayings "You are what you eat" and "Garbage in, garbage out"? What your brain devours makes a difference.

As human beings (what a concept), kids need to be able to communicate with other human beings. Too often, kids who have difficulty doing this prefer to get absorbed in computers — which doesn't help develop their social skills. Existing problems in this department grow worse, leading to more isolation. If you're starting to feel like your child is out of touch and you want to put the machine in its place (and maybe even encourage your child to get her life back), here are some quick self-defense tips:

- ✔ Keep a private log of all the time your child spends in front of the screen during one week. Then ask your child whether this is really how she wants to spend her life.

- ✔ Help your child find a hobby that doesn't involve a screen. Encourage him to join a team, form a band, or create some artwork.

- ✔ Have your child set aside one computer-free day every week.

- ✔ Make your child have meals and conversations with live human beings (that would be you and the rest of your family), face-to-face, in real time.

Surf Safe

Make sure your kids or grandkids know the safety rules for using the Net. Here are some basic guidelines for your kids to start with:

✓ **Never reveal exactly who you are.** Your child should use only his first name and shouldn't provide a last name, an address, a phone number, or the name of his school.

✓ **Never, *ever*, tell anyone your password.** No honest person or organization will ever ask you or your kid for it.

✓ **Be suspicious of strangers who seem to know a lot about you.** Maybe they say they're a friend of yours (the parent) who is supposed to pick up your kid after school or pick up a package from your house. Make sure your kid knows to never go with a stranger or let one into the house without asking a trusted (offline) adult first.

Here are a few more guidelines to help kids sidestep online trouble:

✓ **Think before you give your e-mail address to anybody.** Many websites ask users to register, and many sites require users to provide working e-mail addresses that they verify by sending confirmation messages. Before you let your child register with a website, make sure that it's run by a reputable company from which you won't mind getting junk mail.

✓ **Never agree to talk to someone on the phone or meet someone in person without checking it out with a parent first.** Most people a kid can meet online are okay, but a few creepy types out there have made the Internet their hunting ground.

✓ **Don't assume that people are telling you the truth.** That "kid" who says he's your kid's age and gender and seems to share your child's interests and hobbies may in reality be a lonely 40-year-old. If your kids have younger siblings, impress upon them how important it is to watch out for the safety of their younger "sibs." They may not understand what a stranger is and may believe that everything people tell them online is always true.

✓ **If someone is scaring you or making you uncomfortable — especially if the person says not to tell your parents — *tell* your parents.** If something bothers your child, make sure she knows to ask you to talk to your Internet service provider. Remind your kid that she can always turn off the computer.

Sell, Sell, Sell!

When you spend a lot of time online, you soon notice that everyone seems to be trying to sell you something. Kids, particularly those from middle- and upper-income families, are a lucrative target market, and the Net is being viewed as another way to capture it.

Targeting kids for selling isn't new. Remember Joe Camel of the Camel cigarette campaign that was aimed at kids? Some schools make students watch Channel One, a system that brings advertising directly to the classroom. If you watch TV, you know how TV programs for kids push their own lines of toys and action figures.

Kids should know that big-company marketing departments have designed kid-friendly, fascinating, captivating software to help them better market to you. Delightful, familiar cartoon characters deftly elicit strategic marketing information directly from the keyboard in your home.

You should be aware of this situation and know what to do when someone on the web is asking your kids for information. If your kids have access to credit cards, yours or their own, they can spend big bucks over the Internet. Beware of online stores where you have configured your web browser to remember your passwords, because your kids will be able to waltz right in and start buying. And, your kids should be aware that if they spend your money online without permission, they're going to get into big trouble for it.

The Children's Online Privacy Protection Act (COPPA) limits the information that companies can collect from children under 13 (or at least children who *admit* they're under 13) without explicit parental consent — which, by the way, we think parents should rarely give. We heard of one marketer who said he wanted to use the Net to create personal relationships with all the kids who use his product. Ugh. We have names for guys who want relationships with kids, and they're not nice names.

The FTC (www.ftc.gov/bcp/edu/pubs/consumer/tech/tec10.shtm) has more useful information for teachers about COPPA and online privacy that is useful for parents, too.

Who's Online?

Lots of kids — and grown-ups — are putting up websites about themselves and their families. Social networking sites such as Facebook (see Chapter 10) make it easy. We think that creating websites is cool, but we strongly encourage families who use the Net for personal reasons (distinct from businesspeople who use the Net for business purposes) *not* to use their full or real names. We also advise you and your children never to disclose your address, phone number, Social Security number, or account passwords in online social situations to anyone who asks for this kind of information — online or off. This advice applies especially when people who claim to be in positions of authority ask for them — for example, instant messages from people claiming that they're from America Online (AOL) tech support. They aren't, as we detail in Chapter 2.

People with real authority *never* ask questions seeking highly personal information. For one thing, Internet service providers don't handle member accounts by using instant messages, and they never ask for credit card information by e-mail. It all makes a solid case for knowing how your Internet service provider does its work.

More than ever, children need to develop critical-thinking skills. They have to be able to evaluate what they read and see — especially on the web.

Regrettably, almost anyone with an e-mail address receives their share of junk e-mail *(spam)*. This situation will only get worse until we have effective laws, as well as technology, against unwanted e-mail. In the meantime, remember this important rule: If an e-mail offer sounds too good to be true, it isn't true — and if an ad shows up from someone you don't know, it's also good evidence that it isn't true.

The Internet in Schools

Some schools and libraries use software to filter Internet access for kids. A variety of filtering systems are available, at a range of costs and installation hassles, that promise to filter out inappropriate and harmful websites. It sounds good, but many kids are smart enough to find ways around rules, and extremely smart kids can find ways around software systems designed to "protect" them.

We believe that Internet filtering in schools isn't a good approach. Kids are quicker and more highly motivated and have more time to spend breaking into and out of systems than most adults we know, and this method doesn't encourage them to do something more productive than electronic lock-picking.

Checking out colleges on the Net

Most colleges and universities have sites on the web. You can find a directory of online campus tours at www.campustours.com, with links to lots more info about the colleges and universities.

After you're a little more adept at using the Net, you can use it to take a closer look at classes and professors to gain a better idea of what colleges have to offer.

Not just for kids: School on the Net

Your child's education, as well as your own, isn't over when you finish high school or college or (for those of us seriously dedicated to avoiding real life) graduate school. There's always more to learn. Nothing's quite like learning directly from a first-rate teacher in a classroom, but learning over the Net can be the next best thing to being there — particularly for students who live far from school or have irregular schedules. You can now take everything online from high school equivalency exams to professional continuing education to college and graduate courses leading to degrees. Some courses are strictly online; others use a combination of classroom, lab, and online instruction.

Many institutions rely successfully on students' signed contracts that detail explicitly what is appropriate and what is inappropriate to use. Students who violate these contracts lose their Internet or computer privileges. We recommend the approach of contracts and consequences, from which kids can truly learn.

Many schools use the Internet to post information that students can use in their classes, including a summary of the curriculum, upcoming assignments, and links to websites with useful resources. One such system is Moodle (at www.moodle.org) — ask your kids whether their teachers post assignments and resources online.

A few schools, such as the University of Phoenix (www.phoenix.edu), specialize in online education, but schools all over the world now offer online instruction, and some (such as MIT, at http://web.mit.edu) make all their course material available online for free. If the course is on the Net, it doesn't matter whether the school is across the street or across the ocean. You can find thousands of schools and courses in directories such as these:

```
www.petersons.com/distancelearning
www.online-colleges-courses-degrees-classes.org
```

A Few Useful Websites

Here are a few sites that may be useful for kids and parents (and grandparents).

These sites focus on education and parenting:

✔ **The Global Schoolhouse,** at www.globalschoolnet.org, is an online meeting place for teachers, students, and parents.

✔ **Great Web Sites for Kids,** from the American Library Association, is at www.ala.org/ala/alsc (and then click Great Web Sites for Kids).

✔ **KidPub,** at www.kidpub.com, features book reviews by kids.

✔ **Funbrain,** at www.funbrain.com, has educational games for kindergarten through eighth grade.

These sites are just plain fun:

✔ **Yahoo! Kids,** at http://kids.yahoo.com, is a Yahoo! web portal designed for kids.

✔ **The Yuckiest Site on the Internet,** at http://yucky.discovery.com, is just what it sounds like — the yuckier, the better!

✔ At the **CIA Kids' Page,** at https://www.cia.gov/kids-page, you have to type the https:// part (it's a secure site — that's what the *s* means) because it's, you know, the CIA.

✔ **Netmom,** at www.netmom.com, is run by our friend Jean Polly, who has been looking for online resources for kids even longer than we have.

✔ *Sports Illustrated* **for Kids,** at www.sikids.com, features sports news and games, but no swimsuits.

Part II
Internet, Here I Come!

The 5th Wave   By Rich Tennant

"I don't mean to hinder your quest for knowledge; however, it's not generally a good idea to try to download the entire Internet."

In this part . . .

After you're ready to get started, where do you start? The most difficult part of using the Internet is most likely getting connected. We help you figure out which kind of Internet service is right for you and help you get connected, with plenty of advice for broadband (fast), Wi-Fi (wireless), and mobile (smartphone) users. Then we help you take a test drive on the amazing World Wide Web.

Chapter 4

Assembling Your Gear and Climbing on the Net

"Great!" you say, "How do I connect my computer to the Internet?" The answer is, "It depends." (You'll hear that answer perhaps more often than you'd like.) The Internet isn't one network — it's 100,000 separate networks hooked together, each with its own rules and procedures, and you can get to the Net from any one of them. Readers of previous editions of this book pleaded (they said other things, too, but this is a family-oriented book) for step-by-step directions on how to get on, so we made this chapter as "steptual" as possible.

Here (drumroll, please) are the basic steps:

1. **Figure out which type of computer you have or can use.**

2. **Figure out which types of Internet connections are available where you are.**

3. **Sign up for your connection.**

4. **Set up your computer to use your new connection, and decide whether you like it.**

5. **Install the software you need to protect your computer from viruses and spyware.**

   See Chapter 2 for scary descriptions of the types of Internet dangers you need to protect yourself from.

You need four items to connect to the Internet:

- ✔ A computer, even a tiny computer, such as a phone or an iPad or another handheld device
- ✔ A modem (a piece of computer equipment, which may be right inside the computer) to hook your computer to the phone line, cable system, or mobile phone system
- ✔ An account with an Internet service provider (ISP), to give your modem somewhere to connect
- ✔ Software to run on your computer

We look at each of these items in turn.

If you have more than one computer to connect to the Internet, see Chapter 5. If your computer is a laptop, see the section in Chapter 5 about using your laptop or netbook at home and away.

Internet accounts are easy to use, but they can be tricky to set up. In fact, connecting for the first time can be the most difficult part of your Internet experience. Installing and setting up Internet connection software used to require that you type lots of scary-looking numerical Internet addresses, hostnames, communications-port numbers — you name it. These days, making the connection is much easier, partly because Internet software can now figure out most of the details itself, but mostly because all recent versions of Windows, Macs, and Linux include setup software that can step you through the process.

What Kind of Computer Do You Need?

Because the Internet is a computer network, the only way to hook up to it is to use some kind of computer. But computers appear in all sorts of disguises — including phones, MP3 music players, and toasters (okay, not really) — and they may well already be in your home, whether you know it or not.

Hey, I don't even have a computer!

If you don't have a computer and aren't ready or able to buy one, you still have options.

A likely place to find Internet access is in your public library. Most libraries have added Internet access centers, with clusters of Internet-connected computers among the bookshelves. These computers tend to be popular, so call ahead to reserve time or find out which hours are less crowded.

Another option is your local cybercafé. You can surf the Net while sipping your favorite beverage and sharing your cyberexperience. If you want to check out the Internet, a cybercafé is a great place to try before you buy. Some have computers ready for you to use, whereas others require you to bring your own laptop. (See Chapter 5 for laptop safety tips.)

If you want to use the Internet from your very own home, you're stuck getting some kind of computer. Luckily, almost any newish computer can connect to the Internet, and you can get perfectly usable ones for less than $300.

Yup, I have this old, beige box in the closet

Almost any personal computer made since 1980 is adequate for *some* type of connection to the Internet. But unless you have a really good friend who is a computer geek and wants to spend a lot of time at your house helping you get online, don't bother fooling with that old clunker — unless, of course, you're looking for a reason for the geek to spend a lot of time at your house, but that's your business.

If you can afford it, we strongly encourage you to buy a new computer or at least one that isn't more than four years old. New computers come with Internet software already installed and are configured for the latest in web technology. If you already own an older computer, you will spend more time and energy, and ultimately just as much money, simply trying to get the thing to work the way you want. We think that it's best to buy a brand-new computer.

One problem with old computers is that they tend to run old versions of software. Any version of Windows older than Windows XP or any Mac system older than OS X is more hassle than it's worth to try to use.

Yup, I got a brand-new BitBucket 2012

Ah, you *have* a computer. (Or maybe you're thinking about buying one.) Most Internet users connect by way of a broadband connection, or in a few areas where broadband isn't available, by the computer dialing over the phone line to an Internet service provider. When you first turn on your new computer, or when you run one of the Internet programs that comes installed, your computer offers to attempt to connect right then and there. First read the rest of this chapter. We have some warnings and some options we think you ought to consider first.

Yup, I'm getting a netbook or an iPad

A few years ago, a new category of computer appeared: the *netbook*. It's smaller and lighter than a laptop but bigger than a cellphone or handheld personal organizer. The netbook has a full keyboard, even if its keys are a little smaller than normal, and it's cheaper than most laptops — maybe the same price as an expensive phone (in the $200–$400 range). And, it has built-in Wi-Fi.

If you don't care about having a real keyboard, you can also consider a *tablet computer,* such as the iPad or Galaxy Tab. These flat, magazine-size computers look like oversized cellphones. The screens are larger than those on netbooks, so they're convenient for reading and watching videos, but not so helpful for typing.

The first netbook was the ASUS Eee PC (sounds like a screech), and now laptop, phone, and other manufacturers have gotten into the game. The first tablet computer was the Apple iPad. For information on using netbooks and tablets, see Chapter 5.

Yup, I got this little BlackBerry, iPhone, or Palm

Modern mobile phones have itty-bitty screens and itty-bitty keypads, so industry groups devised a way to show itty-bitty web pages on those screens and navigate around them. *Smartphones* (phones with Internet capabilities) are quite popular in Japan (where teenage girls use them to write novels one screen at a time) and have finally caught on in the United States. Unlike on your PC, a smartphone requires no more setup than what your phone company provides when it sells you the phone.

However, you pay a lot extra for a smartphone. The phone itself costs several hundred dollars, and you also pay extra for Internet use. On some plans, you can pay based on the amount of data you transfer, which can be several dollars per download. If you plan to browse frequently from your phone, call your phone company and sign up for a monthly data plan, which costs between $15 and $50 per month. With some smartphones (including the iPhone), you're forced to buy a monthly data plan.

Before buying a smartphone, consider whether you have a specific use in mind and be sure to try someone else's to see whether you can stand using its teeny screen. The Palm, the BlackBerry, and many other handheld models are designed to display text messages, e-mail, and simple web pages on their small screens. Go to a cellphone store and ask to see a demonstration. If you get a smartphone and you want some tips, see Chapter 5.

You don't need the Internet to send and receive text messages. You can even get information from some web servers by sending text messages. For instructions, see the section in Chapter 13 about searching from your cellphone.

The Types of Internet Connections

If you use a computer at a library, at work, at a cybercafé, or at someone else's house, you don't need to worry about how it connects to the Internet, because someone else has already done the work. But if you have your own computer, you have several options:

- ✔ Connect by using a fast phone line (DSL line).
- ✔ Connect by using your cable TV company.
- ✔ Dial in by using a regular phone line.

(If you're truly in the boondocks, you can also use a satellite to connect, usually via the same company from which you get satellite television.)

TIP

A word about usernames and passwords

More than a billion people are on the Internet. Because only one of them is you, it would be nice if the rest of them couldn't go snooping through your files and e-mail messages. For that reason — no matter which type of Internet account you have — your account has a username and a secret password associated with it.

Your *username* (or *user ID, login name, logon name,* or *screen name*) is unique among all the names assigned to your provider's users. It's usually also your e-mail address, so don't pick a name like *snickerdoodle* unless that's what you want to tell your friends and put on your business cards.

Your password is secret and is the main thing that keeps bad guys from borrowing an account. Don't use a real word or a name. See Chapter 2 for ideas for passwords that you have some hope of remembering.

Never tell anyone else your password. Particularly don't tell people who claim to be from your ISP or your bank — they aren't.

What's in an Account?

An Internet account — fast or slow — comes with

- **That all-important username and password:** You have to be able to connect, after all.

- **One or more e-mail addresses, each with its own mailbox:** Most accounts have from one to five e-mail addresses. If you have a family, every family member can have a separate address.

- **Webmail (a website where you can read your mail):** Webmail is useful when you want to check your mail and you aren't at your own computer with your own e-mail program. You can use a web browser to display your messages from any computer. See Chapter 8.

Your account should also come with a tollfree or local number you can call for support. Every ISP has a website showing prices, sign-up instructions, and support information.

Speedy Connections: DSL and Cable Internet

The most popular way to connect, available almost but not quite everywhere, is a *broadband* (high-speed) connection. Broadband connections can provide greater *bandwidth* — that is, more data transferred in a specific amount of time — than older dialup phone connections. This type of connection can be extremely fast, with downloads (in practice) often exceeding 6 million bits per second.

Broadband connections are now available and affordable by mere mortals in all but the most rural locations in the United States and Canada. (Even rural locations can connect using the same satellite that provides satellite TV.)

After you get used to having a broadband connection, you'll never again be able to tolerate an old-fashioned dialup connection. It's that good.

What is broadband, anyway?

There are two types of broadband Internet connections — DSL and cable:

- A *Digital Subscriber Line* (DSL) is a phone line that you order from your local telephone company, usually shared with the same line that connects your regular phones.

- A *cable* Internet account is provided by your local cable TV company, using the same cable connection that brings you 250 brain-numbing TV channels. Many cable companies also offer phone service as part of a package.

DSL and cable Internet accounts have a lot in common: They're fast and they don't tie up your regular phone line. Some broadband accounts have a permanent connection that works a lot like a connection to a local network in an office. Others require you to log on every time you want to use the Internet. The ISP provides most of the equipment — for example, the modem — and sometimes sends an installer to set it up with your computer. Ask your cable company about its Internet access and ask your phone company about its DSL. Then get one or the other. A few lucky places have competing cable or phone companies, keeping the price down.

High-speed cable or DSL cost about $30 per month depending on your location, plus installation and the cost of the special modem you need, minus whatever discount you receive for buying a package of broadband and other types of services the provider supplies. You usually get the best price with a package combining Internet with some or all of its phone, cable TV, and mobile phone services.

A hidden cost in getting either cable or DSL Internet access is having to take a day off from work to wait for the installers, unless you feel brave enough to install it yourself. Sometimes the installers must make two trips to get things working. Try to make the first appointment in the morning. Also, the cable company or phone company is usually also your ISP unless you pay extra, so you don't have a choice of ISPs. In theory, the phone company provides DSL access on equal terms to all ISPs — but, in practice, its own ISP somehow always seems to be more equal than the others.

Cable and DSL modems

To connect to a DSL or cable account, you use a DSL or cable modem. The phone or cable company provides it (sometimes for a fee). Don't buy one yourself — you need a modem compatible with your provider's equipment, so smart Internauts get their DSL or cable modems from the ISP that provides their Internet service and let someone there install it.

How your computer connects to the modem

DSL and cable modems connect to your computer in one of two-and-a-half ways:

- **Network adapter:** A *network adapter* (or *LAN adapter* or *Ethernet adapter* or *network interface card*) was originally designed for connecting computers to networks. If you have more than one computer in your home or office, you can use network adapters to connect the computers into a local-area network (LAN), as described in Chapter 5. A network adapter has an RJ-45 jack, which looks like a regular phone jack but is a little bigger, into which you plug your modem or network cable. Check the back and sides of your computer for holes that look like overgrown phone jacks. All modern PCs (and all Macs) have network adapters built in.

- **Wireless network adapter:** If your computer isn't located close to a phone or cable outlet or you have a laptop you carry around the house, you can use a wireless network, often called Wi-Fi. It works much the same as a wired network, only without the wires (duh!). All laptops, netbooks, and tablets built in the past five years and many smartphones have built-in Wi-Fi. We cover the ins and outs of Wi-Fi in Chapter 5.

✔ **USB:** Almost all computers come with one or more *USB (Universal Serial Bus,* if you care) connectors, which are used for connecting all kinds of stuff to your computer, from mice to cameras to printers. A USB port looks like a small, narrow, rectangular hole.

Here's some information of interest only to people with very old computers: If your cable or DSL modem installer reports that your computer has no network adapter or USB port that's needed to connect your modem, don't panic. If the installer can't provide the needed adapter, contact a local computer store about adding a network card — it shouldn't cost more than $20. Desktop computers need PCI or PCI Express network adapters, which are printed circuit boards that you install by turning off the computer, opening the case, finding an empty slot, sliding the card in, screwing down the card, and closing the computer. Laptops use various sorts of PC Card network adapters, which look like fat credit cards and simply slide into a slot on the side of the laptop. Several different kinds of PCI and PC Card slots are available; if you buy a card, be sure that it fits the kind of slot your computer has. But before doing all that, consider whether it might be time to bite the bullet and get a newer, faster computer.

Getting your DSL hooked up

DSL service is supposed to use your existing phone line and in-house wiring. But DSL often works better if the phone company runs a new wire from outside your building to wherever you use your computer. (Phone companies call this situation a *home run.*) For most kinds of DSL to work, you have to live within a couple of miles of your telephone company's central office, so DSL is unavailable in many rural areas.

DSL is available at different speeds. The higher speeds cost more (surprise, surprise!). The lowest speed, usually 640 Kbps or more, is adequate for most users.

If DSL service is available in your area, call your phone company to arrange for DSL service. Either it ships you the equipment to install yourself or a phone installer comes with a network connection box that you or the installer hooks to your computer. Some DSL modems connect to a network adapter or USB connector, and most include a router (described in more detail later) that can also provide a Wi-Fi connection.

Avoiding the DSL buzz

One clever thing about DSL is that the DSL connection shares the same phone wires with your phone without tying up the phone line. You can tell that this is the case because on all phones on the line with DSL, you may hear a loud buzz of Data Hornets swarming up and down your phone line. (Well, not really, but it can sound like it.)

To get rid of the buzz, you install a *DSL filter,* which filters out the buzz, between the phone line and all your phones. Filters are available from your DSL ISP, but you can probably find them cheaper at stores like Best Buy or RadioShack. The ideal way to install a filter is to run a separate wire from the box where the phone line enters your house to the DSL modem, and to install one DSL filter in that box into which you plug the wire leading to all the phones. But life is rarely ideal, so most of us install a filter for every phone.

For the phone plug where your DSL modem is connected, you want a *splitter* filter with a filtered jack into which you plug a phone (the one you use to call tech support when your computer doesn't work) and a data-filtered jack for the DSL modem. For all other phones, the filter simply plugs into the phone jack and the phone cord plugs into the filter. For that tidy look, you can also get wall-phone filters (which fit between the phone and the wall plate that the phone is mounted on) and baseboard phone jacks with filters built in.

Getting your cable Internet hooked up

To sign up for a cable account, call your local cable company to open one. Unless you decide to install it yourself (which isn't all that hard), a technician comes and installs a network-connection doozus (technical term) where your TV cable comes into your house, installs a network adapter in your computer if it doesn't already have one (unlikely, these days), brings a cable modem (which can look like a junior laptop computer with a spike hairdo), and hooks them together. Magic.

If you have cable television, the cable is split and one segment goes to your computer. If you don't have cable television, the cable company may have to install the actual cable before it can wire up your computer. When the technician goes away, however, you have a permanent, high-speed connection to the Internet (as long as you pay your bill, about $40 to $50 a month).

Do-it-yourself DSL

Hooking up your DSL modem shouldn't be tough. One side plugs into the phone line, and the other side into your computer. How hard can that be? Well, a few little details are involved.

We assume that you have a DSL modem that connects to a network or USB connector. If you have a network connector, you need a *crossover network cable* that should have come with the DSL modem. (Regular, noncrossover cables plug into a router or network hub, not directly from a modem to a computer.) If you're using USB, you should have a USB cable with a flat connector on one end and a squarish connector on the other. Turn off and unplug both your computer and the modem from the wall socket, plug in the network or USB cable, and then plug everything back in. The modem also connects to the phone line with a regular phone cord. The phone and network jacks on the modem are similar, but the network connector is the bigger one. Your computer setup should look something like the one shown in Figure 4-1. The details may vary a little — John's DSL came with filters that include the two-for-one splitter, and the modem includes a Wi-Fi router, so there's no cable to the computer.

Figure 4-1:
Your
computer,
connected
to a DSL
line.

Now you can skip to the section "After the DSL or cable Internet installer." And be sure to read the nearby sidebars "Avoiding the DSL buzz" and Fast, fibrous FiOS."

Do-it-yourself cable modems

Connecting a cable modem is not unlike connecting a DSL modem, except that you connect the modem to your TV cable rather than to your phone line. If a TV is already attached to the cable, unscrew the cable from the TV and throw away the TV because you'll be having much too much fun with your Internet connection to waste time watching TV. (If you're not yet ready to throw away your TV, move it to another cable outlet or get a cable splitter, available at any store that sells cable accessories.) Screw the cable into the cable modem and plug the network or USB cable from the modem to the computer, just as we describe for a DSL modem in the previous section.

After the DSL or cable Internet installer

The installer (which is you, if you installed the modem yourself) configures your computer to communicate with the Internet. Follow the instructions to connect to your account the first time; some DSL and cable modems come with a software CD you may need to use.

Chances are good, at this point, that you're on the Internet. You should be able to start up a web browser, such as Internet Explorer, and type the name of a website in the Address bar at the top. (Try our `http://net.gurus.org`.) The web page should appear momentarily. If you have a connection with a username, it may ask you whether to connect. (Well, yeah, that's the idea, but sarcasm is lost on machinery.)

If you still can't connect, you can try configuring Windows yourself.

Fast, fibrous FiOS

Cable and DSL network speeds are limited by the old-fashioned copper wire they use. Fiber optics are much faster, and large telephone companies have been making and breaking promises to wire us up with fiber for about 25 years. According to Teletruth, a phone consumers' advocate, if Verizon had kept the promises that its predecessor Bell of Pennsylvania made in 1994, most Pennsylvania homes would be wired with 45-megabits-per-second fiber by now.

Verizon is finally sort of making good on its promises with *FiOS,* a fiber optic package that combines fairly fast Internet (not 45 megabits, though) with home Wi-Fi, phone, and TV. If you want fast Internet and high-definition TV and you're willing to sign up for at least a full year, it's not a bad deal and it costs $45 a month and more. But you might want to consider a few issues before signing up:

✔ **Verizon has some odd rules about the connections it supports.** In particular, it doesn't officially support wireless connections to Macs — only wired.

✔ **There's no going back.** The person who hooks up the fiber often physically rips out your old copper phone line so that you can't switch back without paying for a full new installation.

✔ **It depends on your house power.** Regular phone service powers your phone from the central office, so the phone company's large batteries and professionally maintained backup generators keep the phones working if the power fails. FiOS uses your house power to run your phones as well as your Internet and TV connections. FiOS provides a battery that's supposed to keep your phone going for four hours if the power fails, but the battery lasts only two or three years, and if you don't remember to replace it (Verizon doesn't), you'll have an unpleasant surprise when the power fails and you want to use the phone.

Configuring Windows 7 to connect

Windows 7 detects an Internet connection if one exists, so you may not have to do a thing. It spots Wi-Fi or a connected DSL or cable modem and does the right thing. However, if you need to do it yourself, choose Start➪Control Panel➪Network and Internet➪Network and Sharing Center➪Set Up a New Connection or Network.

Configuring Windows Vista to connect

Windows Vista makes connecting slightly easier. If your network connects with a wired LAN connection and doesn't require a login or password (this includes most cable modems), Vista normally configures itself automagically, so you don't have to do any of this. For connections that require a login, follow these steps:

1. **Choose Start➪Connect To and then click the little Set Up a Connection or Network link.**

   They still don't make it easy to find.

2. **For the Network Connection type, choose Connect to the Internet and click Next.**

3. **Select Broadband (PPPoE).**

   We cover some of the other options for dialup and wireless later in this chapter and in Chapter 5.

4. **Enter the required information in the boxes.**

   In particular, enter the login name and password that your ISP gave you.

Configuring Windows XP to connect

To set up your connection using the Windows XP wizard, follow these steps:

1. **Choose Start➪All Programs➪Accessories➪Communications➪New Connection Wizard.**

   They sure don't make it easy to find.

2. **For the network connection type, choose Connect to the Internet and click Next.**

3. **Select Set Up My Connection Manually.**

   Choose either Connect Using a Broadband Connection That Requires a User Name and Password (if your ISP gave you a username and password) or Connect Using a Broadband Connection That Is Always On.

   If you're worried about your computer being connected to the Internet all the time, you can shut down your computer — when it's turned off, it's definitely hackproof! See the section "Essential Software to Keep Your System Safe," later in this chapter.

4. **Enter the required information in the boxes and accept the suggested check boxes, particularly the Internet firewall.**

Your PC communicates with the Internet by using the TCP/IP protocol, and you should see it listed in the Properties dialog box for the connection (in Windows XP). Don't fool with these settings unless you're sure that you know what you're doing!

Checking your DSL or cable connection

After you're connected, you can check the status of your connection:

- ✔ **Windows 7:** Display the Network and Sharing Center by choosing Start➪Control Panel➪Network and Internet➪Network and Sharing Center. Look in the View Your Active Networks section, shown in Figure 4-2.

- ✔ **Windows Vista:** Choose Start➪Control Panel➪Network and Sharing Center. Broadband connections appear in the upper part of the window.

- ✔ **Windows XP:** Choose Start➪Control Panel➪Network And Internet Connections➪Network Connections. Broadband connections appear in the LAN or High-Speed Internet section.

- ✔ **Macs:** Use the TCP/IP Control Panel in OS 8 and OS 9. For OS X, choose System Preferences from the Apple menu and click the Network icon. Then select the TCP/IP tab.

Figure 4-2:
The Network and Sharing Center in Windows 7 shows how your computer connects to the Internet.

On the other side of the pond

The ISP situation in the United Kingdom is a little different from the one in North America. For broadband, British Telecom (BT) and many competitors provide DSL service with (by American standards) high speeds at a low price as long as you sign up for at least a year at a time. The government forced BT to let other companies share its equipment, so you can often get a better deal on phone and DSL from other companies, using the exact same phone line. Look, for example, at www.greenbee.com, from the John Lewis department store chain.

Cable modem service is also widely available, typically faster than BT and more expensive. You can also get wireless broadband from your mobile phone company, with a little *dongle* that plugs into a USB port on your PC, typically reasonably priced until you exceed the monthly usage cap, after which the price rapidly becomes unreasonable.

Traditionally, all phone calls in the United Kingdom (UK) have been charged by the minute, including even local calls, which can make long dialup online sessions mighty pricey. As a result, the UK now has three different kinds of dialup ISPs:

✔ **Traditional:** These ISPs charge a modest monthly fee and provide access by way of either local numbers or national rate numbers. Unless you're sure that you won't spend much time online or your ISP provides another service you're using, such as web hosting, this type probably isn't what you want.

✔ **Free:** These ISPs charge no monthly fee; they support themselves by splitting the per-minute charges with BT. (BT would rather not, but OFTEL, the regulatory agency for the telecom industry in Britain, insists.) If you only want to try out the Net, free ISPs are a good way to start. We don't recommend them for long-term use because the per-minute split is less lucrative than the ISPs hoped and free ISPs have a disconcerting habit of going out of business on short notice. The tech support system also tends to be weak. (It's free. What do you want — your money back?)

✔ **Flat-rate:** These ISPs charge a monthly fee of about £20 but provide an 0800 or other number you can call without per-minute fees. Most dialup users find this choice the best because it makes the bill predictable. The largest flat-rate ISPs are AOL (yes, *that* AOL) and BT. Be warned that even though access is nominally unlimited, if you "camp" on the phone 20 hours a day, your ISP will invoke small print that you never noticed and cancel your account.

Depending on where you are and where your ISP is, your phone connection may be anywhere from wonderful to dreadful. If you try one ISP and keep getting slow or unreliable connections, try another.

Dialing — the Old-Fashioned Way

A *dialup modem* connects to a normal, everyday phone line — using the same little plug (an RJ-11 jack) and phone wire. You can unplug a phone and plug in a dialup modem in its place. The problems with dialup are that the connection is s-l-o-w and your phone line is tied up while you're online.

Computers used to come with built-in dialup modems — examine your computer carefully for a phone jack and, if you find one, plug a phone wire into it. Otherwise, you have to take your computer to the store and have someone install one. Don't confuse the phone jack with a wired Ethernet jack, which looks quite similar but is wider.

To use a dialup Internet connection, you sign up with an ISP for an Internet account. The features and services that one ISP offers are much like those of another. If you don't know what your local ISPs are, check the phone book or ads in the business section of your local paper.

If you aren't careful, you can end up paying more for the phone call than you do for your Internet account. *Use an ISP whose number is a free or untimed local call* (that is, you aren't paying by the minute). Nearly the entire continent is within a local call of an ISP; if you're one of the unlucky few, see whether your phone company has an unlimited long-distance plan.

Your ISP should give you information to set up your account: your username and password, its dialup phone number, and your e-mail address if it's different from your username. Here's how to set up your computer to dial up your ISP, depending on your version of Windows:

✔ **Windows 7:** Choose Start➪Control Panel➪Network and Internet➪ Network and Sharing Center➪Set Up a New Connection or Network.

✔ **Windows Vista:** Choose Start➪Connect To. In the window that opens, click the little Set Up a Connection or Network link. Click Set Up a Dial-Up Connection.

✔ **Windows XP:** Click the Start button and choose All Programs➪ Accessories➪Communications➪New Connection Wizard.

Enter the phone number as you would dial it on your phone, as 7, 10, or 11 digits. Unless you share your computer with someone you don't trust, select the check box to remember your password.

After your dialup account is set up, your computer should connect automatically whenever you use your web browser or e-mail program. You can also connect at any time. In Windows 7, click the Networking icon on the taskbar (it looks like the connection bars on a cellphone). In Windows Vista and XP, choose Start➪Connect To (in Windows Vista and XP) and then click the dialup connection and the Connect button. If you see a dialog box that asks for your ISP username and password, type them and then click Connect.

I'm In!

When you're connected to the Internet, you can monitor your connection or reconnect or disconnect. There's a Networking icon on the Windows task-bar; it's in the lower-right corner of the screen, to the left of the digital clock. Here's where it is and what it does:

✔ **Windows 7:** A mobile-phone-connection-bars Networking icon appears in the lower-right corner of the screen. Click it to see what you're con-nected to. Click Open Network and Sharing Center at the bottom of its window to see more information (refer to Figure 4-2).

✔ **Windows Vista:** A two-computer-screen icon appears in the lower-right corner of the screen. Right-click the icon to see options.

✔ **Windows XP:** A two-computer-screen icon appears in the lower-right corner of the screen. If you're connected by way of wireless, you see one computer screen with radio waves coming out of it. Double-click this icon to check the speed of your Internet connection.

If you use a broadband account, you never need to disconnect. We love being able to saunter up to our computers at any time to check the weather, our e-mail, a good buttermilk waffle recipe, or which movies Joe E. Brown was in, without having to wait for our computer to reconnect.

If you dial in to the Internet, you eventually want to disconnect (hang up) so that you can use your phone line to talk to actual human beings. You can leave the rest of your programs (such as your web browser and e-mail pro-gram) running even when you aren't connected to the Net. To disconnect a dialup connection, double-click or right-click the Networking icon, which we just described, and choose Disconnect.

Essential Software to Keep Your System Safe

Okay, you're connected. Before you start surfing the web, e-mailing, and instant-messaging, you need to protect your computer from the Terrors of the Internet: viruses and spyware. Chapter 2 describes the concepts behind them, and now is the time to use protection.

Walling out the bad guys

A *firewall* is a barrier between your computer (or computers) and the Internet. In big companies, the firewall may consist of a computer that does nothing but monitor the incoming and outgoing traffic, checking for bad stuff. At your home or office, you have two good options:

- ✔ **Use firewall software built into Windows 7, Vista, and XP.** In Windows 7, choose Start➪Control Panel➪System and Security➪Windows Firewall (shown in Figure 4-3). In Windows Vista, click the little Security Center shield in the notification area at the bottom of the screen and then click Windows Firewall. In Windows XP SP2, choose Start➪Control Panel➪Security Center or Start➪Control Panel➪Network and Internet Connections➪Network Connections, right-click the icon for your Internet account, choose Properties from the menu that appears, click the Advanced tab, and look for the Internet Connection Firewall or Windows Firewall section.

  If it isn't already selected, select the check box to turn on Internet Connection Firewall. When that's done, your computer has basic protection from hackers.

- ✔ **Use a *router*, a small box that sits between your computer (or computers) and your broadband modem.** A router has one plug for a cable to your DSL or cable modem, several plugs (usually four) to which you can connect computers, and usually an antenna for wireless Wi-Fi connections. The router has firewall software running all the time. See Chapter 5 for how to use a router to connect more than one computer to one Internet account. As often as not, your DSL or cable modem includes a router, so you're all set. (If it has a Wi-Fi antenna, or at least four sockets on the back, it's a router.)

Figure 4-3: Windows 7, Vista, and XP come with built-in firewalls, which should be turned on.

Even if you have only one computer that connects to the Internet, we recommend using a router. If your broadband provider didn't give you one, it costs about $40 and we're sure that you'll want to hook a second computer to the Internet before long. The firewall programs included in Windows 7, Vista, and XP work fine, too. Hey, why not use both?

A router is a particularly good idea if you have a broadband connection that is always on (that is, always connected). The router is always on, too.

No viruses need apply

Viruses are sneaky programs that arrive by way of e-mail or in downloaded programs, and immediately get up to no good. (See Chapter 2 for details.) You need to run a virus checker program all the time, and you need to update its list of viruses regularly so that the program can detect the latest viruses.

Many virus checkers are available. The free AVG from the http://free.avg.com website isn't bad, particularly at the price. Microsoft also has an adequate virus checker, named Windows Defender. It comes preinstalled with Windows Vista and 7, and you can download it for free for use with Windows XP. It's at www.microsoft.com/windows/products/winfamily/defender.

The big two commercial programs are McAfee VirusScan, which you can download from www.mcafee.com, and Norton AntiVirus, at www.symantec.com. These programs work fine, but they are large and cost about $50 per year. If you have more than one computer on the Internet, consider F-Prot, at www.f-prot.com, because you have to pay for only one license (at $29 per year) to run the program on as many as five computers in your house. Norton AntiVirus also has a three-pack license if you have several computers.

The commercial programs require that you pay annually for a subscription to updates. Do it — without updates to the list of viruses that it's looking for, your program doesn't spot and block recent viruses. Some bundle the virus checker with other security packages so that you can get all the protection you need in one purchase.

Be sure that your virus checker is set to automatically download updates, which it should do at least several times a week. If you buy a commercial one, you have to renew your subscription every year. If you use Microsoft's (which, honestly, is just as good), there's no charge.

Detecting spyware

Spyware is a class of programs that sneak onto your computer, usually when you're browsing the web, and run unbeknownst to you, doing God-knows-what. (See Chapter 2 for details.) A number of antispyware programs are available for free, although no single program seems to spot all types of spyware. We recommend that you run several antispyware programs from time to time, to sweep your hard drive and look for bad stuff.

Along with Windows Defender, which is built into Windows 7 and Vista and is a free download for Windows 7 and XP, the three free programs we use are

- **Spybot Search & Destroy,** at www.safer-networking.org: It's shareware; donations are appreciated. Note that several unscrupulous programs have started using the word *spybot* in their names, so don't just use a search engine to find the program; from your web browser, type the address shown in this paragraph.

- **Ad-Aware Personal Edition,** at www.lavasoft.com: It's also free, although the developer wants you to buy the fancier, paid version.

- **Malwarebytes Anti-Malware,** at www.malwarebytes.org: It's another free scanning program.

These programs (and many others) are also available for free from www.download.com. For help with downloading and installing a spyware-checking program, see Chapter 2.

In addition, follow a few basic rules, which will make more sense after you read the later chapters of this book. (Don't worry: We mention the rules again in those later chapters, too.) Here they are:

- **Don't use Internet Explorer as your browser.** Most spyware is designed to use features of Internet Explorer to worm its way onto your computer. Instead, use Firefox or Chrome, as described in Chapter 6.

- **Don't use Internet Explorer within other applications.** For example, some e-mail programs have an option to use Internet Explorer to display messages that contain HTML (web formatting). Turn off these options.

- **If you use Windows, turn on Automatic Updates and download and install the updates it suggests.** Microsoft issues security fixes to Windows about once a week. Windows 7 and Vista download and install updates automatically unless you turn off this feature. In Windows 7, you can ensure that Automatic Updates are on by choosing Start⇨Control Panel⇨System and Security⇨Windows Update. In Windows Vista, choose Start⇨Control Panel⇨Security⇨Windows Update. In Windows XP, choose Start⇨Control Panel⇨Security Center or Start⇨Control Panel⇨Performance and Maintenance⇨System. In the System Properties dialog box that appears, click the Automatic Updates tab. Choose the first or second option so that Windows lets you know when updates are available.

Get rid of your Dell or Gateway software

Many computers come with Internet software created by the hardware manufacturers, designed to give you an easier Internet experience. Unfortunately, we find that these programs only give you a more *confusing* Internet experience because each program is renamed to add the name of the hardware manufacturer. (AOL used to do this, too.) If your Dell or Gateway or other new computer comes with Dell or Gateway or other Internet programs, we recommend that you ignore them and use the standard Windows programs described in this book. The polite name for this stuff is *shovelware.* Walt Mossberg of the *Wall Street Journal* has a more descriptive name: craplets.

Our Favorite Internet Setup

You're probably wondering, "The authors of this book have used the Internet forever. What do they recommend as the very best way to connect to it?" Okay, you're probably not wondering that, but we wish you were. And we've got the answer.

The best Internet setup (in our humble opinions) is this:

- ✔ A computer (Windows, Mac, or Linux — they're all good).

- ✔ A DSL or cable Internet account — broadband rocks! FiOS would be even better, but they don't offer it where we live.

- ✔ A *router,* to provide a firewall between your computer (or computers) and the Internet. Our routers also do Wi-Fi, so we can connect wirelessly (as described in Chapter 5).

You're Connected — Now What?

When you connect to your ISP, your computer becomes part of the Internet. You type stuff or click in programs running on your computer and those programs communicate over the Net to do whatever it is they do for you.

You can run several Internet programs at a time, which can be quite handy. You may be reading your e-mail, for example, and receive a message describing a cool, new site on the World Wide Web. You can switch immediately to your web browser program (usually Chrome, Firefox, Internet Explorer, or Safari), look at the web page, and then return to the mail program and pick up where you left off. Most e-mail programs highlight *URLs* (web addresses) and enable you to go straight to your browser by clicking the URL in your e-mail message.

You aren't limited to running programs that your Internet provider gives you. You can download a new Internet application from the Net and begin using it immediately — your ISP just acts as a data conduit between your computer and the rest of the Net.

To find out more about using the web, see Chapter 6. If you want to start off with e-mail, read Chapter 8. Or, just flip through the rest of this book to see what looks interesting!

Chapter 5

Connecting with Wi-Fi, Laptops, and Smartphones

In This Chapter

▶ Setting up a network at home

▶ Connecting all your computers without wires

▶ Hooking up your laptop at home or on the road

▶ Using your smartphone as an Internet device

*T*hese days, lots of families have more than one computer — perhaps one in the office, one in the family room, and one in their teenager's bedroom. Hey, one of us has one in the kitchen for our family's calendar and address book. And that's not to mention the road warrior laptop.

Luckily, you don't need a separate Internet connection for every computer. Instead, you can connect the computers into a network — with cables or through thin air with wireless Wi-Fi connections — and then set them up to share one Internet connection. This chapter shows you how to set up both types of networks.

Maybe you already have a laptop, netbook, or smartphone or just got one — this chapter also talks about ways you can use them on the Internet both at home and on the road. If you set up Wi-Fi for your family or office, you can connect from almost all laptops, all netbooks, and many smartphones, too.

Just One Computer for Internet Access? Naah

Many years ago, back when computers were large, hulking things found only in glass-walled computer rooms, a wild-eyed visionary friend of ours claimed (to great skepticism) that computers would be everywhere, and would be so small and cheap that they would show up as prizes in cereal boxes. We're not sure about the cereal boxes, but it's certainly true that the last time we went to put an old computer in the closet, we didn't have room because of all the other old computers in there. Rather than let them rust in *your* closet, you may as well get some use out of them by connecting them all to the Internet.

With a broadband connection, it turns out to be pretty easy. No more arguing about who uses the phone line next! No more pouting from the computer users who didn't get the cable or DSL hookup! Everyone can send e-mail, receive e-mail, chat, and browse the web — all at the same time.

To share an Internet connection, you connect your computers to each other in a local-area network and then you connect the LAN (rather than an individual computer) to the Internet. A *local-area network* (or *LAN*) is — drumroll, please! — a network entirely contained in one local area, such as one building, and is connected by way of wires or wireless connections, with no phone lines within the LAN. Once the exclusive tool of businesses, LANs have become so cheap that they're showing up in homes. As long as your home is in one building, if you have some computers connected to each other, you have a LAN.

Figure 5-1 shows a typical home network: A cable or DSL modem connects to a *hardware router,* a device that connects your LAN to your Internet connection. Normally, you would connect your PC to a network hub (for a wired network) or an access point (for wireless) — but a hardware router has a hub or an access point built in. Then you connect the LAN to the rest of the computers around the house.

Figure 5-1:
Ready for the whole family to surf.

Internet

Cable or DSL

Hardware router

Wired or wireless LAN

Not all computers on your LAN all have to be running the same version of Windows — or even running Windows. You can connect PCs, Macs, and Linux computers as well as tablet computers and smartphones on the same LAN because they all speak the same networking protocol, the same protocol that the Internet itself uses (TCP/IP, if you were wondering).

First, Make a LAN

LANs come in two basic varieties: wired and wireless. In a wired network, a cable runs from each computer to a central box, whereas a wireless network uses radio signals rather than wires. Either way, you need a central box, which we talk about in a minute. If all your computers are in one room (or you're good at playing home electrician), a wired network is for you; otherwise, wireless is far easier to set up, although the pieces can be more expensive and the resulting network runs slower. Combos are also possible; most wireless equipment has a few jacks for wires to connect to the computers that are close enough to run cables.

The box in the middle — a hub, switch, or router

For any variety of current LAN, you need a special box that connects everything. Here are the main kinds of boxes you have to choose from:

- A *hub* is a book-size box with a bunch of jacks for network cables. It serves as a wired connection point that links all your computers into a LAN.

- A *switch* is the same thing as a hub, but it has a little extra circuitry to speed things up.

- An *access point* is the wireless equivalent of a hub, with a radio antenna or two and only one jack to connect to a wired network.

- A *router* is similar to a hub or an access point (or both) with the addition of Internet-connection smarts, like a firewall (as described in Chapter 4, in the section about walling out the bad guys).

Our advice is to go for a router; it's cheap ($40 to $80), and it saves you days of hair-tearing grief because it keeps most Windows worms out of your network. With a router, none of your computers needs to worry about connecting to the Internet — the router handles it.

Routers come in both wired and wireless versions. The wired versions have varying numbers of jacks, depending on how many computers you plan to connect to your wired LAN; the wireless ones have one jack for the cable to the modem, an antenna for the wireless network, and usually a few jacks for running wires to computers in the same room. For some perverse reason, wireless routers are usually cheaper than wired, even though the wireless ones include everything the wired ones do plus the wireless radio. So get a wireless router.

Setting up a router

A router invariably comes with a short Ethernet cable to connect the router to the cable or DSL modem, so connect your router to your modem, plug in both devices, and turn them on. An *Ethernet cable* (also known as *Category 5,* or *Cat 5*) looks like a fat phone cable, with little plastic connectors that look just like phone plugs but a little larger. (Even their technical names are a little larger; a phone connector is an *RJ-11 jack,* whereas an Ethernet connector is an *RJ-45 jack.*) Many ISPs provide a combined router and DSL modem, which has an RJ-11 jack for the DSL phone line rather than an incoming Ethernet jack.

Configuring routers for DSL connections that require a username and password

For the most part, routers take care of themselves, but if you have the kind of DSL connection that requires a username and password, you need to put those into the router. If your DSL connection doesn't require a username and password, you can probably just skip this section, although you can come back later if a program you're installing requires you to change the router's configuration. Setup instructions for routers are all the same in concept, but they differ in detail from one router to another — so you may have to (gack!) glance at the instructions that came with the router.

Because the router has no screen or keyboard that would enable you to configure it, you use a computer connected to the router instead, by way of a web browser. The router has its own web address, accessible only from the computers on your LAN; the address is usually a strange-looking, all-numeric creation. Even if you plan to have an entirely wireless LAN, the initial setup is a lot easier if you connect a PC (or Mac) to the router by using an Ethernet cable, at least for now, so that the router can figure out which computer it's supposed to be talking to. ("Hey, there it is, at the other end of that wire!") Follow these steps:

1. **Turn off the router and the PC (or Mac).**

   Computers are usually happier if you plug and unplug stuff while they're turned off.

2. **Plug an Ethernet cable into the network adapter on your computer and plug the other end into one of the jacks on the router.**

3. **Turn on the router and then turn on the computer.**

4. **Fire up your web browser and type the address of the router's control page — its home page, with configuration settings.**

Usually this page is at 192.168.0.1 or 192.168.0.254 (special web addresses reserved by the Internet powers that be for private networks such as yours). If those web addresses don't work, check the router's instructions.

5. **If your router's configuration page requires a username and password, check your router's manual to find out what it is and then type it.**

   If you lost the manual, don't panic: Often, the username and password are printed on the bottom of the router. You see the configuration page for your router, similar to Figure 5-2.

Figure 5-2:
Your router has no screen, so you talk with it by using your web browser.

6. **If you have a broadband connection that uses a login and password, find the text box or field to enter your login name and password for your broadband connection.**

   Either follow the instructions in your router manual or try clicking the tabs or links on the page until you find boxes with names such as Username and Password. Connections that use passwords may be named *PPPoE* (Point-to-Point over Ethernet, if you must know). Type them in.

7. **If you see a button or link named Save, Done, or OK, click it to make sure that the router saves your changes.**

   If you see no such button or link, don't worry.

Now your router knows how to log in to your DSL account. (If you will use the router as a Wi-Fi access point, you have more configuring to do, including setting a password. See the section "Forget the Wires — Go Wi-Fi!" later in this chapter.)

Connecting your LAN to the modem

Plug the router into your DSL or cable modem, turn on the modem (if it isn't on yet), restart the router (by unplugging the power cord and plugging it back in), and verify that you can connect to the outside Internet. If you have a combined DSL modem and router, plug the phone line into its DSL jack. (Try a visit to our home page at `http://net.gurus.org`.) If that doesn't work, check the modem cable and ensure that both the username and password setup are correct if your Internet connection needs them. Most routers have reset switches that you can use to return them to their factory settings. It can take a long time, several minutes, for a DSL or cable modem to start the connection, so you might check the little lights to see whether the one that says WAN (for wide-area network) is lit yet.

You can configure a bunch of other router settings that you shouldn't need to worry about unless you're planning to do something exotic. The firewall part of the router watches the Internet traffic as it passes through and blocks the traffic it doesn't like. Routers let through web pages, e-mail, instant messages, and other standard types of Internet communication, but if you're doing something special, like playing certain types of online games, you may need to tell your router to allow additional types of data. If an online game or another program indicates that you need to "open a port" on your router, you need to return to this router configuration web page to make some changes.

Wiring your computers into a LAN

After you have the router set up, if you want to create a wired LAN, you need wires. (Okay, you already knew that.) Specifically, LANs use Cat 5 Ethernet cable with RJ-45 connectors — it looks the same as the cable you use to connect your router to your modem. Cat 5 cable is available at any office supply store, electrical supply store, computer store, or even the occasional drugstore or supermarket, and you can find it in varying lengths, from 10 feet to 50 feet or more. You need one cable to run from the router to each computer.

For every computer — PC, Mac, or whatever — plug one end of a Cat 5 cable into the computer's network adapter jack. (See the section in Chapter 4 about your computer connecting to the modem.) Plug the other end of the cable into the router.

After your computers are connected to the router and, indirectly, to each other, tell every computer about the LAN. Windows 7 and Vista make it easy — as soon as you plug in your network cable, Windows contacts the router and sets up your connection. (The most common problem: The cable isn't plugged in all the way at one end or the other.) If it doesn't, try these steps in Windows 7:

1. **Choose Start⇨Computer⇨Network.**

   You see a window showing the computers and networks that Windows thinks you're connected to.

2. **Click Network and Sharing Center.**

   You see the window shown in Figure 4-2, over in Chapter 4.

3. **Click Set Up a New Connection or Network if this is the first time, or Connect to a Network to connect to a network that already exists (such as someone else's LAN).**

In Windows Vista, try this:

1. **Choose Start⇨Network.**

2. **Click Network and Sharing Center to see which networks Windows thinks you're connected to.**

3. **Click the Diagnose and Repair link to help fix the most common problems.**

On every Windows XP computer on the network, follow this drill:

1. **Choose Start⇨All Programs⇨Accessories⇨Communications⇨Network Setup Wizard.**

2. **Follow the wizard's directions. When it asks what you want to do, choose the option labeled This Computer Connects through a Residential Gateway or through Another Computer on My Network.**

   The residential gateway is your router. On the next page, the wizard asks you to name your computer.

3. **When the wizard asks, give the computer a network name (such as PLAYROOM, OFFICE, or BOB).**

   When the wizard asks for the workgroup name, use the *same* name for all computers on your LAN. (We use WORKGROUP. Windows may suggest MSHOME, which is fine too — just be consistent.)

If you connect a Mac to your LAN, it can probably see the LAN and work without your lifting a finger. If you want (or need) to configure your network connection and you use Mac OS 9 or earlier, choose Apple⇨Control

Panels⇨TCP/IP to access the TCP/IP control panel. Or, run the Internet Setup Assistant by choosing your hard drive and then the Internet folder and then Internet Setup Assistant. In Mac OS X, choose Apple⇨System Preferences and then click the Network icon under the Internet & Wireless heading.

For more details on setting up your LAN, see *Home Networking Do-It-Yourself For Dummies* or *Home Networking All-in-One Desk Reference For Dummies* (both from John Wiley & Sons, Inc.).

Forget the Wires — Go Wi-Fi!

If you have computers in more than one room in the house, using Wi-Fi is easier than snaking wires through the walls or basement.

Most laptop PCs have Wi-Fi built in. For computers that don't, you can get Wi-Fi PC cards, Wi-Fi doozits with USB connectors, and (less often) Wi-Fi add-in cards for desktop computers. Wi-Fi makers do a remarkably good job of adhering to industry standards, so you can expect anyone's 11b or 11g or 11n Wi-Fi equipment to work with anyone else's.

The main practical difference among Wi-Fi equipment is range. Wi-Fi components have one standard feature in common: laughably optimistic estimates of how far away they can be from other Wi-Fi equipment and still work. Bigger antennas bring you more range — as does more expensive equipment. Wi-Fi radio waves use the same band as 2.4GHz cordless phones, so you can expect roughly the same range — like a cordless phone, your Wi-Fi connection will probably work in most parts of your house but not down to the end of your driveway. If your house is an average size, normal Wi-Fi works fine. If you live in a $900,000 mansion, you might have to spring for the $100 Wi-Fi card rather than the $30 one.

Set a password, for Pete's sake!

You would probably notice if a random stranger walked into your house and plugged into your wired network. (At least, we like to think *we* would notice.) However, if you have a Wi-Fi network and a stranger is out on the street with a laptop scanning the area for unprotected wireless access points (a practice known as *wardriving*), he can connect to your Wi-Fi network and you can't easily tell. Some people don't care — at least until they realize that wardrivers can see *all* the shared files and printers on your LAN, and can send spam (and worse) over your network connection. You may well be able to hop on to your neighbors' Wi-Fi networks, and they on yours, which may or may not be okay, depending on how much you like your neighbors.

Fortunately, all Wi-Fi systems have optional passwords. Cryptographers laugh derisively at the poor security of Wi-Fi passwords, but they're adequate to make wardrivers and nosy neighbors go bother someone else. (If you have serious secrets on your network, don't depend on Wi-Fi passwords. A bad guy using a laptop and one of the widely available Wi-Fi password-cracker programs can gather enough data from your network to break any password in less than a week. If you need better cryptographic protection, it's available, but it isn't exactly a do-it-yourself project to set up.)

Those creative Wi-Fi engineers created several flavors of passwords, too. Most new Wi-Fi equipment uses the secure password scheme Wireless Privacy Access (WPA). If all your Wi-Fi equipment can handle it, use WPA. WPA passwords can be almost any length, so you can pick something you can remember. (Don't use your last name or your address, which is likely to be the *only* information that a passerby might know about your house.) Some Wi-Fi equipment arrives configured with a network name and a random password, which you might as well use. It usually includes a card with the network name and password printed on it to help you set up your PCs.

Older Wi-Fi equipment can't do WPA, and you may be stuck using the system named *WEP*, a term that allegedly means Wired Equivalent Privacy (which it's not). WEP passwords come in two sizes: 64 and 128 bits. Use 128 unless you have old equipment that can do only 64, in which case, 64 will do. (Your entire network has to use the same size.) The password can be represented as either a text string or a hexadecimal (base-16, also called *hex*) number — we leave it to you to choose which would be easier for you to type and remember. If you use 64-bit WEP, your password (in text format) must be exactly 7 characters long. For 128-bit WEP, you need a 13-character password. If you want to use a shorter password, pad it out with digits or punctuation.

The easiest way to set the password is to set it up at the same time you set up your network, as described in the next section.

Making the Wi-Fi connection

To create a Wi-Fi system, follow these steps:

1. **Get your router set up, and then set up your computers to connect to it.**

   See the section "Setting up a router," earlier in this chapter. Even if you plan to use an all-Wi-Fi network, to do the setup process, plug in one computer with a cable and use it to set up the Wi-Fi.

2. **Use your web browser to display the router's control page (usually at `192.168.0.1`) so that you can configure the router.**

3. **Find the page where you can configure the router's Wi-Fi settings.**

   What you click depends on your router. On our D-Link router, we clicked Setup and then Wireless Settings to open the page shown in Figure 5-3. Look for a page with settings about wireless, a network name, and wireless security.

Figure 5-3: Configuring your router to do Wi-Fi with a password.

4. **Give your network a name.**

   Every Wi-Fi network has a name. With typical machine imagination, your router suggests a name similar to `linksys` (a router manufacturer) or `dlink` (another manufacturer) or `default`. We suggest a name similar to `FredsHouse` so that any neighbors who happen on it know that it's you.

5. **Turn on Wi-Fi passwords and set one, as described in the preceding section.**

   Your router probably has lots of other options — such as MAC cloning (less pomological than it sounds, and nothing to do with Macintosh computers), all of which you can ignore.

6. **When your router is up and running and your computer can see the Internet (that is, you can display web pages), you're done configuring the router for your Wi-Fi network.**

Now, at last, you can cut the cord and go wireless. You need to tell every PC which Wi-Fi network to use and what the password is. On Windows 7 and Vista, the setup is quick:

1. **In Windows 7, click the Networking icon in the lower-right corner of the screen, to the left of the digital clock. In Windows Vista, choose Start⇨Connect To.**

   You see a window with a list of available networks, one of which is yours. If you have neighbors with Wi-Fi networks, it may show them, too, but don't use your neighbors' networks unless they give you permission.

2. **Double-click your network.**

   In a moment, you see a dialog box that asks for the security key or pass phrase.

3. **Enter the network password, exactly as you did on the router, and click Connect.**

   Windows retrieves network settings from the router, and in a few seconds you're online. If you have trouble typing the password, click the box to display the characters of the password (unless, we suppose, someone you don't trust is looking over your shoulder).

If you're using Windows XP SP2, the process is also fairly painless:

1. **Click Start⇨Connect To⇨Wireless Network Connection.**

2. **After your PC sniffs the airwaves for a moment, Windows shows you a list of available networks, including the one you just set up.**

3. **Click your network's name and then the Connect button at the bottom of the window.**

4. **Windows asks you to type the password, twice. Type the password, whether it's text or hexadecimal, exactly as you did on the router.**

5. **Click OK, and you should be online.**

Windows remembers the wireless setup; in the future, it connects automatically.

For more on wireless networking, check out *Wireless Home Networking For Dummies* (John Wiley & Sons, Inc.).

Using Your Laptop or Netbook at Home and Away

The whole point of having a laptop computer is to take it with you when you travel — and what fun is traveling with a computer if you can't use it to check your e-mail 17 times a day? Almost all laptops and absolutely all netbooks come with built-in Wi-Fi. After you set up your laptop or netbook on a home Wi-Fi network by following the instructions earlier in this chapter, you already know most of what you need to know to use it on other networks when you travel. All the information in this section about laptops applies to netbooks, too.

Home and office setup

Lots of people have laptops they carry back and forth between home and the office. Many variables are involved in doing this successfully, depending on not only your particular laptop but also the networks you use at home and at the office. In general, however, this is how the various setups should work:

- ✓ **If both your home and the office have wired networks,** your computer should work when it's plugged into either network. If your computer doesn't connect at work, talk to your network administrator.

- ✓ **If your office has local shared files and printers and your house doesn't,** or vice versa, Windows complains and sulks if it can't find them. As long as you don't try to print to a printer that's at the other place, though, you can go online just fine.

- ✓ **If both the home and office networks are wireless, or one is wireless and the other is wired,** set up each one as described earlier in this chapter and your PC should automatically recognize whichever is available — that is, the network where you are.

Getting Wi-Fi with your latté

In olden days, people would visit a coffee shop and order cups of coffee, of which there was a maximum of two kinds, regular and decaf, and then chat with people sitting *right next to them*. Now, of course, that situation is hopelessly 20th century. We cruise into the coffee shop with our laptop, order a half-caf single-shot mocha cappuccino grande with 2 percent milk and cocoa drizzle, hold the sprinkles, and put on our Bluetooth earpiece and talk or exchange messages with people thousands of miles away, utterly ignoring the losers at the next table. The magic of Wi-Fi makes this possible, as coffee shops install Wi-Fi *hotspots* (public areas with Wi-Fi Internet access) to which customers can connect.

The amount of effort needed to get online at your coffee shop varies from none to way too much. At some places, the management has enough confidence in its product to figure that if it can get you to stick around, you'll keep buying coffee, so Wi-Fi is free to customers. (The coffee shop where John is sometimes found is in this category.) You turn on your computer; choose the Start⇨Connect To command — if your computer doesn't look for a Wi-Fi network by itself; click the name of the shop's network when it appears; tell it that, yes, you want to connect to that insecure network; and you're on. The next time you come back, your computer remembers the network and connects automatically.

Other places make you pay by the hour or the day. This fee adds an extra, annoying step to the connection process, the one where you pay. After your computer is turned on, fire up your web browser. No matter what your home page is, the network is set up so that your browser shows *its* home page, which allows you to make payment arrangements.

There are about as many ways to pay for Wi-Fi access as there are flavors of coffee. Maybe you buy or are given a ticket at the counter with a code number to enter. More likely, the coffee shop made a deal with one of the large, national mobile phone providers, T-Mobile or AT&T, that makes a sideline of Wi-Fi. In this case, you pay with a credit card, either by the hour (at about $6 per hour) or by buying a package of hours. You sign up via your web browser — the Wi-Fi network lets you connect to the sign-up page for free, but you have to sign up and pay to do anything else. If you plan to drink a great deal of coffee, you can sign up for a monthly flat-rate plan, or in some cases, if you have mobile phone service from the provider, it tosses in a Wi-Fi account for cheap or free.

It isn't hard to get into the Wi-Fi café biz, so you can also find lots of tiny providers. Many of them have reciprocal agreements and alliances, such that (for example) if you sign up with someone who belongs to the iPass group, you can use another iPass member's Wi-Fi hotspot.

Airports, hotels, and beyond

Coffee shops are hardly the only places that offer Wi-Fi. If you spend much time in airports (John does because he's on a lot of advisory boards), you find lots of Wi-Fi — with about the same options as in the coffee shops. The same two providers dominate, with a lot of little local ones as well. After a while, frequent travelers learn Wi-Fi folklore — say that there's free Wi-Fi in the airline club on the mezzanine in Terminal C of Newark airport, and you can use it from the food court downstairs.

Snoops at the coffee shop

Although we think that a lot of concerns about Internet network security are overblown, one place where it's a real issue is on public Wi-Fi networks, like the ones in hotels and coffee shops. These networks frequently have no passwords, which means that *anyone on that network can snoop on your network connection.* Even if everyone in the coffee shop seems nice, a snoop might be sitting in a car out by the curb. And in a hotel, of course, you have no idea who's in all the nearby rooms.

Fortunately, taking a few simple precautions will keep you safe. When visiting websites, make

sure that any site where you type a password or other private information uses *SSL encryption:* The address starts with `https://`, and the little lock in the corner is locked. If the site has no SSL encryption, wait until you return home. For advice on securing your mail program, see the section "The mail problem," a little later in this chapter. If you see a network named Free Public Wi-Fi, do *not* use it, because it is a password-stealing virus running on a nearby infected PC.

Hotels, like cafés, treat Wi-Fi as either a service — like the ice machine on each floor — or a profit center, like your room's minibar full of overpriced beer. Some hotels still offer wired Internet connections (in which case a cable on the desk in your room plugs into your computer), and others go Wi-Fi. If you're at an ice-machine-style hotel, you may just be able to turn on your computer and go online with no fuss, or you may have to sign in through your browser, even though you don't have to pay. Some hotels with Wi-Fi give you a slip of paper with a login code when you register, to deter visitors who would otherwise sit in the lobby and use it for free. In minibar-style hotels, you have to log in through your browser. Most hotels put the charge on the room bill; some want your credit card number so that they can bill you separately. The typical charge is $10 per day, from noon to noon, but we've seen hourly rates, lower rates, and higher rates. Some hotels bundle the rate in a business package with long-distance phone calls and other goodies.

If you encounter a problem with a hotel's Internet service, rarely does anyone at the hotel know anything about it, though they should be able to give you a toll-free number you can call to talk to someone at the company that provides the service.

The mail problem

Wi-Fi connections in coffee shops, airports, and hotels sure are convenient, but remember: *They aren't private.* This situation is a particular problem when you send and receive e-mail, because you usually want your mail to be private *and* because your computer needs to send your network login and password over the Internet back to your mail server to pick up your mail. With a modest amount of advance planning, it shouldn't be hard to get your mail working securely on the road.

The simplest approach is *web mail* — a secure website where you can log in to read and send mail. Check to see whether your mail system offers optional web mail. If so, even if you don't use it at home, you might want to use it on the road, particularly if the web mail offers a secure server. See Chapter 8 to find out how web mail works. Normally, we don't worry about secure websites (`https://` versus `http://`), but public Wi-Fi is one of the few cases where people might actually be snooping, so the https security helps.

If you want to be *truly* paranoid, create an account at Gmail, Hotmail, Yahoo! Mail, or another web mail site, use it during your trip, and then close the account when you return home. Be sure not to use the same password you use for other sites or accounts.

Using Your Smartphone on the Net

The newfangled, Internet-enabled *smartphone* is a tiny computer that happens to have a phone antenna, a microphone, and speakers built in. Some types of phones can also communicate using Wi-Fi, which is faster than a phone connection and doesn't move data over the cellphone system (which you may pay for by the megabyte).

Like computers, which come primarily in Windows, PC, and Linux varieties, smartphones come in several flavors, based on which operating system they run. Most of these types of smartphones allow you to download additional programs *(applications)* from a website. Some applications are free, and others cost 99 cents or more.

The major types of smartphones are

- **Android:** This system is *open source* (anyone can see the code and create compatible software). Because it's sponsored by Google, you can use your Google Apps (such as Gmail, Google Calendar, and Google Maps) on these phones. Android phones are available from a number of manufacturers and work on most cellphone networks.

- **BlackBerry:** The BlackBerry was the first widely used smartphone that made it easy to send and receive e-mail. All BlackBerry phones are made by Research in Motion (RIM).

- **iPhone:** The iPhone is a beautiful thing, and its sleek design created a huge sensation when it debuted in 2007. All iPhones are made by Apple, and none has a keyboard. Figure 5-4 shows an iPhone displaying e-mail.

- ✔ **Palm webOS:** Palm made some of the first smartphones. Palm phones come in both Palm webOS (like the Palm Pre) and Windows Mobile varieties.

- ✔ **Windows Mobile:** A variety of phones use a version of Windows designed for phones and other handheld devices. Windows Mobile phones are available from several manufacturers.

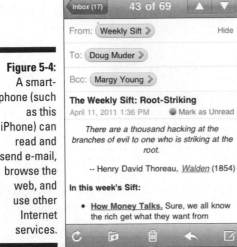

Figure 5-4:
A smartphone (such as this iPhone) can read and send e-mail, browse the web, and use other Internet services.

For each of these smartphone operating systems, you can buy a variety of different phones in different shapes and sizes. Some have little keyboards, some flip open, some have larger screens, some are bigger or heavier, some can connect to the Internet by way of Wi-Fi as well as by using the cellphone system — you get the idea. Shop around. New smartphone models are available every month.

All smartphones come with a web browser and an e-mail program. (Otherwise, what's smart about them?) You can download other programs, including maps (Google Maps has a smartphone version), instant messaging (to communicate with AIM users, for example), and Internet games. Most can also play Internet audio and video files, so you can watch YouTube during your commute, preferably if someone else is driving.

In most cases, each smartphone is available from and will work with only one carrier, so if you have preferences among carriers, you limit your choice of phones. Be sure you understand the monthly plan that comes with the phone and that the monthly data quota matches your usage. If you simply check e-mail a few times a day, an itty-bitty plan is enough, but if you plan to stream video an hour each way on your commute, you need an all-you-can-eat plan.

For much more information on the mobile Internet, see *Mobile Internet For Dummies,* written and published by people you know and trust. For more details on smartphones, go to www.dummies.com and search for specific phone models.

On the road with laptop and MiFi

One of the better new gadgets for road warriors is the portable Wi-Fi hotspot, often known as MiFi after the name of one of the most popular models. You pull a little credit-card-size box out of your briefcase, purse, or pocket; push a button to turn it on; and it's a Wi-Fi hotspot, ready for you to use with your laptop or smartphone, with the connection provided by a mobile carrier. If you find yourself paying $6 here and $10 there for Wi-Fi at hotels, coffee shops, and airports, a MiFi, for which you pay $20 to $50 per month, is a good alternative. Since it is a real Wi-Fi hotspot that can handle several computers, you can also make new friends by letting those envious bystanders share your connection.

All major mobile carriers offer some version of a mobile hotspot, with the same baffling range of prices and plans found with cell phones. Sold in the same places that sell phones, mobile hotspots require a monthly plan; some are pay-as-you-go. John likes Virgin Mobile MiFi (about $150), which you can enable for a month at a time when you need it and disable when you don't. Plans run $20 per month for enough data to check your mail, or $50 per month for no limit.

Chapter 6

Welcome to the Wild, Wonderful, Wacky Web

***P*eople** now talk about the *web* more than they talk about the *Internet*. The World Wide Web and the Internet aren't the same thing — the World Wide Web (which we call *the web* because we're lazy typists) lives "on top of" the Internet. The Internet's network is at the core of the web, and the web is an attractive parasite that requires the Net for survival. However, so much of what happens online is on the web that you aren't really online until you know how to browse the web.

This chapter explains what the web is and where it came from. Then it describes how to install and use some popular web browsers and how to use web browsers to display web pages. If you're already comfortable using the web, skip to Chapter 7.

What Is the World Wide Web?

So what is the web, already? The *World Wide Web* is a bunch of "pages" of information connected to each other around the globe. Each page can be a combination of text, pictures, audio clips, video clips, animations, fill-in-the-blank forms, and other stuff. (People add new types of other stuff every day.)

Linking web pages

What makes web pages interesting (aside from the fact that there seems to be a web page about every topic you can possibly think of) is that they contain *links* that point to other web pages. When you click a link, your browser fetches the page the link connects to. (Your *browser* is the program that shows you the web — read more about it in a couple of pages.) Links can create connections that let you go directly to related information. These invisible connections between pages resemble the threads of a spider web — as you click from web page to web page, you can envision the "web" created by the links.

Figure 6-1 shows a web page. Each underlined phrase is a link to another web page. A lot of non-underlined text is, too — move the mouse pointer around a page and see wherever it turns into a little hand. Anywhere a hand appears is a link, even if it isn't underlined.

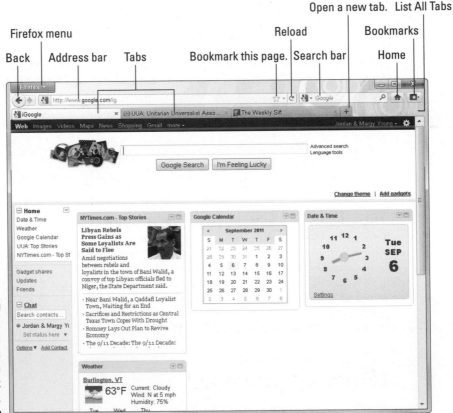

Figure 6-1:
This web page is displayed in the Firefox browser.

Where did the web come from?

The World Wide Web was invented in 1989 at the European Particle Physics Lab in Geneva, Switzerland, an unlikely spot for a revolution in computing. The inventor is a British researcher named Sir Tim Berners-Lee, who is now the director of the World Wide Web Consortium (W3C) in Cambridge, Massachusetts, the organization that sets standards and loosely oversees the development of the web. Tim is terrifically smart and hard working and charming. (Margy met him when he played the part of an amoeba in a church pageant.)

Tim invented *HTTP* (HyperText Transport Protocol), the way web browsers communicate with web servers; *HTML* (HyperText Markup Language), the language in which web pages are written; and *URLs* (Uniform Resource Locators), the addresses used for web pages and most other information on the Net. He envisioned the web as a way for everyone to publish and read information on the Net. Early web browsers had editors that let you create web pages almost as easily as you could read them.

For more information about the development of the web and the work of the World Wide Web Consortium, visit its website at www.w3.org. You can also read Tim's book, *Weaving the Web* (HarperOne, 1999). He was knighted in 2004 and became Sir Tim.

What's remarkable about the web is that it connects pieces of information from all around the *planet,* on different computers and in different databases (a feat you would be hard pressed to match with a card catalog in a brick-and-mortar library). Pages can be linked to other pages anywhere in the world so that when you're on the web, you can end up looking at pages from Singapore to Calgary, or from Sydney to Buenos Aires, all faster than you can say "Bob's your uncle," usually. Most of the time you're only seconds away from any site, anywhere in the world.

Finding the page you want

An important characteristic of the web is that you can search it — all 25 billion or so pages. For example, in fewer than ten seconds, you can find a list of web pages that contain the phrase *domestic poultry* or your own name or the name of a book you want to find out about. You can follow links to see each page on the list to find the information you want. See Chapter 13 to see how to use a search engine to search the web.

Where's that page?

Before you jump onto the web (boing-g-g — that metaphor needs work), you need to know one more basic concept: Every web page has a *web address* so that browsers, and you, can find it. Great figures in the world of software engineering (one guy, actually, named Sir Tim Berners-Lee) named this address *Uniform Resource Locator,* or *URL.* Every web page has a URL, a series of characters that begins with `http://`. (How do you say *URL?* Everyone we know pronounces each letter, "U-R-L" — no one says "earl.") Many URLs include the letters *www,* but not all do. Now you know enough to go browsing. For more entirely optional details about URLs, see the later sidebar "Duke of URL."

Browsing to Points Unknown

It's time to check out the web for yourself, using a *browser,* the program that finds web pages and displays them on your screen. Fortunately, if you have any recent version of Windows, any recent Mac, any netbook, almost any other computer with Internet access, or a smartphone, you probably already have a browser.

Our advice: Switch from Internet Explorer to Firefox, Safari, or Chrome

Internet Explorer, Firefox, Safari, and Google Chrome are all free and downloadable from the Internet, but beyond that, they have some important differences.

The advantages of Firefox, Safari, and Chrome:

✔ They run faster. They're smaller and quicker. Chrome is the fastest, in our experience.

✔ They don't use ActiveX controls, a feature of IE that spyware uses to infect your computer.

✔ If you use a Mac, iPhone, iPad, or iPod touch, you already have Safari.

The advantages of Internet Explorer:

✔ Some websites (mainly sites run by Microsoft itself) require Internet Explorer because they use ActiveX controls.

✔ A few browser add-ins work only with IE.

✔ If you use Windows, you already have IE because it comes bundled with Windows.

Any browser can display and print web pages — don't get us wrong. However, we think that the security issue — avoiding spyware — trumps all other considerations hands down, and we recommend that Windows users install Firefox or Chrome and use it except for the few websites that require Internet Explorer. You can have more than one browser installed at the same time — you can even have two or three running at the same time — so switching to Firefox or Chrome doesn't mean that you can never use Internet Explorer again. Mac users can stick with Safari.

See the later section "Getting and Installing a Browser" for downloading instructions.

Here are the most popular browsers:

✔ **Internet Explorer (IE)** is the browser that Microsoft has built into every recent version of Windows. About 40 percent of people (and dropping) use IE. The latest version is 9, shown in Figure 6-2, which comes with Windows 7 and is available as a free download for many earlier versions of Windows (at www.microsoft.com/ie) but not for the Mac. IE also runs on Windows Mobile smartphones. Previous versions of IE look a little different, but usually try to update themselves to the latest version.

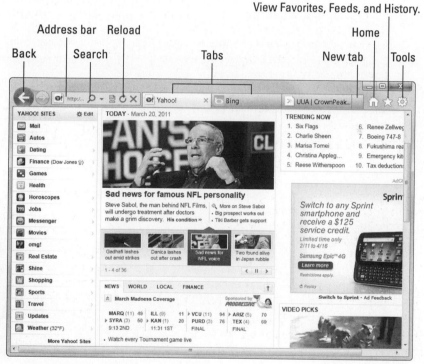

View Favorites, Feeds, and History.

Address bar   Reload

Home

Back   Search   Tabs   New tab   Tools

Figure 6-2:
Your typical web page, viewed in Internet Explorer 9.

✔ **Firefox** (refer to Figure 6-1) is the browser from the open source Mozilla project at www.mozilla.org. You can download Firefox for free for Windows, Macs, and Linux computers; the latest version as of mid-2011 is version 3.6. Firefox is used by about 28 percent of web users, runs faster than Internet Explorer, and is much, much less susceptible to spyware. See the nearby sidebar "Our advice: Switch from Internet Explorer to Firefox, Safari, or Chrome."

✔ **Chrome,** shown in Figure 6-3, is from Google, the company responsible for the www.google.com search site and lots and lots of free, web-based services. About 12 percent of people use Chrome. It's even faster than Firefox, although not as polished, because it's newer. You can download it for free for Windows, Macs, and Linux at www.google.com/chrome. Google appears to have a plan for Chrome to become its own operating system, competing with Windows. This book describes Chrome 13.

✔ **Safari,** shown in Figure 6-4, is the Apple browser for the Mac, iPad, iPhone, and iPod touch. Windows has a version, too, although we've never heard of anyone other than us using it. You can download the latest versions from www.apple.com/safari.

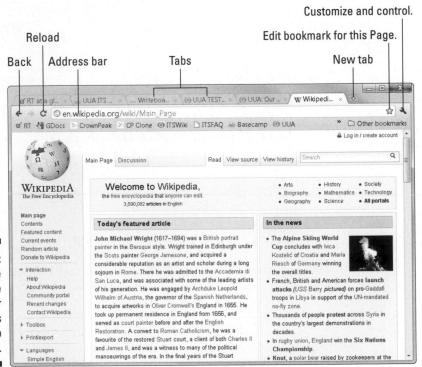

Back   Address bar   Reload   Tabs   Customize and control.   Edit bookmark for this Page.   New tab

Figure 6-3:
The Google Chrome browser displays another web page.

We describe Internet Explorer and Firefox in detail in this book, and we mention Chrome and Safari here and there. All browsers are similar, enabling you to view web pages, print them, and save the addresses of your favorite pages so that you can return to them later. If you want to try a different browser, see the section "Getting and Installing a Browser," later in this chapter.

Show top sites

Add Bookmark

Search bar   Settings menu

New tab

Back   Address bar   Tabs   Reload   Page menu

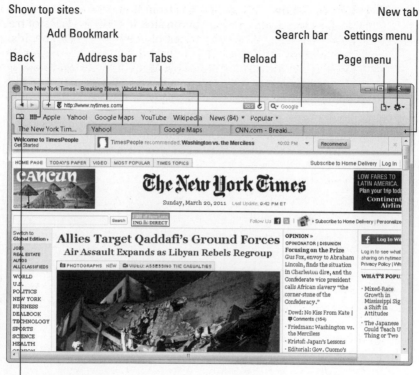

Figure 6-4:
Safari is
Apple's web
browser.

Show all bookmarks.

Web Surfing with Your Browser

When you start your web browser — Internet Explorer, Firefox, Chrome, Safari, or whatever — you see a window that displays one web page, with menus and icons along the top. Figure 6-1 (shown earlier in this chapter) illustrates Firefox, Figure 6-2 shows Internet Explorer, Figure 6-3 shows Google Chrome, and Figure 6-4 shows Safari. Other browsers look similar, but with different menus and icons along the top.

The main section of the browser window is taken up by the web page you're looking at. After all, that's what the browser is *for* — displaying a web page. Which page your browser displays at startup — your *start page* — depends on how it's set up. Many ISPs arrange for your browser to display their home pages; otherwise, until you choose a home page of your own, IE tends to display a Microsoft page, Firefox and Chrome usually show a Google search page, and Safari shows a page from the Apple website. Chapter 7 explains how to set the start page to a web page you want to see.

The buttons, bars, and menus around the edge help you find your way around the web and do things such as print and save pages. Here are some of the most important buttons and menus at the top of your browser window:

- ✔ **Back button:** Click to display the last page you looked at, as described in the later section "Backward, ho!"

- ✔ **Reload button:** Click to reload the page you're looking at now from the web.

- ✔ **Home button:** Click to display your start page (or *home page*), as described in Chapter 7.

- ✔ **Address bar:** Displays the web address (URL) of the current page. You can enter the URL of a page to display, as described in the later section "Going places."

- ✔ **Search bar:** Firefox and Safari have a *Search bar,* to the right of the Address bar, where you can type search terms. IE and Chrome combine the Address and Search bars. See Chapter 13 for details.

The rest of this chapter explains how to use these and other features of your browser.

Getting around

You need two simple skills (if we can describe something as basic as making a single mouse click as a skill) to get going on the web. One is to move from page to page on the web, and the other is to jump directly to a page when you know its URL (web address). Okay, we know that you aren't actually *moving* — your web browser displays one page after another — but browsing feels as though you're cruising (or surfing, depending on which metaphor you prefer) around the web.

Moving from page to page is easy: Click any link that looks interesting. That's it. Underlined blue text and blue-bordered pictures are links, and sometimes other things are, too. Anything that looks like a button is probably a link. You can tell when you're pointing to a link because the mouse pointer changes to a little hand. Clicking outside a link selects the text you click, as in most other programs. Sometimes, clicking a link moves you to a different place on the same page rather than to a new page.

Backward, ho!

Web browsers remember the last few pages you visited, so if you click a link and decide that you're not so crazy about the new page, you can easily go back to the preceding one. To go back, click the Back button on the toolbar. Its icon is an arrow or triangle pointing to the left, and it's the leftmost button on the toolbar, as shown in Figures 6-1, 6-2, 6-3, and 6-4. You can also press Alt+← to return to the previous page.

Duke of URL

The World Wide Web will eventually link together all information in the known universe, starting with all the stuff on the Internet. (This statement may be a slight exaggeration, but not by much.) One key to global domination is to give everything a name so that no matter what a web page link refers to, a web browser can find it and know what to do with it.

Look at this typical URL:

```
http://airinfo.travel/index.
   phtml
```

The first item in a URL, the letters that appear before the colon, is the *scheme,* which describes the way a browser can get to the resource. Although ten schemes are defined, the most common by far is HTTP, which stands for HyperText Transfer Protocol, the web's native transfer technique. HTTP is the language that your browser uses to request a web page from the web server on which it's stored; it's also the language that the web server uses to send you back the page you want to see. (A conversation in HTTP can be translated into English as something like this: "I'd like a web page, please." "Here it is. Enjoy!")

Although the details of the rest of the URL depend on the scheme, most schemes look similar. Following the colon are two slashes (always forward slashes, never backslashes) and the name of the host computer on which the resource lives; in this case, `airinfo.travel` (one of

the many names of John's Internet server). Then comes another slash and a *path,* which gives the name of the resource on that host; in this case, a file named `index.phtml`.

URLs allow a few other optional parts. They can include a *port number,* which specifies, roughly speaking, which of several programs running on that host should handle the request. The port number goes after a colon following the host name, like this:

```
http://airinfo.travel:80/
   index.phtml
```

The standard `http` port number is 80, so if that's the port you want (it usually is), you can leave it out. Finally, a URL can have a *query part* at the end, following a question mark, like this:

```
http://airinfo.travel:80/
   index.phtml?discounts
```

When a URL has a query part, it tells the host computer more specifically what you want the page to display. (You rarely type query parts yourself — they're often constructed for you from fill-in fields on web pages.)

Another useful URL scheme is `mailto`. A `mailto` URL looks like this:

```
mailto:internet13@gurus.org
```

That is, a `mailto` link is an e-mail address. Clicking a `mailto` URL runs your e-mail program and creates a new message addressed to the address in the link.

Sometimes, clicking a link opens the new page in a new browser window or tab — your browser can display more than one web page at the same time, each in its own window or in tabs in one window. If a link opens a new window or tab, the Back button does nothing in that window, but you can still switch back to the old window by clicking it.

Going places

Someone tells you about a cool website and you want to take a look. Here's what you do:

1. **Click in the Address bar, near the top of the browser window.**

   Figures 6-1, 6-2, 6-3, and 6-4 show where the Address bar is in IE, Firefox, Chrome, and Safari. Pressing F6 also gets you to the Address bar, except in IE, where it does nothing. (Another reason not to use IE!) Firefox is trying to rename this box the Awesome Bar, but we aren't buying it.

2. **Type the URL in the box.**

   The URL is similar to `http://net.gurus.org` — you can just type `net.gurus.org`. Be sure to delete the URL that appeared before you started typing.

3. **Press Enter.**

Here are a few shortcuts:

✓ If the entire address in the Address bar is highlighted, when you type, the new URL replaces what was there before. If not, click in the Address bar until the entire old address is highlighted.

✓ You can leave the `http://` off URLs when you type them in the Address bar. Your browser can guess that part! Many web addresses include a name that ends with `.com`, but not all do. See the later sidebar "Why .com?" for more information.

✓ When you start typing a URL, your browser helpfully starts guessing the address you might be typing, suggesting addresses you've already typed that start with the same characters. The browser displays its suggestions in a list just below the Address bar. If you see the address you want on the list, click it — there's no point in typing the rest of the URL if you don't have to!

If you receive URLs in e-mail, instant messages, or documents, you can usually click on them — many programs pass along the address to your browser. Or, use the standard cut-and-paste techniques and avoid retyping:

1. **Highlight the URL in whichever program it appears.**

   That is, use your mouse to select the URL so that the whole URL is highlighted.

2. **Press Ctrl+C (Command+C on the Mac) to copy the info to the Clipboard.**

3. **Click in the Address bar to highlight whatever is in it.**

4. **Press Ctrl+V (Command+V on the Mac) to paste the URL into the box, and then press Enter.**

Why .com?

When you want to put information on the Internet with your own name on it, you register a *domain name* such as `yahoo.com` or `wikipedia.org`. (See Chapter 17 if you're thinking of making your own website with your own domain name.) A domain name for an ISP in the United States usually ends with a dot and a two- or three-letter code (which is the *top-level domain,* or TLD) that gives you a clue to what kind of outfit owns the domain name. The following list briefly explains which type of organization owns which domain for each TLD code:

- **Commercial organizations** typically own domain names ending in `.com`, such as `google.com` (the most popular web search site), `aa.com` (AMR Corporation, better known as American Airlines), and `taugh.com` (John's hard-to-pronounce Taughannock Networks). Because "dot-com" has become a synonym for the Internet itself, lots of other organizations and even individuals have `.com` domains.

- **U.S. colleges and universities** typically own domain names ending in `.edu`, such as `yale.edu`.

- **Networking organizations** typically end with `.net`. These include ISPs, such as `comcast.net`, and companies that provide network services.

- **Government organizations** in the United States typically own domain names ending in `.gov`. For example, the National Do Not Call Registry, run by the Federal Trade Commission, is at donotcall.gov.

- **U.S. military organizations** use domain names ending in `.mil`.

- **Nonprofits** and **special interest groups** typically own domain names ending in `.org`. For example, the Unitarian Universalist Association (where Margy works) is at `uua.org`.

- **Organizations in specific countries** frequently own domain names ending in two-letter country codes, such as `.fr` for France or `.zw` for Zimbabwe. The full list of country TLD codes is at `www.iana.org/domains/root/db`. Small businesses, local governments, and K-12 schools in the United States may end with the two-letter state abbreviation followed by `.us` (such as John's church website at `http://unitarian.ithaca.ny.us`.

Bad guys can easily create e-mail messages where the URL you see in the text of a message isn't the URL you visit; the bad guys can hide the actual URL. Keep this warning in mind if you receive mail that purports to be from your bank — if you click the link and enter your account number and password in the web page that appears, you may be typing it into a website run by crooks rather than by your bank. See Chapter 2.

A great place to start browsing

You find out more about how to find things on the web in Chapter 13, but for now, here's a good way to get started: Go to the Yahoo! News page. To get to Yahoo! News, type this URL in your browser's Address bar and then press Enter:

```
news.yahoo.com
```

The Yahoo! website includes lots of different features, but its news site should look familiar — it's similar to a newspaper on steroids. Just nose around, clicking links that look interesting and clicking the Back button on the toolbar when you make a wrong turn. We guarantee that you'll find something interesting.

For information related to the very book you're holding, go to `http://net.gurus.org`. If we have any late-breaking news about the Internet or updates and corrections to this book, you can find them there. If you find mistakes in this book or have other comments, by the way, please send an e-mail to us at `internet13@gurus.org`.

What not to click

The web has some bad neighborhoods, and it isn't always safe to click whatever you see. For example, clicking a link on a web page can download and install a program on your computer, and that program might not be one you want to be running. So, exercise judgment when clicking.

Here are some links *not* to click:

- ✔ Don't click ads claiming that you just won the lottery or a free laptop or anything else too good to be true.

- ✔ Don't click messages on web pages claiming that your computer is at risk of dire consequence if you don't click there. Yeah, right.

- ✔ Don't click OK in a dialog box that asks about downloading or installing a program, unless you're deliberately downloading and installing a program. (See Chapter 7.)

🖋 Don't click any link that makes you suspicious. Your instincts are probably correct!

If one of these messages appears in a browser window, the safest thing to do is to close the window by clicking the X box in the upper-right corner (or on a Mac, the red Close button in the upper-left corner).

This page looks funny or out of date

Sometimes, a web page becomes garbled on the way in or you interrupt it (by clicking the Stop button on the toolbar or by pressing the Esc key). You can tell your browser to retrieve the information on the page again. Click the Reload button (shown in Figures 6-1, 6-2, 6-3, and 6-4) or press Ctrl+R.

TECHNICAL STUFF

Who makes up these TLDs?

An international group (the Internet Corporation for Assigned Names and Numbers, or ICANN, at `http://icann.org`) is in charge of TLDs (top-level domains). Two-letter TLDs are for entire countries, such as `.us` for the United States, `.ca` for Canada, and `.zw` for Zimbabwe. The newest country domain is `.ss`, for South Sudan.

In 1997, ICANN proposed adding some extra, generic domains, such as `.firm`, `.arts`, and `.web`. After a lengthy detour through a maze of international intellectual-property politics, the first new domains (`.biz` and `.info`) appeared in 2001. The result is confusion that practically guarantees that, more often than not, `whatever.biz` and `whatever.info` are owned by the same group that owns `whatever.com`, and when they're owned by someone else, they're usually sleazy knockoffs. ICANN has since added domain extensions including these:

🖋 `.name`: Personal vanity

🖋 `.coop`: Co-op

🖋 `.museum`: Museum

🖋 `.aero`: Air travel

🖋 `.jobs`: Job offers

🖋 `.travel`: Travel in general

🖋 `.mobi`: For cellphones and other mobile devices

None is widely used, although `.mobi` has a reasonable chance of success because of support from mobile phone companies. However, many websites have versions designed for smartphones (and other devices with small screens) with names that start with `m.`, such as `m.yahoo.com`.

ICANN is planning to throw open the domain floodgates to anyone who fills out the application form and sends it in with a check for a modest $185,000 application fee. By the time you read this sidebar, lots more TLDs might exist. Even if they do, we doubt that any of them will be important.

Some people hardly ever close their browsers, which probably isn't a good idea for their long-term mental stability. (Naturally, we aren't talking about anyone *we* know! Definitely not.) If you're this type of person, however, remember that your browser *caches* pages — it stores the pages temporarily on your hard drive for quick retrieval. If you want to make sure that you're seeing an up-to-date version of a page, reload it.

Get me outta here

Sooner or later, even the most dedicated web surfer has to stop to eat or attend to other personal needs. You leave your browser in the same way you leave any other program: Click the Close (X) button in the upper-right corner of the window (or on a Mac, the red Close button in the upper-left corner) or press Alt+F4. Or, just leave the program running and walk away from your computer. If you have multiple tabs open (described in "Tab dancing," later in this chapter), the program asks whether you want to close them all.

Viewing Lots of Web Pages at the Same Time

When we're pointing and clicking from one place to another, we like to open a bunch of browser windows so that we can see where we've been and go back to a previous page by just switching to another window. You can also arrange windows side by side, which is a good way to, say, compare prices for *The Internet For Dummies* at various online bookstores. (The difference may be small, but when you're buying 100 copies for everyone on your Christmas list, those pennies can add up. Oh, you weren't planning to do that? Drat.) Your browser can also display lots of web pages in one window, by using tabs (as explained in the section "Tab dancing," a little later in this chapter).

Wild window mania

To display a page in a new browser window, click a link with the right mouse button and choose Open in New Window (or Open Link in New Window) from the menu that pops up. To close a window, click the Close (X) button in the upper-right corner of the window frame or press Alt+F4, the standard close-window shortcut. (On a Mac, click the red button in the upper-left corner of the window.)

You can also create a new window without following a link: Press Ctrl+N. (Mac users, press Command+N.)

Tab dancing

We've all heard about how multitasking is a bad idea, but sometimes it's very useful to have several web pages open at the same time. Web browsers have *tabs,* which are multiple pages you can switch among in a window. Figure 6-5 shows a Chrome window with four tabs. The names or addresses of the tabs are shown across the top of the browser window, below the browser's menu and toolbars, like old-fashioned manila folder tabs. One tab corresponds to the page you see; that tab is a brighter color.

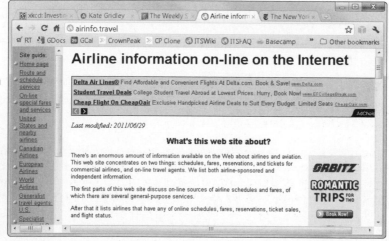

Figure 6-5:
Your web browser can display several web pages at the same time, one in each tab.

Just click a tab to show the page. To make a new, empty tab, click the New Tab (the tiny, blank tab to the right of the other tabs), press Ctrl+T, or right-click an existing tab and choose New Tab from the menu that appears. You can also open a new tab by right-clicking a link and choosing Open in New Tab (or Open Link in New Tab) from the menu that pops up. Click the X on the tab to get rid of it, or right-click the tab and choose Close Tab. (You may have to hover the mouse on the tab to see its X.)

IE normally displays your tabs in the same area as the Address bar, which can make the Address bar rather small. If you'd rather see your tabs below the Address bar, right-click any tab and choose Show Tabs on a Separate Row from the menu that appears. Ah, that's better!

TIP

Short-attention-span tips

If you have a slow Internet connection, use at least two browser tabs or windows at the same time. While you're waiting for the next page to open in one tab or window, you can read the page that opened a while ago in the other tab or window.

While your browser is downloading a big file, it may display a small window in the corner of your screen or an icon at the bottom of the browser window. You can click back to the main browser window and continue surfing while the download continues.

Warning: Doing two or three things at a time in your browser when you have a slow Net connection is not unlike squeezing blood from a turnip — only so much blood can be squeezed. In this case, the blood is the amount of data your computer can pump through your modem. A single download task can keep your Internet connection close to 100 percent busy, and anything else you do shares the connection with the download process. When you do two things at a time, therefore, each one happens more slowly than it would by itself.

For most purposes, we find tabs more convenient than windows, but multiple windows are useful if you want to compare two web pages side by side. You can use both tabs and windows; each window can have multiple tabs. In most browsers, you can drag a tab from one browser window to another, or drag a tab out to the desktop to make a new window.

Browsing from Your Smartphone or Tablet

Internet-connected phones — such as the iPhone and the BlackBerry and phones that run Windows Mobile, Android, or Palm webOS — can browse the web, too. So can the iPod touch, if you have a Wi-Fi connection. Of course, you can see only teeny, tiny web pages on their teeny, tiny screens, but phone-based browsing can still be incredibly useful, especially when you're looking for a good restaurant recommendation. The iPad and other Wi-Fi-connected tablets have browsers, too, and their screens are large enough for a tolerable browsing experience.

The iPhone, iPad, and iPod touch come with Safari; Android phones come with Google Chrome; and Windows Mobile phones come with IE. All these pint-size browsers have Back buttons and Address bars and most of the same basic features as their larger siblings.

Some web pages look great on smartphones, when the page designers create special versions that fit the small screens, dispensing with extraneous columns and graphics. Other pages are practically unreadable. As phone-based browsers become more popular, more websites will have sites customized for mobile devices. If you find a site that's unusable, try adding m. to the domain name (in place of the www.) or change the last part of the name to .mobi to see whether the site has a mobile version. For example, m.netflix.com is the spare, usable version of the Netflix site designed for phones, and yahoo.mobi is the teeny screen version of Yahoo!.

Getting and Installing a Browser

Chances are, a browser is already installed on your computer. If you use Internet Explorer, we think you're better off installing either Firefox or Chrome, for speed and safety reasons. Fortunately, browser programs aren't difficult to find and install, and Firefox, Chrome, and Safari are all free.

Even if you already have a browser, new versions come out every 20 minutes or so. Your browser is probably set to update itself automatically by checking in periodically with its home website. If your browser suggests that it needs to be updated, go ahead and follow its instructions to do so, because occasionally the new versions fix bugs or solve security issues.

Getting the program

To get Firefox (for Windows or Mac or any of the other dozen computers it runs on), visit www.mozilla.com. For Chrome, go to www.google.com/chrome. To get or upgrade Internet Explorer, go to www.microsoft.com/ie. Safari is available at www.apple.com/safari. Use your current browser to go to the page and then follow the instructions for finding and downloading the program. (Take a look at Chapter 7 for advice about downloading files.)

Running a new browser for the first time

To run your new browser, click the browser's attractive new icon. If you use Windows, the default browser also appears at the top of the left column of the Start menu, too.

Hey, how about us Mac users?

Macs have always been famous for their slick, easy-to-use software, and the Internet software is no exception. Macs come with a nice web browser named Safari (refer to Figure 6-4). You use the Command key rather than Ctrl for the keyboard shortcuts, and nearly all the rest of the keys work the way they do in the other browsers we describe.

Or, you can do what we do and use Firefox or Chrome, which work quite nicely on a Mac, just as they do on Windows, with Command rather than Ctrl. You can use Safari to visit `www.mozilla.com` or `www.google.com/chrome` to download and install Firefox or Chrome and then use it instead of or alongside Safari.

Your new browser will probably ask whether you want to import your settings — including your bookmarks and favorites — from the browser program you've been using. If you've already been using the web for a while and have built up a list of your favorite websites (as described in Chapter 7), take advantage of this opportunity to copy your list into the new browser so that you don't have to search for your favorite sites all over again.

The first time you run a new browser, it might run the Internet or New Connection Wizard, which offers to help you connect to the Internet. If it does, see Chapter 4 for details. New browsers may also ask about plug-ins, which are add-on programs that can make your browser smarter (see the next chapter for details).

Chapter 7

Taking Your Browser for a Spin

1 f you've read Chapter 6, you're all set to browse the web. But to be an efficient, downright clever Internaut, you need to know about other browser features, such as printing web pages, displaying more than one web page at the same time, and storing the addresses of web pages you like to visit often. You also need to know how to handle spyware, an Internet menace we describe in Chapter 2. This chapter is your guide to these extra features and how you can make the most of them right away.

Saving Stuff from the Web

Frequently, you see something on a web page that's worth saving for later. Sometimes it's interesting information, a picture, or another type of file. There's not much point to saving an entire page: It's usually made up of several files — one for the text, one for each picture, and sometimes other files — so your browser can't just save the page in a file. However, you can save images and text from a page.

If you want to remember a page and come back to it, bookmark it in your browser, as explained later in this chapter.

Saving text from a page

You can copy and paste text from a web page into a word processing document or another type of file. Select the text with your mouse (click and drag the mouse over the text) and press Ctrl+C (Command+C on the Mac) to save the text on your computer's Clipboard. Then switch to the word processing or other type of program, position the cursor where you want the text to appear, and press Ctrl+V (Command+V on the Mac) to paste it. You'll probably need to do some reformatting once the text is in your document.

Saving an image

To save an image you see on a web page, follow these steps:

1. **Right-click the image.**

2. **Choose Save Image As (in Firefox, Chrome, or Safari) or Save Picture As (in Internet Explorer) from the menu that appears.**

3. **In the Save Image or Save Picture dialog box, move to the folder or directory in which you want to save the graphics file, type a filename in the File Name text box, and click the Save button.**

A note about copyright: Almost all web pages, along with almost everything else on the Internet, are copyrighted by their authors. (A notable exception is U.S. federal government websites, which are all free of copyright.) If you save a web page or a picture from a web page, you don't have permission to use it any way you want. Before you reuse the text or pictures, send an e-mail message to the owner of the site. If an address doesn't appear on the page, write for permission to `webmaster@domain.com`, replacing *domain.com* with the domain name part of the page's web address.

Printing pages

To print a page, press Ctrl+P. Depending on your browser, you can also click something:

- ✔ **Firefox:** Click the Firefox button in the upper-left corner of the window and choose Print from the menu that appears.

- ✔ **Chrome:** Click the Customize and Control button (the little wrench icon at the right end of the Address bar) and choose Print.

✔ **IE:** Click the Tools button (the little gear icon to the right of the Address bar and tabs) and choose Print.

 ✔ **Safari:** Click the Page button (the paper icon to the right of the Search bar) and choose Print.

The browser has to reformat the page to print, which can take a minute, so remember that patience is a virtue. Fortunately, each browser displays a progress window to let you know how it's doing.

 The Chrome browser can print a page to a PDF file, which you can save and open later (as with any other PDF) with the Adobe Acrobat reader. It can be a handy way to save the whole page, images and all.

A Few of Your Favorite Things

You'll find some web pages that you want to visit repeatedly. (Both of us have visited the Google website thousands of times by now.) The makers of fine browsers have, fortunately, provided a handy way for you to remember those URLs so that you don't have to write them on the wall and type them again later.

The idea is simple: Your browser lets you add a web address to a list on your computer. Later, when you want to go back, you just go to your list and pick the page you want. Firefox, Chrome, and Safari call these saved web addresses *bookmarks;* Internet Explorer calls them *favorites*.

Bookmarking with Firefox

 When you're looking at a page you want to bookmark, click the Bookmark This Page icon (a little star) at the right end of the Address bar. The star turns gold — the page is bookmarked.

To see your bookmarks, click the Display Your Bookmarks button that appears near the upper-right corner of the Firefox window. (Logical enough, we think.) A menu of your items appears, including your bookmarks, as shown in Figure 7-1.

To go to one of the pages on your bookmark list, just choose its entry from the menu.

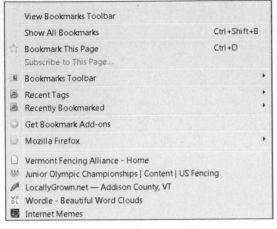

	View Bookmarks Toolbar	
	Show All Bookmarks	Ctrl+Shift+B
☆	Bookmark This Page	Ctrl+D
	Subscribe to This Page...	
	Bookmarks Toolbar	▶
	Recent Tags	▶
	Recently Bookmarked	▶
	Get Bookmark Add-ons	
	Mozilla Firefox	▶
	Vermont Fencing Alliance - Home	
	Junior Olympic Championships	Content	US Fencing	
	LocallyGrown.net — Addison County, VT	
	Wordle - Beautiful Word Clouds	
	Internet Memes	

Figure 7-1:
Your list
of Firefox
bookmarks
can quickly
get out of
control.

If you're like most users, your bookmark menu grows and grows and crawls down your screen and eventually ends up flopping down on the floor, which is both unattractive and unsanitary. Fortunately, you can smoosh (technical term) your menu into a more tractable form. Click the Firefox button and choose Bookmarks (or press Ctrl+Shift+B) to display the Library window, which shows various kinds of items you can save.

When you create a bookmark, it appears in the Unsorted Bookmarks folder. You can click it and double-click any bookmark to see that bookmarked page. (You can leave this window open while you move around the web, or close it by clicking the X in its upper-right corner.) You can also organize your bookmarks into folders and rename your bookmarks with meaningful names — web page titles can be long and uninformative.

If you want to organize your growing list of bookmarks into folders, right-click the Bookmarks Menu folder, choose New Folder, give your folder a name, and click Add. Now you can put bookmarks into this folder, which appears as a submenu on the Bookmarks menu. Drag an item to a folder to put it in that folder's submenu, and click a folder to display or hide that submenu. Because any changes you make in the Bookmarks sidebar are reflected immediately on the Bookmarks menu, you can easily fiddle with the bookmarks until you have them arranged as you like. Firefox starts out your bookmarks with pages that the Firefox developers want you to look at, but feel free to delete those pages if your tastes are different from theirs.

Another way to create a bookmark, and put it where you want it on the Bookmarks menu, is to find the little icon at the left end of the Address bar. (The icon changes depending on the page.) Drag the icon over to the Bookmarks button, which responds by displaying your list of bookmarks. Keep dragging the icon down the list to where you want the bookmark to appear.

Creating one-click bookmarks in Firefox

Okay, you've got the Bookmarks menu, which is what you see when you click the Bookmarks button. You've got the Library window, described in the preceding section. Wait — there's more! The Bookmarks toolbar is a row of buttons that appears just below the Address bar. (If it doesn't appear, right-click just above the Address bar and choose Bookmarks Toolbar from the menu that appears.) This row of buttons gives you one-button access to a bunch of Firefox developers' favorite websites. Wouldn't it be nice if your favorite websites appeared there instead?

No problem! When you organize your bookmarks in the Library window, drag your favorite sites into the Bookmarks Toolbar folder — any sites in this folder automagically appear on the Bookmarks toolbar. Feel free to delete the bookmarks that come with Firefox — the only one we like is the Latest Headlines bookmark, which displays a menu of breaking news stories on the BBC website.

Storing favorites in Internet Explorer

Internet Explorer uses a URL-saving system similar to the one in Firefox, although it calls the saved URLs *favorites* rather than bookmarks: You can add the current page to your Favorites folder and then look at and organize your Favorites folder. If you use Windows, this Favorites folder is shared with other programs on your computer. Other programs also can add things to your Favorites folder, so it's a jumble of web pages, files, and other elements. (To avoid insanity, most people use favorites only for web pages.)

 IE 9 has the Favorites icon — a star — just above the upper-right corner of the web page. To add the current page to your favorites, click the Favorites icon (or press Alt+C) and choose Add to Favorites from the menu that appears. (Or, press Ctrl+D.) The Add a Favorite dialog box, shown in Figure 7-2, displays the page name (which you can edit) and the folder in which the favorite will be saved. Click the Create In box to choose a folder, or click the New Folder button to create a new folder in which to contain the page's address. Click Add when you're ready to save the favorite.

To return to one of your favorite pages, click the Favorites icon to see a menu of your favorites, shown in Figure 7-3. Click an item to view that page. Your Favorites menu can contain folders, too, so that you can organize pages into groups; click a folder to open it and see what's inside.

Creating one-click bookmarks in Internet Explorer

For quicker access to your top favorite pages, IE has a Favorites bar that you can display just below the row of tabs. (If you don't see it, right-click above the Address bar and choose Favorites Bar from the menu that appears.) Click an icon on the Favorites bar to display that page. This feature is seriously handy for websites you visit often.

If you want to reorganize your Favorites menu, click the Favorites icon, click the down arrow to the right of the Add to Favorites button, and choose Organize Favorites. In the Organize Favorites window you can move favorites around, edit them, or delete them. To see what's in a folder, click it. When you're done organizing your favorite items, click Close.

In the Organize Favorites window, the Favorites Bar folder contains whatever you've added to your Favorites bar for instant access. Drag your favorite sites and folders into this folder — any sites in this folder automagically appear on the Favorites bar. Delete any sites in the Favorites bar folder that aren't your favorites. You can also delete icons right from the Favorites bar; right-click one and choose Delete from the menu that appears.

Adding web pages to your Windows taskbar

IE enables you to add an icon for a web page to the Windows taskbar (the icons that run along the bottom edge of your screen, with one for every running program and open document). To create an icon, click and drag a tab in IE to the Windows taskbar.

Bookmarking (including one-click) with Chrome

Google Chrome has a clean, spare look with no menus and only a few icons to clutter its window. But the features we love are there, including bookmarks. To add the current page to your list of bookmarks, click the Bookmark This Page star icon at the right end of the Address bar. A Bookmark Added box pops up so that you can edit the name for the bookmark and choose which bookmark folder to put the web page in. (Click Remove if you clicked this icon accidentally!) After a page is in your bookmarks, the star icon turns gold.

To edit your bookmarks, click the Customize and Control icon, the little wrench to the right of the Address bar, and choose Bookmark Manager from the menu that appears. The Bookmark Manager, shown in Figure 7-4, opens in a new tab. Click Organize to add folders into which you can drag your bookmarks.

When you drag a bookmark into the Bookmarks Bar folder, it appears (where else?) on the Bookmarks bar, between the Address bar and the top edge of the web page in the Chrome window. (If you don't see bookmarks below the Address bar, click the Customize and Control icon, choose Tools, and choose Always Show Bookmarks Bar so that it has a check mark next to it.)

Figure 7-4:
In Chrome,
you can
organize
your book-
marks
on the
Bookmark
Manager
tab.

Bookmarking (including one-click) with Safari

Safari comes from Apple, and Apple always does things a little differently.
Unlike the other three browsers, which use a star icon to indicate bookmarks
or favorites, Safari uses a little Plus Sign icon for creating bookmarks and a
little Book icon for organizing them.

To create a bookmark in Safari, click the Plus Sign icon at the left end of the
Address bar. Safari displays an unnamed dialog box (shown in Figure 7-5)
where you can edit the name of the bookmark (some page names are quite
long) and specify which folder to put it in.

Figure 7-5:
Safari asks
what to
name your
bookmark
and which
folder to file
it in.

Here are some folder options:

✔ The Top Sites folder is where Safari suggests you put your top favorites.

✔ The *Bookmarks bar* is the row of icons that appears just below the Address bar. (If you don't see it, click the Settings button and choose Show Bookmarks Bar.)

✔ The Bookmarks menu is the usual list of bookmarked pages.

Safari uses a visual display rather than a simple list of bookmarks. When you click the Show All Bookmarks button, the Bookmarks bar opens in a tab, shown in Figure 7-6, with the history of the pages you've looked at today. Click Bookmarks Bar to edit the icons on that bar, or click Bookmarks Menu to edit what you've added to that menu.

Figure 7-6:
Safari's History tab shows where you've been recently along with your bookmarks.

Filling In Forms

The web isn't just for reading — it's for buying stuff, signing up for stuff, and expressing your opinion about stuff. To put your two cents into a web page, you usually fill out a form that has boxes to type in, check boxes to select, and maybe other clickable stuff. Then you click a Submit button (or a button with another name) to send in the information you entered. Figure 7-7 shows a typical form.

Check boxes   Radio buttons   Text boxes   List box

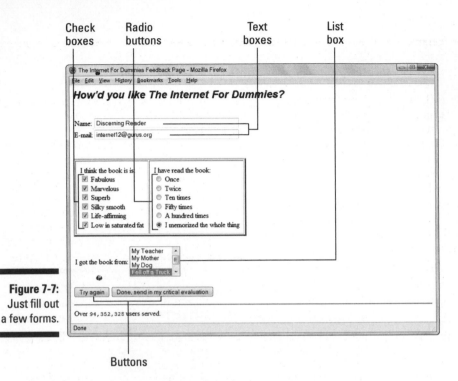

Figure 7-7:
Just fill out
a few forms.

Buttons

Text boxes in a form are white, fill-in boxes in which you type information, in this case, your name and e-mail address. *Check boxes* are little square boxes in which you check whichever ones apply (all of them, we hope, on our sample form). *Radio buttons,* the little round buttons, are similar to check boxes except that you can choose only one of them from each set. In Figure 7-7, you also see a *list box,* in which you can choose one possibility in the box. In most cases, you see more entries than can fit in the box, so you scroll them up and down. You can usually choose only one entry, although some list boxes let you choose more.

Forms also include buttons that determine what happens to the information you enter on the form. Most forms have two of these buttons: one that clears the form fields to their initial state and sends nothing, and one, usually known as the *Submit* button, that sends the filled-out form back to the web server for processing.

Some pages have *Search bars,* which are one-line forms that let you type some text for which to search. Depending on the browser, a Submit button may be displayed to the right of the text area, or you may simply press Enter to send the search words to the server. For example, the Google search page at www.google.com has a box in which you type a word or phrase; when you press Enter or click the Google Search button, the search begins. (See Chapter 13 to find out what happens!)

Your browser can keep a secret

When you fill out a form on a web page, you may need to provide information that you prefer to keep private — your credit card number, for example. Not to worry! Browsers can *encrypt* the information you send to and receive from a *secure web server.* You can tell when a page was received encrypted from the web server by the little padlock icon at one end of the Address bar or in the lower-right corner of the browser window. If the padlock doesn't appear, the page wasn't encrypted.

Typed-in data in forms on secure pages are almost always sent encrypted, making it impossible for anyone to snoop on your secrets as they traverse the Net. Encrypted pages are

nice, but in practice, it's unlikely that anyone is snooping on your web session anyway, encrypted or otherwise. The real security problems are elsewhere (refer to Chapter 2).

Some browsers have the habit of popping up little boxes to warn you about the dangers of what you're about to do. They display a box when you're about to switch from encrypted to non-encrypted (or back again) transmissions. Most of these warning boxes include a check box you can select to tell the program not to bother you with this type of warning again. After you read the warning, select the check box so that your browser stops nagging you.

Your browser can remember the entries, such as your name and address, that you frequently type into web page forms. As you type, your browser may try to spot entries you made earlier and suggest the rest of the entry so that you don't have to type it. If a suggestion pops up from your browser as you're filling in a form, you can click the suggestion to accept it. If you don't like the suggestion, just keep typing.

Knowing Where to Start

When you run your browser, it displays your *start page.* Unfortunately, the people who make browsers usually don't pick pages that we particularly like. Why not tell your browser to start where *you* want to start? You may want to start at the Yahoo! page (www.yahoo.com), which we describe in Chapter 6; or Google (www.google.com); or Wikipedia (http://en.wikipedia.org for the English language encyclopedia); or the home page of your local newspaper. You can even start with more than one page by setting multiple start pages, and your browser can open each one in a separate tab.

 You can also specify a separate *home page,* which is the page you see if you click the Home icon in your browser. Where's the Home icon? Firefox and IE display the Home icon automatically, and we tell you how to display one in Chrome and Safari in the following sections.

The following sections show you how to set both your start page and your home page. Most people set them to the same page (or pages) anyway.

Specifying where Firefox starts

Display the page that you want to use as your start page and home page, and then follow these steps:

1. **Click the Firefox button in the upper-left corner, and choose Options.**

   You see the Options dialog box, shown in Figure 7-8.

Figure 7-8:
In the Options dialog box in Firefox, you can set your favorite website as your start page.

2. **Click the General icon, if it isn't already selected.**

   This icon may already be selected, and its settings appear in the rest of the Options dialog box. The settings you're concerned with are in the Startup section.

3. **Set the When Firefox Starts option.**

   You can choose Show My Home Page (you set your home page in the next step), Show a Blank Page (make Firefox start faster), or Show My Windows and Tabs from Last Time.

Chapter 7: Taking Your Browser for a Spin *121*

4. **Set your home page(s) to the current page(s) by clicking (you guessed it!) the Use Current Pages button.**

5. **Click OK.**

You can set Firefox to display a bunch of pages when it starts up, each on its own, separate tab. For example, you might want to have Firefox open a weather-reporting page, such as Weather Underground (www.wunder-ground.com), the *New York Times* (www.nytimes.com), or even a silly page (such as http://cuteoverload.com) every time you start Firefox. First display the web pages you want to start with. Then follow the preceding instructions to make the entire set of tabs open when you start Firefox.

Configuring Internet Explorer start and home pages

Display the page that you want to use as your start page and home page, and then follow these steps:

1. **Click the Tools icon above the upper-right corner of the web page and choose Internet Options from the menu that appears.**

   You see the Internet Options dialog box.

2. **Click the General tab, along the top of the dialog box.**

   It's probably already selected, but we say this in case you've been looking around at what's on the other tabs.

3. **In the Home Page section, click the Use Current button.**

   The URL of the current page appears in the Address text box. To start with no page, click the Use Blank button.

4. **Click OK.**

Telling Chrome what to display at start-up

Display the page that you want to use as your home page, and then follow these steps:

1. **Click in the Address bar and press Ctrl+C to copy the URL to your Clipboard.**

   You need to paste the address to set your home page. We consider this step to be dim design, and we're hoping that by the time you read this section, the Chrome home page setup has been improved.

2. **Click the Customize and Control wrench icon above the upper-right corner of the web page and choose Options from the menu that appears.**

   You see the Options page in a new tab. (It isn't a web page, but it looks like one.)

3. **In the On Startup section, choose Open the Home Page, Reopen the Pages That Were Open Last, or Open the Following Pages.**

   If you choose the last option, you can click Use Current Pages to set the current page as your start page (or one of several start pages, using tabs).

4. **Set your home page to the current page by choosing Open This Page (in the Home Page section), clicking in the box to its right, and pressing Ctrl+V to paste the URL from Step 1 into this box.**

   Wouldn't you think that Chrome would have a Use Current button here? (Strange.)

5. **Tell Chrome to display a Home icon, if you want one.**

   If the Home icon doesn't appear on the Chrome toolbar, you can tell Chrome to display it by selecting the Show Home Button check box so that it contains a check mark.

6. **Click Close.**

You might consider setting your home page so that it's the New Tab page (as Chrome refers to it), shown in Figure 7-9. This page is pretty cool, actually — Chrome displays a bunch of tiny pages, like thumbnail pictures of the pages, each with a title, showing the pages you've visited most often. It also shows bookmarks you've recently used and pages you've recently closed. Very useful! It's the home page we use.

Figure 7-9:
The New Tab page in Chrome tells you what you visit most often and what you've seen recently.

Setting Safari's home page

Display the page that you want to use as your start page and home page, and then follow these steps:

1. **Click the Settings icon above the upper-right corner of the web page and choose Preferences. On a Mac, choose Safari⇨Preferences.**

   You see the General dialog box.

2. **Set the New Windows Open With option to Home Page.**

3. **Click the Close button in the upper-right corner of the window.**

You can tell Safari to display the Home icon by clicking the Settings icon above the upper-right corner of the web page, choosing Customize Toolbar, and dragging the Home icon to your Safari toolbar. (For example, you can drag it to between the Address bar and the Tools icon.)

Safari has a cool Top Picks page, which shows the web pages you view most frequently. You can tell Safari to display it whenever you open a new tab or window by setting to Top Sites the New Windows Open With or the New Tabs Open With options (or both). It's similar to Chrome's New Tab page (refer to Figure 7-9).

Who Can Remember All Those Passwords?

We certainly can't remember all our passwords. Many websites ask you to enter a username and password. If you're buying an item from an online store such as Amazon (www.amazon.com), you create an account with a username and password that you enter every time you want to buy something. Amazon.com remembers your name, address, and credit card information as part of your account, so you don't need to enter it every time. If you want to read the *New York Times* online at www.nytimes.com, you create an account with a password, too. The account remembers what kinds of news you're interested in reading. After you use the web for a while, you pile up a heap of usernames and passwords.

See Chapter 2 for advice on choosing passwords and keeping track of them safely.

Browsers offer to remember your usernames and passwords for you. Using this feature can be dangerous if other people use your computer or if you use a computer in a public place, such as a library or an Internet café. But if you're the only person who uses your computer, you may want to let your browser do the work of remembering some, if not all, of your usernames and passwords.

When a web page asks for a username and password, your browser may pop up a little window that offers to remember the username and password you enter, or the question may appear just above the top edge of the web page. If you click Yes, the next time you arrive at the same page, your browser may fill in your username and password for you.

Depending on who else has access to your computer, you might let your browser remember only passwords to accounts that don't involve spending money or revealing personal information. For example, if we have an account at a Harry Potter fan site that enables us to participate in online discussions, the danger of having someone break into this account is a lot less daunting than the thought of someone hacking into an online bank account. Unless your computer is in a physically secure place, don't let your browser remember passwords that have any real power.

Storing passwords in Firefox

You can control whether and how your browser stores these passwords. In Firefox, follow these steps:

1. **Choose Firefox⇨Options.**

   You see the Options dialog box, with a list of the categories of options across the top (refer to Figure 7-8).

2. **Click the Security icon and look in the Passwords section.**

3. **Set the Remember Passwords for Sites check box.**

   Click the box to clear the check mark if you want to turn off this feature (or click the box again to turn it back on).

4. **If you want to see the list of usernames that Firefox has saved, click the Saved Passwords button.**

   You can review or delete usernames that Firefox is remembering for you. You can even see the passwords by clicking the Show Password button. (And so can anyone else with access to your computer!) Click Close when you're done.

5. **Select the Use a Master Password check box to set a master password that you need to type only once, at the beginning of every Firefox session.**

   This option reduces the number of passwords you need to remember while maintaining some security.

6. **Click OK to close the Options dialog box.**

Storing passwords in IE

In Internet Explorer, remembering usernames and passwords is the job of the AutoComplete feature, which you set up by following these simple steps:

1. **Click the Tools icon, choose Internet Options, and click the Content tab.**

   You see the Content tab in the Internet Options dialog box.

2. **In the AutoComplete section, click the Settings button.**

   You see the AutoComplete Settings dialog box.

3. **Select the check boxes to control which kinds of entries IE stores.**

   IE doesn't show you a list of the passwords you saved, but you can turn the feature on and off by selecting the Ask Me Before Saving Passwords check box. The User Names and Passwords On Forms check box controls whether IE fills in your stored passwords on forms.

4. **Click OK to close the AutoComplete Settings dialog box, and click OK again to close the Internet Options dialog box.**

Storing passwords in Chrome

The Chrome settings for remembering passwords are more like those in Firefox. Follow these steps:

1. **Click the Customize and Control wrench icon and choose Options from the menu that appears.**

   You see the Options page on a new tab.

2. **Click the Personal Stuff link.**

3. **In the Passwords section, click Offer to Save Passwords or Never Save Passwords.**

    It's your choice, depending on whether you trust the other people who use your computer.

4. **If you want to review the passwords that Chrome has already saved, click Manage Saved Passwords.**

    You see web addresses and the usernames, and you can remove any you don't want saved by clicking the X to its right. To display a password, click the dots that represent it and click Show. Click Close when you're done.

5. **Click Close.**

Storing passwords in Safari

Same old, same old — Safari works similarly to other browsers. Follow these steps:

1. **Click the Setting icon and choose Preferences (Safari⇨Preferences on a Mac).**

2. **Click the AutoFill icon.**

    These settings control which personal information Safari stores and then supplies on web page forms.

3. **Click the User Names and Passwords check box if you want Safari to remember these items.**

4. **To see and edit the usernames and passwords that Safari has stored, click the Edit button to the right of the User Names and Passwords check box.**

5. **Click the Close button in the upper-right corner of the window.**

Cookies Are (Usually) Your Friends

To enhance your online experience, browser makers invented a type of special message, known as a *cookie,* that lets a website recognize you when you revisit that site. They thoughtfully store this info on your very own machine. See Chapter 2 for a full description of cookies and how they compare to more serious security threats. You can control which sites can store cookies on your computer.

Usually, the website that sets a cookie is the only one that reads the cookie. However, *third-party* cookies can be set by one website and read by another. Third-party cookies are used by servers that deliver advertisements and those annoying pop-up and pop-under ads. We recommend that you accept most cookies but block third-party cookies.

Burning cookies in Firefox

Choose Firefox⇨Options, click the Privacy icon, and look in the History section. If Remember History is selected, Firefox stores cookies. If you want more control over which cookies it stores, change it to Use Custom Settings for History. This setting displays these cookie-related check boxes:

- ✔ **Accept Cookies from Sites:** We recommend that you leave this one selected.
- ✔ **Accept Third-Party Cookies:** Click this one to remove its check mark.

You can specify which sites can and cannot store cookies by clicking the Exceptions button. You can enter the web addresses that you definitely trust with your cookies (such as the shopping sites you frequent) or that you don't trust (such as advertising sites).

You can take a look at the cookies on your computer, too. Click the Show Cookies button and scroll down the list of sites. If you see one that you don't recognize or that sounds suspicious, click it and click the Remove Cookie button.

Exploring cookies in Internet Explorer

Click the Tools icon, choose Internet Options, and click the Privacy tab on the Internet Options dialog box that appears. IE displays a slider that you can drag up and down to increase or decrease your level of privacy. By default, Internet Explorer sets your privacy level to Medium, allowing cookies except for third-party cookies. If you want to specify exactly how cookies are saved, click the Advanced button to see the Advanced Privacy Settings dialog box and then select the Override Automatic Cookie Handling check box. The options are

- ✔ **First-Party Cookies:** You can choose to accept or to block or to be prompted to choose, though this option grows tiresome quickly if you encounter a lot of cookies. Some sites can store three or more cookies *per page*. Choose Accept.

- **Third-Party Cookies:** Just say no to (that is, choose Block) third-party cookies.

- **Always Allow Session Cookies:** This check box lets through all *session* cookies, a type of cookie used to track a single instance of your visit to a website. These cookies are commonly used by shopping sites such as Amazon.com and are harmless. Select this option so that it contains a check mark.

Cookies and Chrome

 Click the Customize and Control wrench icon, choose Options from the menu, and click the Under the Hood tab on the Options page that appears. In the Privacy section, click the Content Settings button to display the Content Settings dialog box. In the Cookies section, select the setting labeled Allow Local Data to Be Set. (In our humble opinion, it's your best bet.)

Safari with cookies

 In Safari, click the Settings icon, choose Preferences, and click the Security icon in the window that appears. Set the Accept Cookies option to Only from Sites That I Visit.

Where Have You Been?

Browsers keep a *history list* of the websites you've been to. No, your browser isn't spying on you; the history list remembers pages you went to earlier, even days ago, so that you can find them again.

Your browsing history

You can see your history list, and you can return to any page on it by clicking it. Here's how:

- **Firefox:** Click Firefox⇨History to display the Library window with the History list selected. You can also press Ctrl+H to display the list down the left side of your browser window, arranged by day. Close the History list by clicking the X in its upper-right corner.

- ✔ **Internet Explorer:** Click the Favorites icon, click the History tab on the menu that appears, and then click a day (for example, Today).

- ✔ **Chrome:** Click and hold the Back button (or right-click it) to see a list of the pages you've been to recently. Or, click and hold and then choose Show Full History from the bottom of the menu. You see a new tab with a list of web pages by day, with the time you viewed each page.

- ✔ **Safari:** Click the Settings icon and choose History (or press Ctrl+H) to see the History tab (refer to Figure 7-6).

Oh, nowhere, really

Some of our readers have asked us how to clear out their browsing, presumably because they meant to type www.disney.com but their fingers slipped and it came out www.mega-xxx-babes.com instead. (It could happen to anyone.)

If you're using someone else's computer, and especially if you're using a public computer in a library or Internet café, you should delete your browsing history and any other information about your session that might be stored on the computer. Otherwise, the next person to sit down at the computer might find your browsing history rather interesting, especially if the browser has thoughtfully stored the usernames and password you entered.

Whether you, um, mistyped web addresses or you don't want to leave your personal information on someone else's computer, follow these procedures:

- ✔ **Firefox:** Choose Firefox⇨Options and click the Clear Your Recent History link. Choose how far back to forget and click Clear Now.

- ✔ **Internet Explorer:** Click the Tools icon, choose Safety, and choose Delete Browsing History from the menu that appears. (Hmm, it's right at the top. There must be a lot of sloppy typists out there.) In the Delete Browsing History dialog box, decide which information to clear (by selecting check boxes), and click Delete.

- ✔ **Chrome:** Press Ctrl+H to display the History tab and click the Edit Items link in the upper-right corner. Click Clear All Browsing Data, or click the check boxes next to the web pages that you inadvertently or accidentally visited and click Remove Selected Items.

- ✔ **Safari:** Press Ctrl+H to see the History tab. The pages you visited are arranged by day; click a day to see the pages you viewed. To remove one page from the list, right-click it and choose Delete.

Some browsers let you browse in a kind of "stealth mode," which leaves no trace:

- ✔ **Firefox:** Choose Firefox⇨Start Private Browsing.
- ✔ **IE:** Click the Tools icon, choose Safety, and choose InPrivate Browsing.
- ✔ **Chrome:** You can browse incognito. (Don't forget your trench coat and fedora.) Click the Customize and Control icon and choose New Incognito Window. Or, you can right-click any link or bookmark and choose Open Link in Incognito Window.

- ✔ **Safari:** Click the Settings icon, choose Private Browsing, and click OK.

Blocking Pop-Up Windows

Pop-up windows, as described in Chapter 2, are browser windows that open without your asking for them, usually at the command of the website you're viewing. Some websites display so many pop-ups that your computer becomes unusable until you can close them all. If you've encountered these sites, you'll be glad to hear that your browser can block most (though not all) pop-up windows.

No pop-ups in Firefox

Choose Firefox⇨Options to open the Options window, click the Content icon, and you see the Block Pop-up Windows check box. We leave it selected.

Blocking all pop-ups makes a few websites stop working. In particular, some shopping sites pop up small windows in which you have to type credit card verification information. Online help sometimes appears in pop-ups, too. Firefox thoughtfully includes an Exceptions button that lets you specify websites whose pop-ups are okay with you.

When a website tries to display a pop-up, you see at the top of the web page a message saying "Firefox prevented this site from opening a popup window." Click the Options button and choose from the menu that appears:

- ✔ **Allow Popups from *Sitename*** puts this site on your Allowed list.
- ✔ **Enable Popup Blocker Options** displays the Allowed Sites dialog box so that you can edit your list of sites.
- ✔ **Don't Show This Message When Popups Are Blocked** continues to block pop-ups, without asking each time it blocks one.

Click the red X at the right end of the message to make the message go away.

Blocking pop-ups in Internet Explorer

Microsoft finally added a pop-up blocker in response to the growing popularity of Firefox. Click the Tools icon, choose Internet Options to display the Internet Options dialog box, click the Privacy tab, and click the Turn On Pop-Up Blocker check box to turn this feature off or back on. (We leave the check box selected.) You can tell IE to allow pop-ups from specific sites by clicking the Settings button and adding web addresses to a list.

The IE pop-up blocker displays a "Pop-up blocked" message at the top of the web page whenever it blocks a pop-up window, and clicking the message displays a similar set of options.

Chrome and pop-ups

Chrome includes a pop-up blocker, too. When Chrome blocks a pop-up, you see a message in the lower-right corner of the browser window. You can either click the message and choose the first option (the exact address of the pop-up) to display it or choose Always Allow Popups to allow pop-ups from the site. To set up Chrome to block all pop-ups, follow these steps:

1. **Click the Customize and Control icon and choose Options.**

2. **Click Under the Hood in the left-hand column.**

3. **Click the Content Settings button in the Privacy section at the top of the page and scroll down to the Pop-ups section.**

4. **Select the Do Not Allow Any Site to Show Pop-ups check box. Click the Manage Exceptions button to allow specific websites to display pop-ups.**

Safari stops pop-ups

In Safari, click the Settings icon and choose Block Pop-Up Windows from the menu that appears to turn the pop-up blocker on or off.

When Browsers Go Bad

If your browser looks odd, try these tricks:

- ✔ **If the web page looks garbled,** click the Reload or Refresh icon (the circular arrow) to load the page again. Maybe it was damaged during its arduous trek across the Net.

- ✔ **If the whole top of the window is gone** — you have no window title bar or menu bar — you're in Full Screen mode. Press F11 to return to normal.

- ✔ **If the browser restarted and is telling you which fabulous new features it now has,** it probably just downloaded an updated version of the program and had to restart itself to complete the installation. Read the message appreciatively and then close the tab or window.

- ✔ **If your browser is just acting weird,** close all your browser windows, take a few deep breaths, and run your browser again. If the situation is ugly, try restarting the computer. (Save any unsaved work first.)

- ✔ **If your browser, particularly IE, still looks strange,** especially if it's showing a lot of ads that you didn't ask for, your computer is probably infected with spyware. See Chapter 2 for a definition of spyware, and see the section in Chapter 4 about detecting spyware for advice on getting rid of it.

Getting Plugged In with Plug-Ins

Web pages with text and pictures are old hat. Now web pages must have pictures that sing and dance or calendars that let you create events or games such as chess that play against you. Every month, new types of information appear on the web, and browsers have to keep up. You can extend your browser's capabilities with *plug-ins* — add-on programs that glue themselves to the browser and add even more features. Internet Explorer can also extend itself by using *ActiveX* controls, which are another (less secure) type of add-on program.

What are you to do when your browser encounters new kinds of information on a web page? Get the plug-in program that handles that kind of information and glue it to the browser program. *Star Trek* fans can think of plug-ins as parasitic life forms that attach themselves to your browser and enhance its intelligence.

When you restart your browser, maybe because it updated itself, it may display messages about add-ons that are installed or that need to be updated. You can display a list of your plug-ins at any time:

- **Firefox:** Choose Firefox⇨Add-ons to see a page about all kinds of add-ons and extensions. Click the Plugins tab to see a list of which ones are installed. You can click the More link for more information and click the Disable button if you don't want to keep the plug-in.

- **IE:** Choose Tools⇨Internet Options, click the Programs tab, and click Manage Add-ons. To disable a plug-in, select it and click the Disable button at the bottom of the Manage Add-ons dialog box.

- **Chrome:** Click the Customize and Control icon, choose Options, click Under the Hood, click the Content Settings button in the Privacy section at the top of the page, scroll down to the Plug-ins section, and click the Manage Exceptions button. If you don't like the look of a plug-in, point your mouse at it on the list, and click the X to delete it.

- **Safari:** On the Mac, you can choose Help⇨Installed Plug-Ins.

Three essential plug-ins

Here are three useful plug-ins you may want to add to your browser:

- **Flash Player:** Plays both audio and video files in addition to other types of animations. Widely used on web pages, it's available at www.adobe. com/products/flashplayer. Using Flash, you can view videos on YouTube (see Chapter 14). Flash can also play *streaming* sound and video files while you download them. Our favorite site with streaming audio is the National Public Radio website (www.npr.org), where you can hear recent NPR radio stories. Another favorite is the BBC at www. bbc.co.uk, with news in 43 languages (really) and other BBC programs 24 hours a day.

- **QuickTime:** Plays videos in a number of formats. Download it from www. apple.com/quicktime/download.

- **Adobe Acrobat:** Displays Acrobat files formatted exactly the way the author intended. Lots of useful Acrobat files are out there, including many U.S. tax forms (at www.irs.gov). You can find Acrobat at http://get.adobe.com/reader.

How to use plug-ins

After you download a plug-in from the web, run it (double-click its icon or filename) to install it. Depending on what the plug-in does, you follow different steps to try it out — usually, you find a file that the plug-in can play and watch (or listen) as the plug-in plays it.

After you install the plug-in, you don't have to do anything to run it. It fires up automatically whenever you view a web page containing information that requires the plug-in.

Plug-ins, particularly Flash and Acrobat, are subject to security problems, and they often aren't automatically updated by Windows Update or Apple's Software Update. Drop by the Flash and Acrobat websites from time to time to see whether they have new versions. Visit www.adobe.com and click Downloads (at the top).

Down it comes!

Downloading means copying files from a computer Up There on the Internet "down" to the computer sitting on or under your desk. By far the easiest way to download any kind of file is by using your browser. Follow these steps:

1. **Find the file on the web.**

   Search the web for it, as described in Chapter 13.

2. **Follow the instructions on the web page to download the file.**

   This step usually just means clicking a Download button.

3. **If your browser displays a Save or Save As dialog box, choose where to put the file.**

   Put it on your desktop, where it's easy to find later. Or, put it in the folder where you want the file to end up. Or, your browser may display a Downloads window where the file appears, or the downloaded file may appear as an icon at the bottom of your browser window.

4. **Open the file with its matching program, usually by double-clicking the filename or icon.**

If you downloaded a Word document, it opens in Word or WordPad (or, maybe OpenOffice, a nice freeware office suite you can download from www.openoffice.org).

5. **If it's a program file, it runs.**

   The file should open itself and walk you through a wizard-style set of windows to collect any needed setup info — and then install itself. A box may pop up to ask whether you are an administrator to complete the installation. If you're sure that you trust the source of the program, click OK. The setup program probably creates an icon for the program on your desktop. In Windows, it may also add the program to your Start menu.

Lots of the programs that this book recommends can be downloaded from the web, often for free. But watch out! Any program can contain viruses and spyware, so don't run an executable file unless you're sure that you know what's in it! Stick with the software libraries we recommend in this book because they scan their files for viruses and spyware. And make sure that you are running a virus-scanner, as described in Chapter 4.

Part III
Hanging Out with Friends Online

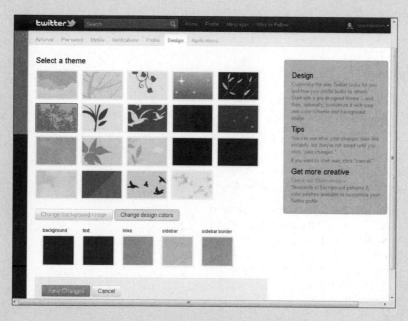

Keep in touch and up to date
with Twitter.

In this part . . .

Now we turn to the part of the Internet that only *slightly* resembles talking on the phone, because you're talking (or typing) to other people. We start with e-mail, one of the oldest but still most useful Internet services, for one-to-one conversations *and* discussions among larger e-mail communities. You'll find advice about how to use e-mail and how to stay safe from e-mail-borne spam and viruses. We finish with faster-paced modern alternatives, such as instant messages, online chat, Twitter, Internet phones (VoIP), Google+, and Facebook, the final solution to free time.

Chapter 8

It's in the Mail: Sending and Receiving E-Mail

....

....

*E*lectronic mail, or *e-mail,* is without a doubt the most popular Internet service, even though it's one of the oldest and least glitzy. Although e-mail doesn't have the flash and sparkle of the World Wide Web, more people use it. Every system on the Net supports some sort of mail service, which means that no matter what kind of computer you're using, if it's on the Internet, you can send and receive mail. Even some systems that aren't technically on the Internet — think mobile phone — can do e-mail.

Regardless of which type of mail you're using, the basic tasks of reading, sending, addressing, and filing mail work in much the same way, so skimming this chapter is worthwhile even if you're not using any of the mail programs we describe here.

Young whippersnappers are alleged to think that e-mail is for old people, and that the cool way to send messages is by using text messages on their phones, instant messaging (covered in Chapter 12), or messages within Facebook or another social networking site. However, e-mail is still *the* way that businesses communicate with each other and with customers, and that most people send messages over the Internet. Not everyone is on Facebook, LinkedIn, or whatever the new website is, but almost everyone who has ever used the Internet has an e-mail address. Don't worry: E-mail is still cool! (And anyway, nearly all those sites send you mail when someone sends you a message, so you just need to check your mail, not all umpteen websites, to see what's new.)

What's My Address?

Your *e-mail address* is the cyberspace equivalent of a postal address or a phone number. When you send an e-mail message, you type the addresses of the recipients so that the computer knows where to send it.

Before you can do much mailing, you have to figure out your e-mail address so that you can give it to people who want to get in touch with you. You also have to figure out some of their addresses so that you can write to them. (If you have no friends or plan to send only anonymous hate mail, you can skip this section.)

E-mail addresses have two parts, separated by the @ (*at*-sign). The part before the @ is the *username* or *mailbox,* which is, roughly speaking, your personal name. The part after that is the *domain.*

The domain part

The domain (the part after the @) indicates where your mailbox is stored. Mailboxes usually live in one of four places:

- ✔ **Your Internet service provider (ISP):** If you sign up for a DSL account at Verizon, the domain is `verizon.net`. If you use AOL, it's `aol.com`.

- ✔ **Your school, employer, or other organization:** If you attend Tufts University (Go, Jumbos!), the domain is `tufts.edu`. If you work for Microsoft, it's `microsoft.com`.

- ✔ **Your own domain, such as** `gurus.org`: (That's one of ours.) You can own your domain name, as described in Chapter 17. You need to arrange for your domain to live somewhere, which is probably where your mailboxes will be stored, too.

- ✔ **A web-based e-mail service, or** *webmail:* If you don't have an ISP (say, you connect from the public library), all is not lost. Years ago, some genius had the idea of creating a website where you can sign up for an e-mail account and then log in to read and send messages. Your e-mail mailbox lives on the website's mail servers, and you use your browser, rather than a regular e-mail program, to read and send messages. Many websites now provide free mailboxes — try Google Gmail at `www.gmail.com`, Windows Live Hotmail (formerly just Hotmail) at `http://mail.live.com`, Yahoo! Mail at `http://mail.yahoo.com`, or AIM Mail at `http://webmail.aol.com`. See the later section "The Web Is a Fine Place to Read Your E-Mail" to find out how to sign up for a webmail account.

Even if your ISP or employer offers mailboxes, you may want to sign up for a webmail account. Some of us prefer to separate our work-related e-mail from our personal ones. Another advantage of webmail is that if you change ISPs, your e-mail address doesn't change. When our local cable Internet company changed its domain from verizon.net to myfairpoint.com, all its customers had to let their friends know about their new e-mail addresses, and many chose to switch to webmail addresses instead.

The username part

Your *username* is the name assigned to your particular mailbox. For example, you can write to the president of the United States at president@whitehouse.gov. The president's username is president, and the domain that stores his mailbox is whitehouse.gov — reasonable enough.

If you're lucky, you get to choose your username; in other cases, ISPs standardize usernames and you get what you get. You may choose (or be assigned) your first name as your username — or your last name, your initials, your first name and last initial, your first initial and last name, or a completely made-up name. At the major webmail sites, the best 20 million or so usernames have already been taken, so you may need to get creative, by adding numbers or other information to create a username that isn't already in use.

Many organizations assign usernames in a consistent format for all users, most often by using your first and last names with a dot (.) between them or your first initial followed by the first seven letters of your last name. In these schemes, your e-mail address may resemble elvis.presley@bluesuede.org or epresley@bluesuede.org. (If your name isn't Elvis Presley, adjust this example suitably. On the other hand, if your name *is* Elvis Presley, please contact us immediately. We know some people who are looking for you.)

When you sign up with an ISP, the provider creates a mailbox for each of your usernames. Although some ISPs offer only one username per Internet account, many ISPs offer as many as five mailboxes with five different usernames for a single account so that every person in your family can have a separate mailbox.

Don't share an e-mail account with anyone else — you deserve your own. Many Internet services use your e-mail address as your account identifier, send a message to your address to confirm your identity, and assume that anyone with access to your account is you. Webmail addresses are free, so if you don't already have your own e-mail address, get one.

TIP

Whaddaya mean you don't know your own address?

It happens frequently: You know the e-mail address you requested for your new account, but you aren't absolutely positive that it was approved. Before you give out your address to everyone you know, test it out by sending a message to a friend or two. Tell them to reply to your message when they receive it and to let you know which address your message came from. Or, send yourself a message and use your

e-mail login name as the mailbox name. Then examine the return address on the message.

Better yet, send a message to *The Internet For Dummies* Mail Central, at `internet13@ gurus.org`, and a friendly robot will send back a message with your address. (While you're at it, tell us whether you like this book, because we authors read that mail and write back when time permits.)

Putting it all together

Whenever you set up a mail program, you need to enter information about your e-mail mailbox. People switch mail programs from time to time (new versions often come out with swell new features), so write in Table 8-1 your e-mail address and other info that your ISP, employer, or school or another e-mail provider gave you (and fold down the corner of this page so that you can find it again later). Capitalization never matters in domains and rarely matters in usernames. To make it easy on your eyes, therefore, most domain and mailbox names in this book are shown in lowercase. (Don't worry about the parts of the table you don't understand right away — we explain *servers* later in this chapter.)

Table 8-1   Information Your Mail Program Needs to Know

What You Supply	Description	Example
Your e-mail address	Your username followed by @ and the domain name	`internet13 @gurus.org`
Your e-mail password	The password for your e-mail mailbox (usually the same as the password for your account)	`dum3myBook`

What You Supply	Description	Example
Webmail URL	The web address where you can check your mail	`https://mail.google.com`
POP/IMAP server	Computer where your mail program picks up your mail (not for webmail)	`pop.gurus.org`
POP/IMAP account	Log in to pick up your mail, often but not always your username (not for webmail)	`Internet13` or `internet13@gurus.org`
SMTP server	Computer where your mail program sends outgoing mail (not for webmail)	`smtp.gurus.org`

And I Would Read My Mail How?

How you read and send e-mail depends on which kind of e-mail account you have:

- **Mailbox at your ISP or school or your own domain:** Most ISPs expect you to use a *mail program* to read your e-mail — a program that displays incoming messages and allows you to send messages. You can use any of a long list of mail programs, including Thunderbird, Outlook, Windows Mail, or Apple Mail, as well as mail programs on your smartphone. We talk about the most popular mail programs in the rest of this chapter. Most of these providers also have webmail options; see the next section.

- **Corporate account:** If you use e-mail at work, your organization may use a different type of mail server: Microsoft Exchange. In addition to providing mail services, Exchange also provides shared calendars, to-do lists, and other nifty features. The most popular program that works with all Exchange features is Microsoft Outlook, so your organization probably insists that you use it, despite its security flaws. To read about Outlook, see *Outlook 2010 For Dummies* (John Wiley & Sons, Inc.). Exchange provides a web-based system, too; see the next section. Check with your organization's information technology support group if you have trouble setting up your e-mail.

- ✔ **AOL:** If you have an AOL account, you get as many as seven mailboxes as part of the AOL service. You have three options for using AOL mail:

  - *The AOL e-mail program:* An all-in-one program provided by AOL, mostly used by people who use AOL for their basic Internet connections.

  - *Another mail program:* You can use almost any Windows or Mac mail program. We recommend that you use Thunderbird, which we describe later in this chapter.

  - *Your web browser:* Webmail at the AOL website `www.aol.com`. You can use any web browser from any computer. See the next section.

- ✔ **Webmail:** The whole point of webmail is that you can read it on (drumroll, please) the web. Any web browser will do, as described in the next section.

See also the section "Reading Your E-mail on Your Smartphone," later in this chapter.

The Web Is a Fine Place to Read Your E-Mail

No matter which type of e-mail account you have, even if you normally use an e-mail program such as Thunderbird or Outlook to read your messages, your mailbox provider most likely has a web-based mail system. On a webmail system, you can read your mail from any computer on the Internet, including computers at your friends' houses, at public libraries, and at Internet cafés. For example, if you have a cable Internet account with Fairpoint, you can use its website to read and send messages at any computer on the Net; go to `http://myfairpoint.net` and click the Email link.

To find out whether your ISP provides webmail, go to its website and look around or write to its support e-mail address. Most ISPs have a Mail or similar link on their home pages. You log in with the same account name and password that you may have jotted down in Table 8-1.

A cool thing about webmail systems such as AIM Mail, Gmail, Hotmail, and Yahoo! Mail is that you can read and send messages from any computer on the Net. Your mailbox is stored on the webmail server, and any computer with a browser can access it — you can check your mail from a friend's computer, at a cybercafé, or from the computer at the public library. Of course, no one should be able to read your messages, or send messages as you, without typing your password. One downside is that reading and sending messages tends to be slower with webmail than with an e-mail program because you have to wait for a new web page to open every time you click a new message.

If you use a computer on a wireless connection, particularly a connection without a password (see Chapter 5), people who are not your friends can snoop on your session. Fortunately, most webmail systems offer *https* sessions, which are encrypted so that snoops see only undecipherable noise. Start the web address with *https://,* as in `https://gmail.com`, and look for the Lock icon next to the address before logging in.

Setting up a webmail account

If you don't have a webmail account and you want one, follow these steps:

1. **Using your web browser, go to the webmail service's website.**

   Try AIM Mail at `http://webmail.aol.com`, Google Gmail at `www.gmail.com`, Windows Live Hotmail at `http://mail.live.com`, or Yahoo! Mail at `http://mail.yahoo.com`. See Chapter 6 for help starting your web browser.

2. **Look for a link named Click Here to Get a Free E-Mail Account or Create Account or a link with similar wording and follow the instructions to create your account.**

   They don't ask anything too nosy. Be sure to click the links to read the *terms of service* (rules of the game) and *privacy policy* (what they plan to do with the information you give them).

3. **In Table 8-1, write down your e-mail address and your password.**

   Your e-mail address ends in `@aim.com`, `@gmail.com`, `@hotmail.com`, `@live.com`, or `@yahoo.com`, depending on which service you choose.

You'll end up with a username and password that you can use for other services provided by these websites. You're ready!

Reading webmail

You can read webmail — where else? — on the web, whether your mailbox is at a webmail site listed in the previous section or is hosted by your ISP. Almost every ISP has a website where you can read your mail.

To access your webmail mailbox, go to the website and log in:

1. **Go to the same website where you created your account.**

   If you created a webmail mailbox at AIM Mail (`http://webmail.aol.com`), Google Gmail (`www.gmail.com`), Windows Live Hotmail (`http://mail.live.com`), or Yahoo! Mail (`http://mail.yahoo.com`), log in at that website. If your mailbox is provided by your ISP, employer, or school or another organization, go to its website.

2. **Sign in with your new username and password.**

    You see a web page that may have ads and news and all kinds of other information, but somewhere is an Inbox link or another link for reading and sending mail. For example, Figure 8-1 shows the part of the Comcast home page where you can log in to myComcast to read your mail.

Figure 8-1:
Somewhere on your ISP's home page is probably a place to log in and read your e-mail.

3. **Click the Inbox or another mail-related link.**

    You see your inbox, which might look something like Figure 8-2. You may not have any e-mail yet, or you may have a welcome message from the webmail service. If so, you see the sender and subject line of the message.

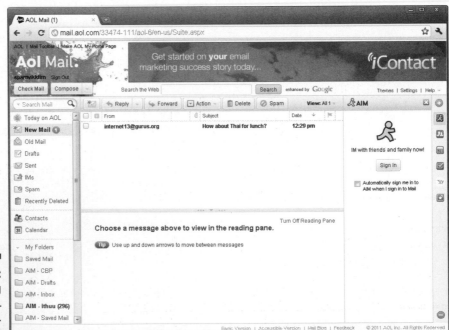

Figure 8-2:
Reading mail in AOL Mail.

4. **Click the message to read it.**

   Then you can click the Reply, Forward, or Delete button or link to deal with the message.

Sending e-mail with webmail

To send an e-mail message using webmail, follow these steps:

1. **Sign in.**

   See Steps 1 and 2 in the previous section to find out *where* to sign in.

2. **Click the Compose button or New button or any link that seems to be about writing and sending a message.**

   Your browser displays a form with boxes for To (the address) and Subject and a large, unlabeled box for the text of the message, as shown in Figure 8-3.

3. **Type one or more addresses in the To box.**

   If you want to send your message to more than one address, separate every address with a comma.

4. **If you see a Cc box, you can enter addresses there, too.**

   The Cc (carbon *copy*, for you historians) is for people to whom the message isn't directly addressed but who might want to be aware of your message.

Figure 8-3:
Sending
mail from
Yahoo! Mail.

5. **Type a subject line in the Subject box.**

6. **Type your message in the big box.**

7. **Click the Send button.**

   If you want to check your spelling first, which is the polite thing to do, look for a Spelling button or Spell Check button to click before clicking Send.

That's all it takes!

Be sure to log out from the webmail site when you're done reading and sending mail, especially if you're using a friend's computer or a computer in a public place. Otherwise, someone else can come along and read or send messages using your account.

Reading Your E-Mail on Your Smartphone

Regular old cellphones can't send or receive e-mail, but so-called *smartphones* can. (To find out what a smartphone is, see the section in Chapter 4 about getting a little Android, BlackBerry, Phone, or Windows phone.) Here are some tips for reading and sending mail depending on which kind of smartphone you have:

- **Android phones:** Phones that run Android software come with one e-mail program for Gmail and one for POP accounts. Use the web browser to read webmail. Otherwise, configure Android to read and send e-mail by choosing Menu, and then Accounts, and then Menu⇨Add Account. Enter your e-mail address and password.

- **BlackBerry:** You get an e-mail address at BlackBerry.com when you set up your phone. Ask your phone store to help.

- **iPhone:** An iPhone can read and send mail from one or several accounts. Choose Settings⇨Mail Contacts Calendars⇨Add Account. You see a list of popular mail providers, including AOL, Gmail, Microsoft Exchange (used by many corporations and other organizations), and Yahoo! Mail. If your mail is somewhere else, choose Other⇨Add Mail Account and enter your name, e-mail address, e-mail password, and a name for the account. Click Save. Choose IMAP or POP, fill in the names of your incoming (IMAP or POP) and outgoing (SMTP) mail servers, and click Save.

✔ **Windows Mobile phones:** If your phone runs Windows Mobile (a teeny-tiny, slow version of Windows), you can read and send e-mail from one or more accounts. Press the Start button and choose Messaging to start the e-mail program. To set up a new account, press Menu, choose Tools➪New Account, enter your e-mail address, and follow the instructions on the screen.

If you see an option similar to Leave Messages on Server, we recommend that you select it. If you have a choice between POP and IMAP as the account type, choose IMAP. (These two types of mail servers are described in the next section of this chapter.) Although checking e-mail on a phone is cool, you *also* want to be able to check it on your computer!

If you don't have a smartphone, you aren't necessarily out of luck. Other service providers (such as US Cellular) offer proprietary web browsers that are capable of retrieving webmail. Check with your cellphone provider.

Reading Your E-Mail in a Mail Program

Although reading your mail on the web is convenient, it's usually slower than using a *real* mail program. Mail programs have more features than many webmail sites, too. Many mail programs are available. Many businesses and other organizations use Outlook, which comes with Microsoft Office. Our favorite free mail program is Thunderbird, from the same people who make Firefox, an excellent free web browser.

If you want to use a mail program (we do!), you need to figure out which mail servers it uses for sending and receiving mail, choose a program (download it if you don't already have it), and set it up. This section walks you through the process.

When your computer is on a public wireless connection, people who are not your friends can snoop on your session. (See Chapter 2.) Fortunately, most mail systems can encrypt the traffic between the program and the server by using the same technology as `https` web sessions. When setting up your mail, look for TLS or SSL options (they do the same thing, with minor technical differences you don't care about) for the outgoing and incoming servers.

Webmail and mail programs, together at last

You can use a mail program (such as Thunderbird or Outlook) with most webmail systems. If you have a mail program you like, you can use it to read mail at home and read the webmail when you're elsewhere:

- **AOL** provides an IMAP server (imap.aol.com), a POP server (pop.aol.com), and an SMTP server (smtp.aol.com). Use your AOL or AIM username and password to connect.

- **Gmail** (at gmail.com) provides IMAP (imap.gmail.com), POP (pop.gmail.com), and SMTP (smtp.gmail.com) servers for all its users. You enable them by clicking Settings at the top of any Gmail page, clicking Forwarding and POP/IMAP, and clicking either Enable POP or Enable IMAP. If you use IMAP, your entire e-mail address (including @gmail.com) is your username and you choose SSL as the connection type. For your outgoing mail, change the port for the SMTP server from 25 to 587 and choose TLS as the connection type.

- **Windows Live Hotmail** (at http://hotmail.com or http://mail.live.com) provides a POP server (pop3.live.com, TLS/SSL security required) and an SMTP server (smtp.live.com). Your entire address is your username. If you use Outlook, you can download the Microsoft Office Outlook Connector to read your Hotmail mail from Outlook. (From http://microsoft.com/downloads, search for *Microsoft Office Outlook Connector*.)

- **Yahoo! Mail** (at http://mail.yahoo.com) provides only webmail for basic free accounts. If you sign up for its premium Yahoo! Plus service at $20 per year, it also provides IMAP (imap.mail.yahoo.com — be sure to select SSL or TLS), POP (pop.mail.yahoo.com), and SMTP (smtp.mail.yahoo.com — also be sure to select TLS).

Mail servers galore

If you use a mail program to read your e-mail, one option you have to specify in your mail program is the *incoming mail server,* which holds your mail until your mail program picks it up. (Webmail users can skim this section.)

The usual way to pick up mail is known as *POP* (Post Office Protocol, sometimes also written as *POP3* because it's version 3). All ISPs offer POP as the standard way to receive your mail. To send mail, your mail program reverses the process and sends messages to your *outgoing mail server* (or *SMTP server,* for the badly misnamed Simple Mail Transfer Protocol).

Write the names of your incoming (POP or IMAP) and outgoing (SMTP) mail servers in Table 8-1. If you don't know what to write, ask your ISP or whichever organization hosts your e-mail mailbox. With luck, your mail program has the server names set automatically, but when the setup gets screwed up, you'll be glad that you know how to restore its settings.

Which mail program do you like?

You can easily make a specific e-mail program do what you want — after all, dealing with mail is what these programs are for. Popular e-mail programs include:

- **Outlook:** Organizations use Outlook, which comes with most editions of Microsoft Office (but not the Home and Student Suite, as of 2011). It's helpful in organizations because it connects to Microsoft Exchange servers and provides e-mail, shared calendars, and other features that are useful in offices. See *Outlook 2010 For Dummies,* by Bill Dyszel (John Wiley & Sons, Inc.).

- **Thunderbird:** This mail program comes from the people who created Firefox, the web browser we describe in Chapter 7. It works with regular Internet accounts as well as with AOL accounts and some web-mail accounts. You can download Thunderbird from `www.mozilla messaging.com/thunderbird`.

- **Windows Live Mail:** Windows Live Mail is part of Windows Live Essentials (see the sidebar of that name, earlier in this chapter).

- **Apple Mail:** Mac OS/X comes with the creatively named Apple Mail. It's not bad, and has the advantage of already being there on your Mac. If your mail system uses Microsoft Exchange, it's one of the few alternatives to Outlook.

Before you can use your mail program, you need to tell it two things:

- **Where your mailbox is stored:** Usually on a POP server or an IMAP server at your ISP

- **Where to send outgoing mail:** Usually to the same or another mail server at your ISP

Follow the instructions in the following sections to get your mail program up and running. Later sections describe how to send and receive mail with each program.

IMAP: Mail anywhere and everywhere

When you use POP to pick up your mail, the messages are downloaded to your PC and stored there and are deleted from your mailbox on the mail server. If, like most people, you build up large files of saved messages, the saved messages are on your PC and accessible only from your mail program on that PC. Often, that's good enough, but if you read your mail in more than one place (say, at home and at work), it can be a pain if you're one place and the saved message with a crucial work-related item (a recipe for Killer Tequila Nachos, for example) is in the other. IMAP solves this problem by storing all your mail on a mail server so that you can access it from any mail program, and you have the same set of mailboxes no matter which computer you use. Many mail systems offer both IMAP and webmail, in which case you see the same mail in your mail program as you see in the webmail.

To use IMAP, you need a broadband connection at each place you read your mail, because IMAP is unusably slow on dialup. Because all your mail folders are on your ISP's computer, see how much mail you're allowed to store there because folders can get pretty big. One or 2 megabytes is tight, whereas 100 megabytes should be plenty unless you mail around a lot of video files.

Setting up Outlook

Outlook comes with most editions of Microsoft Office. If you're using Outlook at your office, check with your information technology support folks to set up Outlook. To tell Outlook about your e-mail account, follow these steps:

1. **Choose File⇨Info⇨Account Settings⇨Account Settings (Outlook 2010) or Tools⇨E-mail Accounts (in Outlook 2007).**

   You see a series of dialog boxes asking you about your account.

2. **Under E-mail, choose New (in Outlook 2010) or Add a New E-mail Account (in Outlook 2007) and click Next.**

3. **Choose the type of e-mail account.**

4. **Fill in your name, your e-mail address, and the server names from Table 8-1.**

5. **Click Next and Finish.**

Outlook now retrieves any messages and displays them in your Inbox folder.

Setting up Thunderbird

The Mozilla Foundation, which creates free, open source software, has written Thunderbird to complement its excellent Firefox browser. This chapter describes Thunderbird 6.0. To download it and set it up, follow these steps:

1. **Download and install Thunderbird from** www.mozillamessaging.com/thunderbird.

2. **Start Thunderbird by clicking the desktop icon or choosing Start⇨All Programs⇨Mozilla Thunderbird⇨Mozilla Thunderbird.**

   The first time you run Thunderbird, the Account Wizard runs, asking for information about your mail account.

3. **Type your information, copying the information from Table 8-1.**

   When you're done, you see your new account in the Account Settings window, which you can close.

If you need to change your e-mail account information later or set up Thunderbird to work with a different e-mail account, choose Tools⇨Account Settings. To run the Account Wizard again, click Account Actions (in the lower-left corner of the Account Settings window) and choose Add Mail Account. To change the settings for an existing account, choose the account, click the settings categories below the account name, and change the settings that appear.

The Thunderbird window looks like the one shown in Figure 8-4. A list of your mailboxes (mail folders) appears in the upper-left corner. To the right is a list of the messages in that mailbox and the text of the selected message.

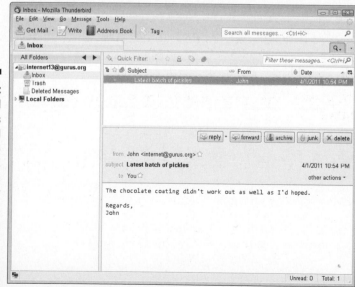

Figure 8-4:
Thunderbird displays your mail folders to the left, messages to the upper right, and the selected message to the lower right.

Windows Live Essentials

Windows 7 doesn't come with all the free programs that earlier versions of Windows did. The reason might be the Microsoft response to various antitrust suits, in which the makers of competing programs (other web browsers, e-mail programs, and chat programs, for example) pointed out that Microsoft took advantage of sales of Windows itself to push its other products. Or, maybe Microsoft had other reasons.

Instead, Windows 7 encourages you to download the Windows Live Essentials package, which includes several Internet-related programs:

- Windows Live Mail, described in this chapter

- Windows Live Toolbar, an add-on to the Internet Explorer web browser (It includes a Mail button that displays your Hotmail inbox page in your browser.)

- Windows Live Messenger, an instant messaging program described in Chapter 12

- Windows Live Photo Gallery, a photo-editing and -organizing program described in Chapter 17

- Windows Live Writer, a blogging program described in Chapter 18

- Windows Live Family Safety, an Internet filtering program for families with small children

These programs work with Windows XP (with Service Pack 2), Windows Vista, and Windows 7. To download Windows Live Essentials, follow these steps:

1. Go to `http://download.live.com` and click Download.

2. Save the file in your Downloads folder.

3. Open or run the file you just downloaded.

4. Choose which Windows Live Essential programs you want to download. You can download others later.

5. During the installation, the program asks to set Live Search as your default search provider; Chapter 13 describes ways to search the web. We recommend deselecting this option because you might prefer another search site.

6. If the installation program asks to make MSN your browser's home page, which we doubt you will enjoy, deselect that one, too.

7. Finally, the installation program suggests that you sign up for a Windows Live ID. This free account gives you a Hotmail webmail mailbox and lets you participate in instant messaging. You can click Sign Up to sign up now, or you can sign up at any time at `http://signup.live.com`.

Setting up Windows Live Mail

You can download Windows Live Mail along with any other Windows Live Essentials programs you might want to use. Follow these steps:

1. **Follow the steps in the "Windows Live Essentials" sidebar, earlier in this chapter, to download Windows Live Mail.**

   You can download other Windows Live programs, too, if you want them.

2. **Choose Start⇨Windows Live Mail.**

   You see the Add an E-Mail Account window.

3. **Enter your e-mail address, password, and name and click Next.**

   Or, if you want to sign up for a free Hotmail account, click the link.

4. **Enter the specs for your incoming mail server and outgoing server, copying the information from Table 8-1.**

   If you have an account at any of the popular webmail systems (including AOL, Gmail, Hotmail, or Yahoo! Mail), you can skip this step because the system already knows how to set it up. Windows Live Mail downloads the folders and mail from the mail server.

5. **If the program displays a list of your folders (usually just Inbox and Trash and a few other folders, unless you've created more), click OK.**

The Windows Live Mail layout looks a little different from the other mail programs, with a lefthand column of tasks and features, a middle column that lists your messages, and a righthand column that shows the selected message.

Setting up Apple Mail

Apple Mail is already installed on all OS X Macs, so just fire it up and tell it about your account.

1. **Start Apple Mail by clicking on its icon, which looks like a postage stamp.**

   If this is the first time you've run it, it immediately starts the new account process. Otherwise, choose File⇨Add Account.

2. **It asks you for your full name, e-mail address, and password.**

   Your full name is your actual name, which is displayed on the From line of mail you send. The address and password are assigned by your mail provider. With any luck, you already wrote them down in Table 8-1. Click Continue.

3. **Tell Apple Mail about your incoming mail server.**

   Apple Mail tries to guess the appropriate mail server, and it usually guesses correctly. If it doesn't, enter the account type, which is POP, IMAP, or Exchange, and the information about your incoming mail server from Table 8-1. The Description box is just a comment to remind you which account it is, if you configure more than one. Click Continue, and it ensures that it can connect to your server.

4. **Tell Apple Mail about your outgoing mail server, if it hasn't already figured it out.**

If it's the same as the incoming mail server, click the little arrow to the right of the Outgoing Mail Server box and select that server. Otherwise, fill in the specs from Table 8-1. Click Continue, and again it checks to ensure that it can connect.

5. **Check the Account Summary page.**

   Assuming that all the information is correct, click Create to create the mail account on your computer and fetch any waiting mail.

Sending Mail Is Easy

Whether you use an e-mail program or webmail, sending messages is easy enough that we show you a few examples rather than waste time explaining the theory. It works much the same way in all e-mail programs.

Follow these steps to write an e-mail message and send it off:

1. **Click the Write, New, or New Message icon or button.**

   A window (either the Compose or New Message window) opens. In webmail, your composition area appears in the web browser.

2. **Fill in the recipient's address (or recipients' addresses) in the To box.**

   You can send this message to more than one person at a time by entering more than one To address. This feature works a little differently in different programs. In Thunderbird, press Enter (rather than Tab) to move down a line to enter another address. In Windows Live Mail or Apple Mail, just type a comma between the addresses. In Outlook, type a comma or semicolon between addresses.

   Remembering people's e-mail addresses is annoying (or, for those of us at a Certain Age, just plain impossible). See the section in Chapter 9 about keeping track of your friends to find out how to add people to your address book and use it when sending messages.

3. **Add any Cc or Bcc addresses that you want the messages to go to.**

   See the later sidebar "CC and BCC" if you're wondering what we're talking about. In Outlook, enter addresses in the appropriate To or Cc box. In Thunderbird, after you enter an address, click the To button next to the address and select Cc or Bcc from the list that drops down. In Windows Live Mail, click Show Cc & Bcc to see boxes in which you can enter those addresses in the New Message window. In Apple Mail, click the little three-line icon to the left of the From line to see the Bcc line.

4. **Type the subject in the Subject box.**

   Make it specific. If you want help, don't type Help! as the subject. Type **Need help getting my cat not to spit out his pills**.

Press Tab to move to the message box.

5. **Type the message in the big box.**

   The cursor should be blinking in the *message area,* the large, empty box where you type the message.

6. **Click the Send icon or button to send the message.**

   In Thunderbird and Outlook, you can also press Ctrl+Enter. In Windows Live Mail and Windows Mail, you can press Alt+S.

7. **If the message isn't sent right away, tell your mail program to send all waiting messages by clicking the Get Mail icon (in Thunderbird), clicking the Send/Receive icon (in Outlook), or pressing F5 (in Windows Live Mail).**

When you send a message in which you use formatting (such as boldface or italics, by using the toolbar buttons in the Compose window), your e-mail program may ask whether you truly want to send the message using formatting. See the sidebar "To format or not to format," later in this chapter, to find out when to send formatted messages.

Spell-checking your message is a good idea; avoid the embarrassment of spotting your typos only after it's too late to fix them. You can ask your mail program to check the spelling in your message before you send it. Click the Spell icon to see which typos your program finds. In Thunderbird, you can also press Ctrl+K or choose Options⇨Check Spelling; in Outlook, press F7 or choose Tools⇨Spelling and Grammar; in Windows Live Mail, press F7 or choose Tools⇨Spelling; and in Apple Mail, choose Edit⇨Spelling and Grammar⇨Check Document Now.

After your mail program sends a piece of e-mail to the outgoing mail server, you can't cancel it!

CC and BCC

The term *carbon copy* should be familiar to those of you who were born before 1965 and remember the ancient practice of putting sheets of carbon-coated paper between sheets of regular paper to make extra copies when using a typewriter. (Please don't ask us what a typewriter is.) In e-mail, a *carbon copy* is simply a copy of the message you send. All recipients, on both the To and Cc lines, see who's receiving the message — unless a recipient's e-mail address is typed in the BCC field instead. *Blind carbon copies* (BCCs) are copies sent to people without putting their names on the message so that the other recipients are none the wiser. You can figure out why you may want to send a copy to someone but not want everyone to know that you sent it.

To format or not to format

Years ago, someone grew tired of e-mail's plain, unformatted appearance. When almost all computers could display boldface, italics, different fonts, and different font sizes, someone wondered, why not use them in e-mail? And formatted e-mail was born.

Very old e-mail programs may not be able to display formatted e-mail. All programs described in this chapter, including webmail, can. The formatting usually takes one of two forms: *MIME,* in which the formatted text is sent like an attached file with the message, and *HTML,* in which web page formatting codes are included in the text. If your mail program can't display formatted mail and you receive a formatted message, you see all kinds of gobbledygook mixed in with the text of the message, rendering it unreadable.

A big problem is that any HTML-formatted mail can potentially contain viruses, hostile web pages that take over the screen, and other annoying or dangerous content. Some people turn off HTML mail, both the nice mail you send and the nasty kind, to avoid having to deal with the nasty kind.

Boldface, italics, and color can add emphasis and interest to your messages, although they're no substitute for clear, concise writing. Some people (including John) prefer mail without formatting. To be sure that a message has none of that tatty-looking formatting, do this in either the New Message window or the Compose window when you're writing your message:

- **Outlook:** On the Format Text or Message Options tab, set Format to Plain Text.

- **Thunderbird:** Choose Options⇨Format⇨ Plain Text Only.

- **Windows Live Mail:** Press Alt to display the hidden menus, and then choose Format⇨Plain Text.

- **Apple Mail:** Choose Format⇨Make Plain Text.

Mail Coming Your Way

If you send e-mail, and in most cases even if you don't, you most likely receive it also. The arrival of e-mail is always exciting, even when you receive 200 messages a day. (It's exciting in a depressing kind of way, sometimes.)

A helpful feature of mail programs (not webmail) is that you can compose messages while you're offline. On the other hand, when you want to check your mailbox for your most current messages, you have to connect to the Internet. Webmail users have to be online to do anything. (That's not quite true: Gmail can do some work in your browser while offline.)

Reading your messages

To check your e-mail in almost any e-mail program, follow these steps:

1. **Start your e-mail program, if it isn't already running.**

   If you use webmail, start your web browser and go to your webmail website.

2. **If your program doesn't retrieve mail automatically, click the Check Mail, Sync, or Send/Receive button on the toolbar to retrieve your mail.**

   If you have a full-time Internet connection, your mail program may retrieve your mail automatically, in which case you only have to start the program to fetch your mail. In addition, if you leave your mail program running, even hidden at the bottom of your screen as an icon, it may automatically check for new mail every once in a while. Most mail programs can even pick up mail while you're reading or sending other messages.

   The program may play a tune or display a message when you receive messages. The mail appears in your inbox (usually in a window or folder named In or Inbox), showing one line per message. If you don't see it, double-click the In or Inbox mailbox in the list of mailboxes that usually appears on the left side of the window.

3. **To see a message, double-click the line or click the line and press Enter.**

   You see the text of the message, along with buttons for replying, forwarding, and deleting the message. Figure 8-5 shows an e-mail message as it appears on the iPhone.

4. **To stop looking at a message, click the Close (X) button in the upper-right corner of the message window (the standard way to get rid of a window) or press Ctrl+W or Ctrl+F4.**

   On a Mac, click the red Close button in the upper-left corner.

Here are some tips for displaying your inbox in specific e-mail programs:

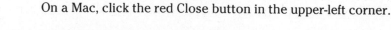

- ✔ **Outlook:** The left side of the window usually displays your folders, and the Inbox appears at the top of the list.
- ✔ **Thunderbird:** To display your inbox, click your e-mail address, account name, or inbox in the Mail Folders list.

✔ **Windows Live Mail:** If you've clicked Calendar (to see an appointment calendar), Feeds (to see articles from newsfeeds or blogs to which you have subscribed), or Newsgroups (to participate in online discussion groups, described on the web at `http://net.gurus.org/usenet` or `http://groups.google.com`), you may need to click Mail to return to the Mail part of the program.

To tell Windows Live Mail to check for new messages, click the Sync or Send/Receive button on the toolbar. If you don't see it, your Windows Live Mail window is too narrow (ours usually is); make your window wider.

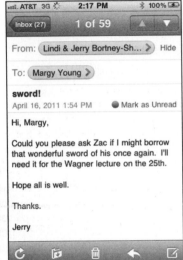

Figure 8-5:
The iPhone displays an e-mail message.

Deleting messages the quick-and-easy way

You don't have to read every single message before you delete it; sometimes, you can guess from the sender's name or the Subject line that reading the message would be a waste of time. If you subscribe to e-mail mailing lists or newsletters, certain topics may not interest you. And, of course, you may receive messages that are obvious spam.

One-click surfing

Most e-mail programs display web addresses as links. That is, if the text of a message includes a web address (such as http:// net.gurus.org), the address appears underlined and perhaps in blue. Just click the link to display the page in your browser.

When you send messages, you don't have to do anything special to display a web address as a link — the recipient's mail program should do it automatically.

Buttons on the e-mail program's toolbar at the top of its window let you dispose of your mail. First, click once to highlight the message. Then (in most mail programs) click the Trash or Delete button on the toolbar to discard the message.

In webmail, on the web page that displays messages, is a Delete button of some sort. Some webmail systems have a check box next to every message in your inbox folder and a Delete button at the bottom of the list. To delete a bunch of messages, select their check boxes and then click Delete.

When you delete a message, most e-mail programs don't throw it away immediately. Instead, they file the message in your Trash or Deleted Messages mailbox or mail folder or just mark it as deleted. From time to time (usually whenever you close the e-mail program), the program empties your trash, truly deleting the messages. Until then, you can undelete it if you deleted it by mistake.

To Whom Do I Write?

As you probably have figured out, one teensy detail is keeping you from sending e-mail to all your friends: You don't know their addresses. In this chapter, you find out lots of different ways to look for addresses. Start out with the easiest, most reliable way to find out people's e-mail addresses:

Call them on the phone and ask them.

TIP

Top ten reasons *not* to call someone to find an e-mail address

10. You want to surprise a long-lost friend.

9. You want to surprise a long-lost *ex*-friend who owes you a large amount of money and thinks that she has given you the slip.

8. Your friend doesn't speak English. (That happens — a majority of Internauts are outside the United States.)

7. You don't — or your friend doesn't — even speak. (That happens, too — networks offer a uniquely friendly place for most people with handicaps; nobody has to know or care whether someone has a disability.)

6. It's 3 a.m. and you need to send a message right now or else you'll never get to sleep.

5. You don't know the phone number, and, because of an unfortunate childhood experience, you have a deathly fear of calling directory assistance.

4. The pay phone takes only quarters; nobody around can break your $100 bill.

3. Your company has installed a new phone system, no one has figured out how to use it, and no matter what you dial, you always end up with Dial-a-Prayer.

2. You inadvertently spilled an entire can of soda into the phone and can't wait for it to dry out to make the call.

1. You called yesterday, didn't write down the answer, and forgot it. Oops.

Pretty low-tech, huh? For some reason, this technique seems to be absolutely the last thing people want to do. (See the nearby sidebar "Top ten reasons *not* to call someone to find an e-mail address.") Try it first. If you know or can find out the phone number, this method is much easier than any of the others.

Another way to find a person's e-mail address is by using an online directory. Wouldn't it be cool if an online directory listed everybody's e-mail addresses? Maybe, but the Internet doesn't have one. For one thing, nothing says that somebody's e-mail address has any connection to her name. For another, not everybody wants everybody else to know his e-mail address.

Another approach is to go to a search engine, such as Google (www.google. com) or Yahoo! Search (www.yahoo.com), and type the person's full name, enclosed in quotes. You see a list of pages that include the name — of course, many people may have the same name if your friend is named Allen Johnson or Bob Smith. Or, try Yahoo! People Search at http://people.yahoo.com, which enables you to search by name and state. Try searching for your own name and see what you find!

If you're in contact with someone by way of Facebook or another social networking site (described in Chapter 10), you can send them messages through that site to ask for an e-mail address.

Avoiding Viruses, Malware, and Other Mailborne Annoyances

A virus or another type of malware arrives on your computer as an attachment to an e-mail message. (Refer to the section in Chapter 2 about viruses and malware arriving by e-mail for a description of how viruses work.) In most mail programs, programs contained in attachments don't run until you click them — so *don't* open programs that come from people you don't know. Don't even open attachments from people you *do* know if you weren't expecting to receive them. Many successful viruses replicate themselves by sending copies of themselves to the first 50 people in an address book, so a message that appears to be from a friend is actually from a virus in the friend's computer.

It used to be that only an attachment that looked like a program (for example, a file with the filename extension .com or .exe) could contain a virus. Then the bad guys (aided by software written without security in mind) came up with ways to hide viruses in word processing documents, PDF files (print-ready formatted documents), and even pictures. Bad guys can also hide malware in web pages (more of a problem if you use Internet Explorer than other browsers), so if you receive an unexpected message with a link, think twice before clicking on it.

One-click surfing, but no phishing

Most e-mail programs convert URLs (website addresses) in your e-mail messages into links to the actual websites. You don't have to type these addresses into your browser. All you have to do is click the highlighted link in the e-mail message and — poof — your browser opens and you're at the website. If your e-mail program has this feature (all programs mentioned in this chapter do), URLs in e-mail messages appear underlined and in blue — a nice feature.

Unfortunately, this feature is abused by phishers. *Phishing* is sending faked e-mail that claims to be from your bank or another official organization to trick you into revealing personal information, and we describe it in Chapter 2. If you click one of these links and it opens a website that asks for a password or credit card number or the like, don't give it any information!

Most webmail and e-mail programs have phish detection features. The features aren't perfect, but if either one says that a link looks phishy, you probably shouldn't click it.

Chapter 9

Putting Your Mail in Its Place

• •

In This Chapter

▶ Following the rules of e-mail etiquette

▶ Throwing away spam automatically

▶ Responding to mail, or not

▶ Keeping an e-mail address book

▶ Forwarding and filing mail

▶ Sending and receiving exotic mail and mail attachments

▶ Sorting and filtering your messages

• •

After you get used to using e-mail, you start sending and receiving enough messages that you had better keep it organized. This chapter describes how to delete, reply to, forward, and file messages in Outlook, Thunderbird, Windows Live Mail (which comes with Windows Live Essentials), Apple Mail (which comes with Mac OS X), and webmail systems such as AOL Mail, Gmail, Hotmail, and Yahoo! Mail. (Refer to Chapter 8 to find out how to get started using these programs.)

After you read (or decide not to read) an e-mail message, you can deal with it in a number of ways, much the same as with paper mail. Here are your usual choices:

✓ Throw it away (as described in Chapter 8).

✓ Mark it as spam so that your program and sometimes your mail provider can learn to identify spam before you even have to see it.

✓ Reply to it.

✓ Forward it to other people.

✓ File it.

You can do any or all of these things with any message. If you don't tell your mail program what to do with a message, it usually stays in your mailbox for later perusal.

Smartphones have simpler e-mail programs that don't have all the features described in this chapter.

A Few Words from the Etiquette Ladies

Sadly, the Great Ladies of Etiquette, such as Emily Post and Amy Vanderbilt, died before the invention of e-mail. Here's what they may have suggested about what to say and, more important, what *not* to say in e-mail.

E-mail is a funny hybrid, something between a phone call (or voice mail) and a letter. On one hand, it's quick and usually informal; on the other hand, because e-mail is written rather than spoken, you don't see a person's facial expressions or hear her tone of voice.

A few words of advice:

- ✔ When you send a message, watch the tone of your language.
- ✔ Don't use all capital letters — it looks like you're SHOUTING.
- ✔ If someone sends you an incredibly obnoxious and offensive message, as likely as not it's a mistake or a joke gone awry. In particular, be on the lookout for failed sarcasm.

Flame off!

Pointless and excessive outrage in e-mail is so common that it has a name of its own: *flaming*. Don't flame. It makes you look like a jerk.

When you receive a message so offensive that you just *have* to reply, stick it back in your inbox for a while and wait until after lunch. Then . . . don't flame back. The sender probably didn't realize how the message would look. In about 20 years of using e-mail, we can testify that we have never, ever, regretted *not* sending an angry message (although we *have* regretted sending a few — ouch).

When you're sending e-mail, keep in mind that the person reading it will have no idea what you *intended* to say — just what you *did* say. Subtle sarcasm and irony are almost impossible to use in e-mail and usually come across as annoying or dumb instead. (If you're an extremely superb writer, you can disregard this advice — but don't say that we didn't warn you.)

BTW, what does IMHO mean? RTFM!

E-mail users are often lazy typists, and abbreviations are common. Here are some of the most widely used:

Abbreviation	What It Means
AFAIK	As far as I know
BTW	By the way
DR	Didn't read — write something shorter next time
FWIW	For what it's worth
IANAL	I am not a lawyer, (but. . . .)
IMHO	In my humble opinion
LOL	Laugh out loud
ROTFL	Rolling on the floor laughing (or ROFL)
RSN	Real soon now (that is, any time in the next century)
RTFM	Read the manual — you could have and should have looked it up yourself
TIA	Thanks in advance
TLA	Three-letter acronym (for a three-letter acronym)
TL	Too long — write something shorter next time
YMMV	Your mileage may vary

Another possibility to keep in the back of your mind is that it's technically easy to forge e-mail return addresses. If you receive a totally off-the-wall message that seems out of character for the person who sent it, somebody else may have forged it as a prank. (No, we don't tell you how to forge e-mail. How dumb do you think we are?)

Smile!

TIP

A *smiley* or an *emoticon* such as :-) means "This is a joke." (Try tilting your head to the left if you don't see why it's a smile.) In some communities, <g> or <grin> serves the same purpose. Here's a typical example:

```
People who don't believe that we are all part of a warm,
caring community who love and support each other are no
better than rabid dogs and should be hunted down and shot.
:-)
```

In our experience, any joke that needs a smiley probably wasn't worth making, but tastes differ. For more guidance about online etiquette, see our `http://net.gurus.org/netiquette` web page.

Spam: Kill, Kill, Kill!

Spam, unsolicited and unwanted bulk mail, is a scourge on the Internet. By most measures, upward of 90 percent of all mail is spam, which means that your mail provider has to filter out ten spam messages for every message it delivers. Spam filters work pretty well, but they aren't perfect. Here are some suggestions about how to make your mail's filtering closer to perfect.

Filtering spam in webmail

Webmail systems try to identify spam and move it to a Junk or Spam folder. (In Gmail, you may need to click the More link to see the Spam folder.) Take a look in this folder from time to time to look for any real messages that might accidentally have gotten marked as spam.

If you see spam messages when reading your incoming mail, you can mark them as spam, which helps the webmail service identify this type of message in the future. From the list of messages, select the message and click the Spam, Report Spam, or Junk icon or link. If you find misfiled real mail in your junk folder, you can usually click a Not Junk or similar icon to "unreport" it.

You can sometimes adjust how aggressively your webmail service looks for spam, and determine what it does with the spam it finds. In AOL Mail, click Settings and then Spam Controls. In Hotmail, choose Options⇨More Options⇨Filters and Reporting. In Yahoo Mail!, choose Options⇨Mail Options and then click Spam to see the spam settings. (As of 2011, Gmail has no spam controls you can set. It sure filters out a lot of spam, though.) The controls adjust how stringently the system filters out spam and determines what it does with suspected spam.

Filtering spam in Thunderbird

Thunderbird 6 has its own filter that works pretty well after you give it some examples of what your spam looks like. Usually, your mail provider's filters do all the filtering you need, but if stuff leaks through, this can be an extra layer to catch the leaks.

Telling Thunderbird to start filtering

First, set up your spam filtering configuration settings, like this:

1. **Choose Tools⇨Account Settings. In the new window, click Junk Settings under your e-mail account.**

   You see the Junk Settings dialog box, shown in Figure 9-1.

2. **Select the Enable Adaptive Junk Mail Controls for This Account check box if it isn't already selected.**

3. **Select the check box labeled Personal Address Book if it doesn't already contain a check mark in it.**

   Usually, people you know don't spam you.

4. **Click to select the Move New Junk Messages To check box if it doesn't already contain a check mark. Choose where to move your spam.**

   The default setting is a Junk folder, which sounds good to us.

5. **Clear any check mark from the Automatically Delete Junk Messages Older Than ___ Days check box.**

   Until your filter is well trained, don't let Thunderbird delete suspected spam before you have a chance to review it. It's terribly embarrassing to tell someone that you threw away their important message because your program thought it was spam.

Figure 9-1:
Configuring
Thunderbird
to can your
spam.

6. **Click OK.**

   If you have set up more than one account, repeat this set of steps for every account in the Account Settings window.

Now Thunderbird is ready to distinguish the spam from the ham — the bad messages from the good. As you read the messages in your Inbox folder, every time you receive a spam message, click the Junk button on the toolbar. The message vanishes from your inbox and Thunderbird analyzes the words in the message and makes a note that they're likely to appear in spam. The more spam messages you mark with the Junk button, the more Thunderbird knows about what spam looks like.

Checking your Junk folder for real mail

From time to time (every week or so), open the Junk mail folder (or whatever folder you told Thunderbird to put suspected spam into in Step 4 in the previous section). The Junk mail folder appears on your list of folders, below your Inbox, Templates (form letters you send out), and Sent folders. Click the Junk folder to see the list of messages. You don't need to open every message — reviewing the sender names and subjects is usually enough to find any good messages mixed in there.

If you see a good message in your Junk folder, select it and click the Not Junk button on the toolbar. (It's where the Junk button usually is — the button turns into Not Junk when you open the Junk folder.) This button tells Thunderbird to look at this message and to adjust the filters accordingly. Then drag the message back into your Inbox. When you're sure that all messages in your Junk folder are indeed junk, delete them. An easy way to do it is to click the first message and then scroll down and Shift+click the last message — now all messages in the Junk folder are selected. Press the Del key or click the Delete button on the toolbar to trash them.

Filtering spam in Outlook

Outlook has a Junk E-mail folder into which it puts anything it thinks is spam. You can look at what's in it just as you use any other folder, by clicking it in the folder list in the left pane of the Outlook window.

When you get a spam message, right-click the message and choose Junk⇨Block Sender. Future messages from that sender will automatically move into the Junk folder.

Be sure to check your Junk folder every few days, in case a good message gets misfiled there. If you see a nonspam ("ham") message in your Junk folder in Outlook 2010, select the message and click the Home tab. Then choose Delete⇨Junk⇨Not Junk. In Outlook 2007, select the message and choose

Actions⇨Junk E-Mail⇨Add Sender to Safe Senders List to whitelist the sender so that no future messages from that person are considered to be spam. You can whitelist an entire domain, too, by choosing Actions⇨Junk E-Mail⇨Add Sender's Domain to Safe Senders List. This command can be useful if you're doing business with an organization and you want to receive mail from anyone with an address at that organization's domain.

Filtering spam in Windows Live Mail

Windows Live Mail (which comes with Windows Live Essentials) has no adaptive filters but has a number of other spam-fighting features:

- ✔ **Junk E-Mail Options:** You can adjust the built-in spam filters.
- ✔ **Blocked Senders list:** If you receive a message from anyone on this list, the message is moved directly into the trash.
- ✔ **Safe Senders list:** Messages from people on this list *aren't* marked as spam, even if the message looks like spam.

The following sections describe how to use these features.

Configuring your junk e-mail options

To configure the built-in junk mail filter, follow these steps:

1. **Click the Menu button (to the left of the Home tab on the Ribbon) and choose Options⇨Safety Options.**

   You should see the Safety Options window.

2. **Select Low to pick the normal junk filter setting.**

   You can try High, but we find that it catches too much real mail.

3. **Click the Phishing tab.**

4. **Select Protect My Inbox from Messages with Potential Phishing Links if it isn't already set.**

   This feature is useful, but it raises some privacy concerns. Because it checks any web URLs in the message against a list of known phishing sites maintained by Microsoft, the link information in your mail is sent to Microsoft for checking.

5. **Click OK.**

You can use the Safe Senders and Blocked Senders tabs to list addresses of people whose mail you always want or never want, respectively. On the Options tab of this window, click Safe List Only to accept mail only from people listed on the Safe Senders tab. This setting is way too restrictive for adults, but is appropriate for children, so you can set up a list of the friends and relatives from whom you expect them to be receiving mail.

The International tab lets you block mail from addresses from certain top-level domains (the part of the e-mail address after the last dot) and in certain language encodings. We don't recommend the domain blocking, which tends to block more mail than you want, but if you don't speak Korean (or Arabic, Chinese, Greek, Vietnamese, or another language in the list) and don't know anyone in Korea, you can somewhat safely tell it to block mail encoded as Korean. Don't tell it to block US_ASCII or Western European or else you'll block most of your real mail.

Blocking messages by sender

In Windows Live Mail, right-click the message in the message list and choose Junk E-Mail⇨Add Sender to Blocked Senders List. If you've opened the message in a separate window, click Junk.

The message you opened is still in your inbox; the program will block *future* messages, but doesn't do anything about this one. Just delete it! Blocking by sender is occasionally useful to deal with real people who send mail that's never interesting, but it's useless for spam because spammers never use the same address twice.

Viewing your Blocked Senders list

You can look at or edit the Blocked Senders list later, in case you add a friend accidentally or you want to type a bunch of spammer addresses. In Windows Live Mail, click the Menu icon (to the left of the Home tab on the Ribbon) and choose Options⇨Safety Options. Click the Blocked Senders tab to see the list of senders you have blocked. Messages from any addresses on this list are shunted straight to your Deleted Items folder.

You can add more addresses to your Blocked Senders list by clicking the Add button and typing or pasting the address in the dialog box that appears. If you decide to accept messages from an address after all, you can delete it from the list by choosing the address and clicking Remove.

Blocking messages from entire domains

The Blocked Senders list can include entire domains. (A *domain* is the part of an e-mail address after the @ character.) For example, if you don't want to receive *any* mail from the White House, you can block all messages that come from `anything@whitehouse.gov`. Follow these steps to block all messages from an entire domain:

1. **Display the Blocked Senders list, as described in the preceding section.**

2. **Click the Add button.**

   You see the Add Sender dialog box.

3. **Type the domain name and click OK.**

   When you click OK, the new entry appears on your Blocked Senders list.

Reviewing your spam

From time to time, be sure to skim the messages that have been identified and filed as spam. Perfectly innocent messages may have been mislabeled as spam.

To look in your Junk E-Mail folder, click it on the folder list. The list of messages in that folder appears. Scroll the messages; unread messages appear in bold. (Any spam you've never seen should appear in bold.) If you see any good messages, select them all and click Not Junk to put them back in your Inbox.

Filtering spam in Apple Mail

Apple Mail has a simple but usable spam filter. To use it, follow these steps:

1. **Choose Mail⇨Preferences. Click the Junk Mail icon at the top of the panel.**

   You should see the Junk Mail window.

2. **Check Enable Junk Mail Filtering, if it isn't already checked.**

   You have your choice of leaving junk mail in your inbox marked as junk or moving it to the Junk mailbox. We suggest using the Move It to the Junk Mailbox option.

3. **Select the message types to exempt from filtering.**

   Select the box to exempt senders in your address book. Deselect the other two boxes, Previous Recipients and Messages Addressed Using Your Full Name — leaving these two boxes selected has caused plenty of junk to come our way.

4. **Select Trust Junk Mail Headers Set by My Internet Service Providers.**

   Some providers mark junk but leave it in your inbox. This option tells Mail to use the markings to recognize junk.

5. **Close the Preferences panel.**

Back to You, Sam: Replying to Mail

Replying to mail is easy: Choose Message⇨Reply in Thunderbird, choose Actions⇨Reply in Outlook, click Reply in Windows Live Mail, or click Reply in Apple Mail. Pressing Ctrl+R (Command+R on the Mac) works in most mail programs, too. In webmail, you usually see a Reply button. On the iPhone, touching the left-pointing curved arrow icon at the bottom of the e-mail message displays a menu from which you can choose Reply.

After you open the reply message, ask yourself two important questions:

✔ **To whom does the reply go?** Look carefully at the To line, which your mail program has filled out for you. Is that whom you thought you were addressing? If the reply is addressed to a mailing list, did you truly intend to send a message to the entire list, or is your reply of a more personal nature, intended only for the individual who sent the message? Did you mean to reply to a group? Are all the addresses that you think you're replying to included on the To list? If the To list isn't correct, click it and edit it as necessary.

Occasionally, you may receive a message that has been sent to a zillion people and their addresses appear in dozens of lines in the To section of the message. If you reply to a message such as this one, make sure that your reply isn't addressed to the entire huge list of recipients.

Some mail programs have a separate Reply All command or button that addresses your reply to the people that the message was from *and* the people who received copies of the message (the "To" people and the "Cc" people). Thunderbird, Windows Live Mail, and Apple Mail all have the Reply All button on their toolbars.

✔ **Do you want to include the content of the message to which you're replying?** Most mail programs include the content of the message to which you're replying, usually formatted to show that it's a *quotation* or *quoted text*. Edit the quoted text to include only the relevant material, so as not to bore or confuse the recipient with unrelated stuff. If you don't provide some context to people who receive a great deal of e-mail, your reply makes no sense, so including part of the original message can be helpful. If you're answering a question, include the question in the response. You don't have to include the entire text, but give your reader a break. She may have read 50 messages since she sent you mail and may not have a clue what you're talking about unless you remind her.

When you reply to a message, most mail programs fill in the Subject field with the letters *Re:* (short for *re*garding) and the Subject field contents of the message to which you're replying. Type your message above the quoted text from the original message and click Send.

Keeping Track of Your Friends

After you begin using e-mail, you quickly find that you have enough regular correspondents that keeping track of their e-mail addresses is a pain. Fortunately, every popular e-mail program provides an *address book* or *contacts list* in which you can save your friends' addresses so that you can send mail to Mom, for example, and have it automatically addressed to chairman@ exec.hq.giantcorp.com. You can also create address lists so that you can send mail to family, for example, and it goes to Mom, Dad, your brother, both sisters, and your dog, all of whom have e-mail addresses.

All address books let you do the same things:

✔ Save in your address book the address from a message you have just read.

✔ Use addresses you have saved for outgoing messages.

✔ Edit your address book.

Some address books also provide space for you to store other information about your friends and coworkers.

Who's who

Click the Address Book or Contacts icon or link to see your address book. Apple Mail uses the standard Address Book, which you can open by clicking the book icon in your dock. Most programs open a new window for your contacts list. In most address books, you double-click a contact's name to edit the person's information.

Here's how to add people to your address book:

✔ **Thunderbird:** Click New Contact and fill out the form. To edit an entry, select it and click the Properties button on the toolbar. You can also create a *list* — that is, an address book entry that sends a message to a bunch of people (for example, the members of a committee or of your family). To create a mailing list for your use, click the New List button, which creates an empty list, and then type the addresses you want.

When you're reading a message, you can add the sender's address to your address book by clicking the sender's name or address on the From line and choosing Add to Address Book from the menu that pops up.

✔ **Outlook:** Click the Contacts button in the left pane of the Outlook window, or choose Go⇨Contacts. You see Outlook's Contacts list, showing people alphabetically by last name. Click the New button to display a dialog box with spaces for all the information you could possibly want to store about someone. Then click Save and Close.

- ✓ **Windows Live Mail:** Click Contacts in the lower-left corner of the window to see your Contacts list, and then click Contact in the New section of the Home tab on the Ribbon to create a new contact. Fill out the information and click Add Contact. When you're reading a message and want to save the sender's name in your Contacts list, right-click the person's name and choose Add to Contacts from the menu that appears.

- ✓ **Apple Mail:** Click the + character under the name, enter as much info as you have about the person (at least name and e-mail address), and then click the little Edit button to say that you're done editing.

- ✓ **Webmail:** Click the Contacts, Contacts List, Addresses, or Address Book link to display your address book. Click the Add Contact, Create Contact, or New button or the little plus sign or similar icon or link to add someone. Fill out the form that appears, and be sure to enter a *nickname* for the person: You can type the nickname when addressing an e-mail message rather than type the person's whole e-mail address. The form may include fields for the person's postal address and phone numbers, but you can leave them blank. Then click the Save or Save Contact button. (These instructions are approximate because webmail sites change their designs all the time.)

Addressing messages the easy way

Composing a message is a good time to use your address book, because who can remember all those weird e-mail addresses your friends pick? When you're writing a new message (or replying to or forwarding a message, as described later in this chapter), here's what to do after you click the Write, New, or New Message icon or button:

- ✓ **Thunderbird and Outlook:** Just start typing the person's name in your new message. As soon as Thunderbird sees a name that begins with the same letters as an address book entry, it displays the person's name. If more than one entry matches, you see a list you can choose from.

- ✓ **Windows Live Mail:** Start typing a name into the To box, and the contacts that match appear.

- ✓ **Apple Mail:** Click the Address icon at the top of the message composition window to open the address book. Click the address you want, and then click To, Cc, or Bcc to add it to one of the address lines. Close the address book when you're done.

- ✓ **Webmail:** Webmail systems provide several ways to address a message to someone in your address book. In Yahoo! Mail, you can display a list of your contacts. When composing a message, try typing the person's nickname to see whether a matching entry appears in the window of address book entries or click the To or Cc button to see a list of contacts from which to choose.

Hot Potatoes: Forwarding Mail

You can forward e-mail to someone else. It's easy. It's cheap. Forwarding is one of the best things about e-mail and at the same time one of the worst. It's good because you can easily pass along messages to people who need to know about them. It's bad because you (not *you* personally, but, um, people around you — that's it) can just as easily send out floods of messages to recipients who would just as soon not hear *another* press release from the local Ministry of Truth or another joke that's making the rounds. Think about whether you will enhance someone's quality of life by forwarding a message to him. If a message says "Forward this to everyone you know," do everyone you know a favor and delete it instead.

Forwarding a message involves wrapping the message in a new message of your own, sort of like putting sticky notes all over a copy of it and mailing the copy and notes to someone else.

Forwarding mail is almost as easy as replying to it: Select the message and click the Forward button on the toolbar, the Ribbon, or the message window, or choose Message⇨Forward or Action⇨Forward. Pressing Ctrl+L (Command+L on the Mac) also works in Thunderbird, and Ctrl+F forwards in Windows Live Mail. In webmail systems, the Forward button usually appears whenever you view a message. The mail program composes a message that contains the text of the message you want to forward; all you have to do is address the message, add a few snappy comments, and send it. On the iPhone, touching the left-pointing curved arrow icon at the bottom of the e-mail message displays a menu from which you can choose Forward.

The text of the original message appears at the top or bottom of the message, usually formatted as quoted text and preceded by a line that specifies whom the original message was from, and when. You then get to edit the message and add your own comments.

Cold Potatoes: Saving Mail

Saving e-mail for later reference is similar to putting potatoes in the fridge for later. (Don't knock it if you haven't tried it — day-old boiled potatoes are yummy with enough butter or sour cream.) Lots of your e-mail is worth saving, just as lots of your paper mail is worth saving. Lots of it *isn't,* of course, but that's what the Delete icon is for.

You can save e-mail in a couple of different ways:

- ✔ Save it in a folder full of messages.
- ✔ Print it and put it in a file cabinet with paper mail. (Spare a tree; don't use this method.)

The easiest method usually is to stick messages in a folder. E-mail programs usually come with folders named In (or Inbox), Outbox, Sent, and Trash, and perhaps others. But you can also make your own folders.

People use two general approaches in filing mail: by sender and by topic. Whether you use one or the other or both is mostly a matter of taste. For filing by topic, it's entirely up to you to come up with folder names. The most difficult part is coming up with memorable names. If you aren't careful, you end up with four folders with slightly different names, each with a quarter of the messages about a particular topic.

Gmail takes a different tack: It saves all your mail in one huge folder. When you want to find an old message, you search for it by sender or by some text in the message. This method sure saves filing!

You can save all or part of a message by copying it into a text file or word processing document. Select the text of the message by using your mouse. Press Ctrl+C (Command+C on a Mac) or choose Edit⇨Copy to copy the text to the Clipboard. Switch to your word processor (or whatever program in which you want to copy the text) and press Ctrl+V (Command+V on the Mac) or choose Edit⇨Paste to make the message appear where the cursor is.

Filing messages in Thunderbird

Thunderbird lists your mail folders down the left side of the window, starting with Inbox. Thunderbird provides folders named Inbox, Drafts, Sent, Trash, and Outbox, but you can create your own folders. If you have a *lot* of messages to file, you can even create folders within folders to keep things organized. To make a new folder, follow these steps:

1. **Choose File⇨New⇨Folder.**

   You see the New Folder dialog box.

2. **Type a name for the folder in the Name text box.**

   Make one named Personal, just to give it a try.

3. **Set the Create As a Subfolder Of drop-down box to the folder name in which you want the new folder to live.**

   Usually, you want your folder to be a subfolder of Local Folders, so set it to Local Folders and click Choose This for the Parent. Or, choose another folder; for example, you can have a folder named Personal, and inside it can be a folder for every friend you receive messages from.

4. **Click OK.**

The new folder appears on the list of folders on the left side of the Thunderbird window. You can see the list of message headers for any folder by clicking the folder name.

You can save a message in a folder by dragging the message to the folder name — easy enough. Or, right-click the message, choose Move To from the menu that appears, and choose the folder from the list that appears.

When you compose a message, you can tell Thunderbird to save a copy of your message in a folder. While writing the message, choose Options⇨Send a Copy To and then choose a folder.

Filing messages in Outlook

Outlook starts with a bunch of folders, including Inbox, Deleted Items, Drafts (messages you haven't sent yet), Junk E-Mail, and Sent Items. They appear indented under your mailbox name (the name you gave when you configured Outlook for your e-mail account; for example, Mailbox – Margy Levine Young). You can create a new folder by right-clicking the mailbox name and choosing New Folder from the menu that appears. You can also make folders within folders: Right-click *any* folder to make a folder inside it.

To move a message from one folder to another, just drag it from its current location onto the name of the folder where you want to store it.

Filing messages in Windows Live Mail

You usually start out with folders named Inbox, Sent Items, Drafts, Deleted Items, Junk E-Mail, and Outbox. (If you start using Windows Live Mail with an account that already contains other folders, you'll see them instead.) To make a new folder, click the Folder tab on the Ribbon and then click New Folder.

Give the folder a name and choose which folder to put this new folder in. (You can have folders within folders — very convenient.)

Move messages into a folder by clicking a message header and dragging it over to the folder name or by right-clicking the message on the message list and choosing Move to Folder.

Filing messages in Apple Mail

What other people call folders, Apple calls mailboxes. To make a new one, choose Mailbox⇨New Mailbox. You might be able to choose the location of the mailbox (on your Mac, or with the rest of the mail in your mail account). Enter the name of the new mailbox and click OK.

To move a message, click on the message in the message list and drag it to the mailbox where you want it to go.

Filing messages in webmail systems

Webmail systems change every time the company decides to redesign the website, but here's how the popular webmail system worked the last time we checked.

Your folders appear in the list of folders down the left side of your browser window, under the My Folders heading. Your folders include names such as Inbox, Sent, Draft, Spam, and Trash. Click a folder name to see the messages in that folder. To save a message in a folder, drag the message from the list of messages into the new folder, as in a real mail program. To create a new folder, click the Add link to the right of My Folders; or in Hotmail, click Manage Folders and then click New.

In Gmail, rather than put mail into folders, you label it. All mail with the same label acts sort of like a folder. Click the Labels button and choose from the list. If you're creating a new label, click the Labels button, choose Manage Labels, click the Create New Label button, type a name, and click the Create button.

Handling Exotic Mail and Mail Attachments

Sooner or later, just plain, old, everyday e-mail isn't good enough for you: Someone will send you a picture you just have to see, or you will want to send a video clip of Fluffy to your new best friend in Paris. To send stuff other than text through the mail, a message uses special file formats. Sometimes the entire message is in a special format, and sometimes people *attach* things to their plain text mail.

When you receive a file that's attached to an e-mail message, your mail program is responsible for noticing the attached file and doing something intelligent with it. Most of the time, your program saves the attached file as a separate file in the folder you specify. After the file has been saved, you can use it just like you use any other file. If you see a picture in a message and you aren't sure where it's saved, most programs let you right-click the picture and choose Save Image As to put the picture in the folder of your choice.

These types of files are often sent as attachments:

- ✔ Compressed files, such as zip files
- ✔ Movies, in video files
- ✔ PDF files (printable, viewable formatted documents)
- ✔ Pictures, in image files
- ✔ Programs, in executable files
- ✔ Sounds, in audio files
- ✔ Word processing documents

E-mail viruses often show up as attachments. If you receive a message with an unexpected attachment, even from someone you know, **DO NOT OPEN IT** until you check with the sender to make sure she sent it deliberately. Viruses often suck all addresses from a victim's address book so that the virus can mail itself to the victim's friends. A few kinds of attachments can't carry viruses — notably, GIF and JPG images.

Your ISP or webmail service may place a limit on the size of your mailbox (the place on its server where your messages are stored until you pick them up). Google Gmail and Yahoo! Mail have high limits, so other mail systems have been increasing their limits to match, but you may still run into a size limit if someone sends you a truly gigantic file, such as a video file.

When you receive a picture as an attachment, it's sometimes so large that all you see in your message window is one corner of a picture that would measure about 4 feet by 6 feet if viewed in its entirely. When this happens, right-click the picture and save it as a separate file, and then view it using another program.

If you receive an attachment on your smartphone, you may want to wait to open it until you're reading the message on your computer, where you're more likely to have the program required to open the attached file.

Thunderbird attachments

To attach a file to the message you're composing, click the Attach button or choose File⇨Attach. Then select the file you want to send. Or, just drag the file from an Explorer window or the desktop into the message composition window. You can insert a picture directly into the text of the message by positioning the cursor where you want the picture to appear, choosing Insert⇨Image, and specifying the filename.

For incoming mail, Thunderbird displays any attachments that it can display itself (web pages and GIF and JPEG image files). For other types of attachments, it displays a little description of the file, which you can click. Thunderbird then runs an appropriate display program — if it knows of one — or asks you whether to save the attachment to a file or to configure a display program, which Thunderbird then runs in order to display the attachment.

Outlook attachments

To attach a file to your message, just drag the file from the Windows Explorer window and drop it on the message. Or, choose Insert⇨File or click Attach File on the Message tab on the Ribbon.

If you receive a message with attached files, Outlook displays the filenames at the top of the message, just below the To and Cc headers. You can double-click a filename to open it and then save it where you want it.

Windows Live Mail attachments

In Windows Live Mail, create a new message and then attach a file to the message by clicking the Attach File button on the Message tab or the Insert tab on the Ribbon. Then select the file to attach. Or, just drag the file into the New Message window. Then send the message as usual.

When an incoming message contains an attachment, the Paper Clip icon appears in the message on your list of incoming messages and in the message header when you view the message. Click the paper clip to see the filename — double-click and you may be able to see the attachment.

Microsoft has "solved" some chronic security problems by making Windows Live Mail refuse to show you certain attachments, including a lot of benign ones, such as attached text messages and PDF files. You can sort of fix this problem by choosing the Menu button (the leftmost tab on the Ribbon) and then choosing Options⇨Safety Options. Then click the Security tab and deselect Do Not Allow Attachments to Be Saved or Opened That Could Potentially Be a Virus. Now the program lets you open your attachments, although of course when someone *does* send you a virus, it cheerfully opens that one, too.

Apple Mail attachments

In Apple Mail, to attach a file to a message you're writing, either click the Attach button and select the file to attach or drag the file into the message composition window.

When you're reading a message with attachments, Apple Mail shows them under the message headers, above the text of the message. Click Quick Look to see what the attachment looks like, or Save to save it to a file.

Webmail attachments

To attach stuff at most webmail sites, compose a message as usual. Then click the Attach button and select the file. (You might need to click Browse first, to find the file.) Your web browser, amazing beast that it is, copies the file right off your hard drive and sends it to the mail system to include in your message. When the file is done uploading, the filename appears just below the Subject line. Send the message as usual.

When you receive a message with attachments, a paper clip may indicate that a file came along for the ride. If the file is a picture, the browser usually displays it directly in the message, or you might have to click a Show Images button. The filename of the attached file also appears, and you can click the filename or a View or Download link to open or save the file.

Chapter 10

Getting Social with Facebook and Google+

- -

In This Chapter

▶ Getting started with Facebook

▶ Making your own Facebook page look just right

▶ Making amazing numbers of Facebook friends

▶ Staying in touch with all your Facebook friends

▶ Google+ gets started

- -

A *social networking* site lets you easily create an online profile about yourself and browse the online profiles of other people. You can add basic information about yourself, photographs, and announcements to your personal profile. You can also use social networking sites to communicate with friends, organize events, create groups, and meet new people.

Facebook Isn't the Only Social Network

Social networking sites have become hugely popular with all kinds of people. Facebook (www.facebook.com) was started for college students and expanded to teenagers in general. But Facebook has now attracted a large and diverse user base of more than 700 million people. And the percentage of older people using social networks has increased significantly. Facebook is used by everyone from grandmothers seeking to connect with their grand-children to coworkers sharing conversations outside of work to politicians looking to update their supporters and gain new ones.

Before Facebook's ascendance, MySpace (www.myspace.com) was perhaps the leading social network. In addition to facilitating connections with friends and family members, MySpace carved out a niche as a site where rock bands and other musical groups can easily market to fans. MySpace is still active, but Facebook has left it in the dust.

Enter Google, with Google+ in early 2011. As of this writing, you still need an invitation to join Google+, but by the time you read this, the testing will be done and Google+ will probably be opened up to everyone. Go to `http://plus.google.com` to find out.

Though Facebook, Google+, and MySpace serve the purpose of connecting users to as many people as possible for all sorts of purposes, other social networks are intended for a specific audience and purpose.

For example, LinkedIn (`www.linkedin.com`) is designed for professional networking and can be particularly useful for job searches. After you connect with your business contacts on LinkedIn, you can post news about your work, write recommendations for colleagues, and see who your contacts know at other organizations. Many people use LinkedIn to make personal connections at places where they are applying for jobs. One feature lets you post and answer questions. The idea is to write useful answers so that people looking for employees or contractors will see your profile and decide to contact you by way of a mutual connection.

Since their creation, these sites have been a way for people to keep in touch with contacts and reach new people, for free. (In a few cases, including LinkedIn, sites provide basic service for free and more advanced services for pay.)

You can find a bunch of social networking sites on Wikipedia (`http://en.wikipedia.org`); search for *list of social networking sites.* Facebook is the most popular in North America, so we describe it in detail here. How do you decide which social network to join? Ask your friends and colleagues which networks they belong to.

Because social networking is trendy, you can find a vast number of sites, most of which will never amount to anything. Some sites are popular in specific niches, such as Google's Orkut (`http://orkut.com`) which has been inexplicably popular among Brazilians. But if you've never heard of a site, nobody else you'd be interested in has likely heard of it, either.

Before joining a site, think of people you'd expect to find there, and search for them. If you don't find at least a few of them, the site isn't likely to interest you. Some sleazier wannabe sites scoop all the addresses out of members' address books and send invitations "from" them. So if you receive an invitation you weren't expecting, first write back to the alleged sender to see whether they intended to invite you.

Different sites have different age restrictions for users, along with rules that apply to all users regardless of age. Facebook, like most networking sites, requires users to be 13 or older.

It's entirely possible to join several social networks — and sometimes sensible to do so. We know many people who use LinkedIn for business contacts and use Facebook for everyone else. Remember that the main reason to use a social network is to stay in touch with people, so there isn't much point in joining a network unless you already know people there.

Getting Started with Facebook

The best way to discover Facebook is to set up an account. Social networking sites want to have as many users as possible, so they make it easy to join.

Start by opening your browser and visiting www.facebook.com. You see a form requesting basic information — including name and e-mail address — that is required to set up an account on Facebook.

When you finish signing up for a Facebook account, Facebook sends you an e-mail asking you to confirm your registration by clicking a link in the message. If you don't click the link, after several days you can no longer use your Facebook account.

Figure 10-1 shows a typical Facebook page (okay, it's the page of one of the authors of this book), also known as a *profile*. Your page can include photos, videos, announcements, and other elements to present the Real You (or, optionally, the Fake You).

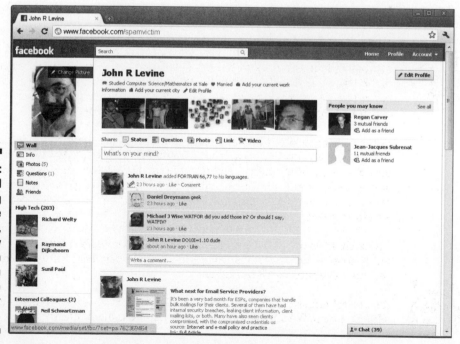

Figure 10-1: Social networking sites, like Facebook, display information about you and make links to your friends.

Expanding Your Profile

After setting up your account, Facebook invites you to add information to your profile. You also have the opportunity to upload your photograph. Photographs are optional, but they help your friends recognize you on Facebook and help distinguish your profile from those of other people with the same name.

Connecting with your friends

The whole point of social networking sites is, believe it or not, social networking. Your site isn't complete until it includes links to lots of friends and, preferably, people you actually know. (We don't try to explain the difference between a Facebook friend and an actual friend.)

Facebook offers multiple ways for you to find other people you know on the site.

After signing up for Facebook, it prompts you to allow Facebook to access your e-mail address book. Facebook can then identify people you know who are also on Facebook and with whom you may want to become friends. This feature is entirely optional; if your address book is like ours, with a lot of addresses of people you barely know, this can be a way to annoy a lot of near strangers *very quickly.*

Based on the other information you add when setting up your profile, Facebook generates a list of other Facebook users whom you might know in real life and invites you to become their Facebook friend. In our experience, it does a creepily good job of finding possible friends.

You can also use the Search bar at the top of any Facebook page to search for a friend by name or e-mail address. Just be careful to select the See Results For option that appears underneath the Search bar as you're typing a friend's name; you can then see the full list of people who have that name. If you click the People link in the left sidebar, you can filter the list by education, location, or workplace in order to narrow the list.

After you see your friend's profile listed, simply click the Add As Friend button to the right of her name. Facebook asks you to confirm this request by clicking the Send Request button. Before sending your friend request, you can also add a personal message. Social norms do not require you to include a personal message when making a request to someone who knows you, but if your name has changed or the person might not recognize you for another reason, it can be helpful.

After you click the Send Request button, you just sit back and wait for your friend to (hopefully) accept your request.

Do you want the whole world to see this?

To edit your privacy settings, click the Account link in the upper-right corner of the page and then select Privacy Preferences.

Facebook's privacy settings are in two parts: Connecting on Facebook and Sharing on Facebook. Make sure to visit both sections to choose your privacy settings.

In the Connecting on Facebook section, shown in Figure 10-2, you see options to select how wide a circle of people can see your friend list or send you messages or otherwise view your information and interact with you. Every action listed in the Connecting on Facebook section has a different menu of restrictions associated with it.

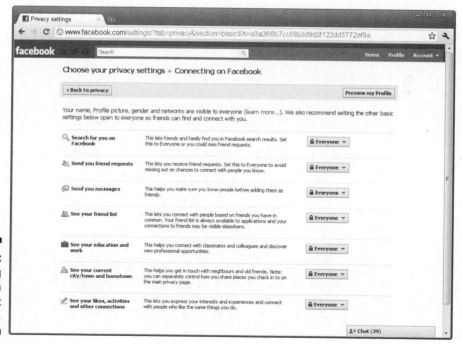

Figure 10-2: Specifying who can connect with you.

In the Sharing on Facebook section, shown in Figure 10-3, you can simplify matters by picking one of the four settings that Facebook has already configured and applying it to all actions in that section.

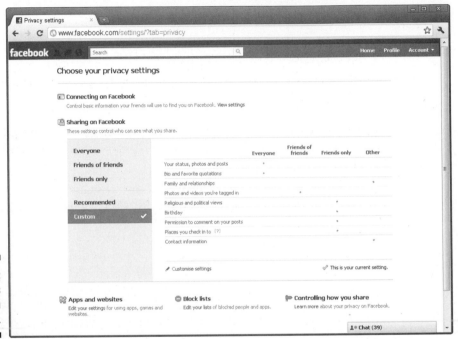

Figure 10-3:
Sharing is
good, within
limits.

For example, if you choose the Everyone configuration, your updates and certain information associated with your profile are visible to the general public, and anyone on Facebook can comment on your posts. If you choose Friends Only, only people you've connected with directly on Facebook can see your information. But, if you choose Friends of Friends, you're in for a surprise: This setting makes some of your information visible to the wider circle of your friends' connections, but still restricts other information to your inner circle of direct connections.

You can also choose the Recommended configuration, which automatically designates different levels of privacy for different pieces of information. For example, photos you post are visible to the general public, your birthday is visible to your friends and your friends' friends, and your contact information is visible only to your friends.

If you prefer to have even more control, choose the Custom option. You can then handpick which types of information have which level of visibility. For example, you can decide to make your posts available only to your friends but your bio and favorite quotations available to everyone.

Three other useful custom settings are available. You can

- ✔ Choose specific subsets of your friends, or specific individuals, who can see particular types of information
- ✔ Choose specific people to "hide" different types of information from
- ✔ Make some of your information visible only to you

To implement any of these three options from within the Custom settings section, click the button next to the type of information you want to control and then select the Customize option.

In addition to setting overarching privacy controls for your account, you can specify who can see particular updates as you're adding content to Facebook.

An ounce of prevention

If you take a little extra time to become familiar with the Facebook privacy settings, you can exercise a lot of control over how your wall posts, photos, and other information are seen (or not seen) by the world. But keep in mind that nothing is totally private on the Internet, particularly on Facebook.

Even if you choose settings so that only your friends can see your announcements and photographs, and even if you become friends with only your immediate family, there's sadly no guarantee that they won't share those announcements and photographs with their friends and coworkers. Neither are you guaranteed that their accounts won't be broken into or otherwise used by someone else.

Facebook has an unfortunate history of changing its privacy options to show ever more of your information to ever more people. The option that gives you maximum control over your information is to think before you post. If you would be mortified to have your snarky comment or silly photograph shared widely, don't post it on Facebook.

Sharing Your News

Sharing appropriate information is what makes Facebook fun and worthwhile for millions of people.

Some people log in to Facebook once a week to see whether new comments or messages are posted online. Others feel the need to update their accounts several times a day. (Perhaps these people check their voice mail every hour, too.) It's all up to you.

You can also receive updates from Facebook via e-mail so that you don't need to log in to see whether anyone has sent you a message, written a comment on your wall, or otherwise interacted with you on Facebook. To change your e-mail notification settings, go to the Notifications tab in the Account Settings section.

Posting status updates, photographs, and links are three especially popular ways of sharing news on Facebook.

Every time you log in to your Facebook account, you see your News Feed page. Directly underneath the words *News Feed* is a list of Share options, inviting you to share a status, question, photo, link, or video.

Updating your status

Your Facebook *status* is simply a written update from you that is displayed to your friends and on your profile. To write a status message, click in the What's On Your Mind box (underneath the Share options). The question disappears from the box and you're free to enter whatever text you want. In this box, you might write *Making chocolate chip cookies for a friend's birthday* or *Took a walk by the river today since the weather was so beautiful!*

Pointing out an online news article

If you want your friends to check out an online news article that you just read (or any other web page), follow these steps:

1. **Click the link labeled Link in the Share options.**

   A box appears with the text `http://` inside.

2. **Click inside the text box.**

   The text disappears and you can type or paste in the link to the web page you want to post.

3. **Click the Attach button.**

   Don't be confused by the Attach label, which makes most people think of attaching a document to an e-mail. You're simply sharing a link.

   The article or web page you've linked to appears.

4. **If you want to add commentary of your own before posting the link to your profile and sharing it with your friends, type your commentary in the box labeled Say Something about This Link.**

   Or skip this step if you want to post the link without additional remarks.

5. **Click the Share button.**

Posting photographs

To put your photographs on Facebook, follow these steps:

1. **Click the Photo link in the Share options.**

   You see three options: Upload a Photo, Take a Photo, and Create an Album.

2. **Choose Upload a Photo (to share a single photograph), Take a Photo (for using a camera on your computer), or Create an Album (to share a group of photographs, usually related to a particular theme or event).**

3. **Follow the instructions to choose or take photos and add comments about them.**

4. **Click Share.**

Making them live!

After you write your update, prepare your link, or upload a single photograph, the last step is to click the Share button to post it. Your update appears on your profile and may show up in the News Feeds of your friends.

The little Lock icon that appears next to the Share button gives you the opportunity to override your current privacy settings and restrict or expand the range of people who can see this particular post.

Networking on the go

Considering the increased popularity of smart-phones, you have multiple ways to use social networks on your smartphone.

If you have an iPhone or iPod touch or an Android phone, the free Facebook, Google+, and MySpace mobile applications let you view and update your site from that cute little device. The Facebook app, shown in this sidebar, enables you to post profile updates and photos, read messages, and look at your friends' pages.

Mobile applications are fun, but not necessary, for smartphone users. You can access Facebook, Google+, LinkedIn, and MySpace using the web browser on your smartphone.

Keep in mind that just because you post an update that all your friends can see doesn't necessarily mean that all your friends will notice and read your update. Don't be surprised if you show up to a party and your friend doesn't know that you just got a new dog or walked in the park earlier that day. A Facebook user with lots of friends can't possibly keep up with everyone's updates (unless they have an extraordinary amount of free time).

Responding to and Arguing with Your Friends

After you have your hundreds of Facebook friends, you have lots of ways to keep up with them and to let them know what you're doing and thinking.

Keeping an eye on the News Feed

The News Feed is displayed on Facebook's home page when you log in. If you scroll down the page, you can see posts from your friends and announcements about their activities on the site. The default setting for the News Feed is Top News, which provides a sampling of updates based on Facebook's guess about which posts will most appeal to you.

If you click the Most Recent option instead, you see your friends' updates in reverse chronological order (starting with the newest updates at the top of the page).

In the News Feed, you can not only read your friends' updates but also "like" those updates and comment on them. For example, if your friend posts that she has gotten a new job, you might click the Like link underneath her post, as a way of expressing congratulations. Or, you can click the Comment link and write a few sentences in response.

To see more of what's been going on in your friend's life, click her name to visit her profile. From her profile, you can read her past updates, view her photos, look at her friends, and (depending on people's privacy settings) look at her friends' pages.

You can also see on your friend's profile the Write Something box (underneath the Share options), similar to the What's On Your Mind box on your home page. If you type an update in this box, it appears on your friend's profile as a note from you to her, a process known as *writing on someone's wall;* it's a kind of digital graffiti.

Sending messages

If you want to write a note to your friend that only she can see, send her a message. Start by visiting her profile and clicking the Message button in the upper-right corner. Type a subject and the message body, as you would in an e-mail. You also have the option to add a photo, video, or link to your message.

To see your sent messages, and to read messages you have received, click the Messages link in the upper-left corner of your Facebook home page.

Hiding and unfriending

Every one of us has that friend who is fun to spend time with in real life but who continually posts random, uninteresting updates. After the fourth time in one afternoon that this person's update appears in your News Feed, you may be tempted to unfriend the poor soul, regardless of the consequences for your relationship. But there's a better way.

Hover your mouse over the person's latest post. A light blue *x* appears in the upper-right corner of their update. After you click the *x*, you have several options, including Hide All By. When you select this option, updates from this person no longer appear in your News Feed.

Your friend will never know the difference. Hiding a friend doesn't limit her access to your information, but it prevents her information from popping up in your News Feed.

But relationships end in real life, and sometimes when that happens, the online friendship also ceases. The easiest way to *unfriend* someone (so that she's no longer your Facebook friend) is to go to her profile and scroll down to the bottom of the left sidebar. Underneath the list of her friends, you see several links in blue text. Click Unfriend.

Facebook asks you to confirm your decision by clicking the Remove from Friends button. Your former friend doesn't receive a notification. However, she may notice if she decides to check in on you sometime by visiting your profile (where she will see an Add As Friend button next to your name) or by looking for your name on her list of friends (where you will no longer be included).

Google Goes Social with Google+

Google+ is Google's answer to Facebook. It has many of the same features as Facebook (friends, messages, photo-sharing, and chat), but it makes it easier for you to control who can see what parts of your online material. Sign up at `http://plus.google.com` when the service has gone public. As of late 2011, accounts were available only by invitation.

In Google+, you organize your friends into *circles,* as shown in Figure 10-4. When you post a comment, photo, or other information, you can choose which circles will be able to see it. This is useful when posting a message about how bored you are at work, if perhaps you don't want your work colleagues to know it.

Figure 10-4:
Google+
enables you
to organize
your count-
less friends
into circles.

Chapter 11

Tweeting about Your Life

*T*he Internet can let the world know the details of your life as it happens. How can you tell your friends right away that you found an outstanding purchase at the mall? Or that you have something stuck in your teeth? And how can you receive these vital messages from your friends even when you're not at home? Twitter (at `http://twitter.com`) is the answer. The service lets you post updates as often as you want, no matter where you are. This level of detail can, of course, be a mixed blessing. A friend of ours likens Twitter to a continuously updated Christmas letter.

When you create a free Twitter account, you create a blog that allows only very short entries, no more than 140 characters each, known as *tweets*. You can send as many tweets as you want, and some people send many indeed. The simplest way is to log in to Twitter and type a line in the box at the top of the page, but you can also tweet from any of a vast number of Twitter-compatible programs, plug-ins on websites such as Facebook, as well as from your mobile phone. (See the section "Tweeting via text message," later in this chapter.)

Every user's tweets are visible on a web page; for example, President Barack Obama's tweets are visible at `http://twitter.com/barackobama`. Because it would be tedious to have to check every page of every person you're interested in, you can *follow* other Twitter users. Then on your Twitter home page, you see, in one chaotic list, all the tweets from everyone you're following. Twitter saves and indexes all tweets, and you can search for words and phrases to find recent tweets of interest.

Getting Started

To get started using Twitter, visit `http://twitter.com/signup`. The website invites you to provide your name (which helps your friends find you on Twitter) as well as your username, password, and e-mail address. Your username is your nickname on Twitter, and other Twitter users refer to you by it. You can choose a name that's fun and different from your given name. In fact, unless your given name is rather unusual, you *have* to choose a different one because your username has to be different from the names of all 175 million existing Twitter accounts.

Don't forget to check the e-mail address that you've provided during registration; Twitter sends an e-mail to that address with a confirmation link.

Reading Tweets and Following Twitterers

To get started, read Twitter for a while to get the idea. Most people use Twitter to find out what's going on right now. Wait to tweet until you have the general idea and have something of interest to say.

Searching the universe of tweets

You can search for people you know by entering their names into the Search box. A surprising number of people and organizations use Twitter to send out announcements and updates. They range from pop stars (try username *LadyGaga*) to politicians *(Schwarzenegger).* Even the fictional Lord Voldemort *(Lord_Voldemort7)* is on Twitter.

You can also enter a keyword (such as *soccer* or *quilting*) into the Search box to find people who tweet about these subjects. Or you can click on the list of possible interests suggested by Twitter after you set up your account. For example, right after the Japanese earthquake and tsunami, you could read up-to-the-minute tweets from Japan by searching for *Japan, earthquake,* or *tsunami.*

What's with all this weird punctuation?

As you read Twitter, you see a number of punctuation marks thrown in, apparently at random. Believe it or not, they mean something:

✔ **A hash mark (#),** (or what we still refer to as a sharp sign) appears at the beginning of a word to indicate that it's a *hashtag,* or a subject or keyword that people can search for. As you read tweets, look at their hashtags. If they appear in tweets that interest you, you can search for that hashtag to find other tweets about it.

✔ **An at-sign (@)** appears in front of someone's Twitter username. For example, mentions of the U.S. president look like *@BarackObama.*

Hey, I like this person's tweets

As you're browsing lists of twitterers, you may see a person or an organization whose tweets you want to receive. Click the Follow button next to their name.

If you choose to follow a twitterer whose profile is private, she must approve your request before you can see her tweets. Otherwise, your request is approved automatically. Keep in mind that just because you're following someone doesn't necessarily mean that she's following you.

Another way to find your friends on Twitter is by using the Find Friends feature: Click Who to Follow and then click Find Friends. Twitter displays a bunch of buttons for widely used webmail and social media accounts, such as AOL, Gmail, Hotmail, LinkedIn, and Yahoo!. You can click on them to give Twitter access to your address book for that account and then identify people that you know on Twitter.

You can see a person's Twitter profile page by clicking their @username. Or, go to `twitter.com/#!/username` in your browser.

Twitter has a culture all of its own, but it's easier to simply watch the tweets scroll by and see the style rather than try to explain it.

How to Not Become Overwhelmed by All Those Tweets

After you read Twitter for more than about 15 minutes, you see that the volume of "tweetage" (accent on the second syllable) is immense and that some of it is a lot more interesting than the rest.

Lists

When you log in to Twitter and view your home page, the Timeline tab shows a list of all tweets from everyone you follow, with the tweets in reverse chronological order, most recent first. Eventually, you may be following so many other twitterers that it's hard to keep track of them all. This is when it's helpful to group Twitter accounts into lists.

For example, you may decide to have one list for your close friends, another list for your colleagues, and a third list for news organizations. The beauty of having lists is that they allow you to see all tweets from one group of people in one place.

To set up a list, click the Lists tab and choose Create a List. Choose a list name and description. You can also choose whether your list is public or private. Choose Private to make your list completely invisible to the outside world. For example, if you're setting up a list named My Real Friends, you can set that list to private so that no one else can see who is on the list, or even that the list exists.

Many people enjoy creating public lists to help other people with similar interests. If you make your Favorite Mystery Authors list public, other mystery readers may come across the list and choose to follow it. If someone follows your list, your list is added to her collection of lists and she can easily visit it.

To add a twitterer to your list, visit the profile and then click the little head-and-shoulders button. Click Add to List and select the check box next to the list(s) to which you want to add them.

Saved searches

Saved searches provide another way to sort through the avalanche of tweets and find the news you truly want. To create a search, enter one or more search terms into the Search box at the top of the page on Twitter. When viewing your search results, click the Save This Search button in the upper-right corner to create a saved search. From the Twitter home page, you can click the Searches tab (under the What's Happening box) at any time and select a saved search to see its latest results.

Preparing to Tweet

Reading tweets doesn't reveal much information about you to the world. But before you start tweeting, be sure to set your privacy settings, and others, to control who can see what.

Your Twitter profile

When you sign up for a Twitter account, you have the bare bones of a profile in place. But there's much more to add. To write additional information about yourself and to choose a look and feel for your profile, follow these steps:

1. **Click the Profile tab at the top of the web page (unless Twitter has redesigned its pages since we wrote this chapter).**

   You see a page with your Twitter username and recent tweets (and retweets).

2. **Click the Edit Your Profile link below your name.**

   You see a page of profile settings that looks like Figure 11-1. You can upload a photograph of yourself, enter your location, write a brief bio, and add the URL of your website, such as to your blog or Facebook profile.

   Click another link on the header menu to change another type of information that Twitter knows about you.

3. **Make your changes and click Save.**

You also can control how your Twitter profile looks. Click the Design link in the Settings section to choose a recommended design that's available from Twitter. You can also upload your own picture for the background of your profile and select your own color scheme for your profile, as shown in Figure 11-2.

Private tweeting

Normally, your Twitter account is public, so anyone can view and follow your tweets. If you're one of the rare people who would rather not have every random person in the world watching what you say, click the Account link on the Settings page, scroll down, and select the Protect My Tweets check box to limit the visibility of your tweets to people you approve.

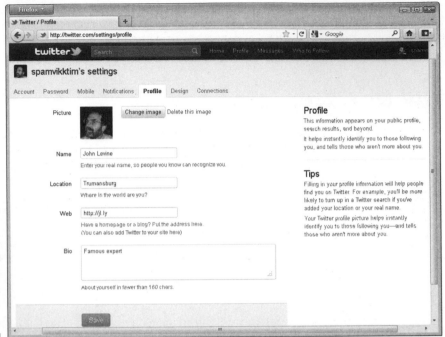

Figure 11-1:
Profiles
in self-
promotion.

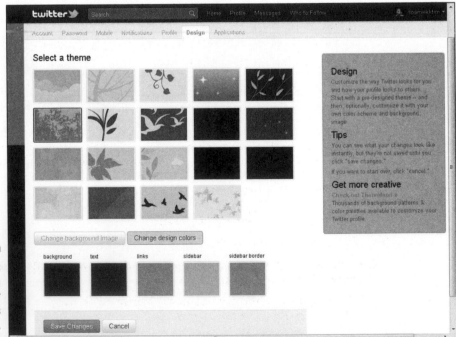

Figure 11-2:
Making
your Twitter
pages
beautiful.

Whether or not you approve someone to read your tweets, she can still see that your account exists. For example, if you follow someone, she can see you on her list of followers, along with your username, full name, photo, and bio.

How to Tweet

The simplest way to send a tweet is by visiting the Twitter home page at `http://twitter.com` and typing a message of 140 characters or fewer into the What's Happening box. Click the Tweet button to publish your tweet. That's it!

Be sure to proofread your tweet before publishing it. And never tweet in anger. After a tweet is out there, it's out there forever.

Hashtags identify keywords

To help people find a particular tweet, insert a *hashtag* (a word starting with the # pound sign character) into a tweet to specify that it's related to other tweets with the same topic tag. For example, include *#green* in your tweets about saving the planet.

Including a web address in your tweet

When all you want to do is share a few words, sending a tweet by way of Twitter is the simplest way. But what about when you want to include a link in your tweet?

Web addresses can be long, and tweets have to be short. What to do? A number of URL-shortening websites can provide a shorter web address that redirects to the real web address. The most popular URL shortener is `http://bit.ly`. Another is `http://tinyurl.com`. Here's how to make a short URL for use in your tweets:

1. **Go to `bit.ly` in your web browser.**

   (Don't insert *.com* at the end.)

2. **In the text box, type or paste the web address you want to include in a tweet. Click the Shorten button.**

   Bit.ly displays a short web address (starting with `http://bit.ly`) that redirects to the address you provided.

3. **Click the Copy button to copy the shorter address to your Clipboard.**

4. **Paste (or type) the address into your tweet.**

   Or, use the address anywhere else you want to use a shorter web address, such as in an e-mail message.

 Some common Twitter applications automatically shorten URLs or allow you to designate a URL shortener during setup so that you don't have to visit a URL-shortening website every time you tweet a link. To find tools to make the URL-shortening process, uh, shorter, visit `http://bit.ly/pages/tools`.

Using @replies and direct messages

Sometimes, you may want to reply to another user's message. If you start a message with the @ sign and the name of a user, the message is a reply to that user. Or, you can insert @*user* in the middle of a tweet, as a mention. In either case, the user you reply to or mention sees your message whenever she clicks the @Mentions link (under the What's Happening box) on the Twitter home page.

You can also send a *direct message* by typing the letter *D,* a space, the user-name, and the message. A direct message isn't visible to anyone else — only to the person that you sent it to.

Retweeting someone else's tweets

If you see a tweet from a friend that you want to share with your own follow-ers, go for it! Just give her credit by starting your tweet with `RT @username` and then repeating her words. Don't be shy about retweeting — people love that kind of shout-out.

Marking your favorite tweets

If you particularly like someone's tweet, you can mark it on your Twitter home page as a Favorite by clicking the star that appears when you hover the mouse cursor underneath the tweet.

Even More Ways to Tweet

Web browsers are so 20th century — far too antiquated for today's modern tweeters. Fortunately, you have plenty of other ways to let the world know what you're up to.

Desktop programs

Twitter is so popular that many programs are available to make it simpler to send tweets, follow people, and find tweets on specific topics. Here are a few:

- **HootSuite (http://hootsuite.com):** This popular Twitter application can be accessed from a browser window and used as a desktop application.

- **Pidgin (http://pidgin.im):** John likes this all-in-one desktop messaging program, which handles Twitter via a free plug-in.

- **TweetDeck (www.tweetdeck.com):** This program (provided by Twitter itself) runs on Windows and Macs (and on Google Chrome), and you can configure it to display tweets from people you follow, tweets that mention specific topics, tweets from Twitter lists, and more.

Both HootSuite and TweetDeck also let you view updates from your friends on Facebook, LinkedIn, and other social networks. To find more Twitter-related programs, search the web for *Twitter applications*.

Mobile applications

Mobile applications aim to make Twitter easier to use on your smartphone. They generally do not require you to use text messaging, but instead let you access Twitter by using simplified layouts designed for small screens.

Official Twitter applications are available for the iPhone and for Android and other types of devices.

Tweeting via text message

If you don't have a smartphone but still want to tweet on the go, you can post to Twitter by text-messaging from your mobile phone.

To tweet via text message, first link your phone number to your Twitter account:

1. **Click the Profile link and then click Edit Your Profile.**

2. **Select the Mobile tab.**

3. **Follow the instructions, which include sending a text message to prove that the number is yours.**

4. **If you want to receive tweets on your phone, select the check box labeled Tweets from People You've Enabled for Mobile Notifications.**

   The Mobile tab also lets you control whether you receive text messages alerting you to direct messages or mentions and replies. You also have the option to specify certain times of day (for example, while you're asleep) that you do not want to receive text messages.

Now whenever you send a text to the special phone number 40404 in the United States or 21212 in Canada, Twitter posts the message as a tweet from you.

Reading tweets by text message

After you connect your phone to Twitter, you have the option to not only send tweets from your phone but also receive them. You probably don't want to receive tweets from random strangers on your phone, especially if you pay by the text message, but you can tell Twitter to send tweets from specific people.

To see all tweets from a particular Twitter user, visit the user's profile by clicking their username in a tweet. Or, go to `http://twitter.com/#!/ username` in your browser. Then click the Mobile Phone icon underneath her username and bio in the righthand column, next to the Follow (or Following) button. The icon turns a different color to indicate that you will start receiving this person's tweets by text message. You can click the button again to turn off this option.

The Twitter service is free, but Twitter can send you a lot of text messages. If you receive as few as five messages a day, that's 150 messages a month. Be sure that you have a monthly plan or bundle that includes enough messages, or you may find yourself paying ten cents per tweet.

Chapter 12

Typing and Talking on the Net

E-mail is pretty fast, usually arriving in less than a minute. But sometimes that just isn't fast enough. Instant-message (IM) systems let you pop up a message on a friend's screen in a matter of seconds. You can also tell your instant-message program the usernames of your friends and colleagues so that the program can alert you the instant that one of your buddies comes online and you can instantiate an instant message to them. (Excuse us — this topic gives us a headache. Wait just a moment while we get some instant coffee. Ahh, that's better.)

The good thing about instant messages is that you can stay in touch with people as fast as by talking to them on the phone. The bad thing about instant messages is that they also offer an unparalleled range of ways to annoy people. Instant message systems usually have about 2 features to send and receive messages and about 12 features to reject, denounce, erase, and otherwise deal with unwanted messages. (This may say more about IM users than about the technology, of course.)

Gregarious people can chat with a whole bunch of people at once, by either typing at the same time, like a party line, or sending messages to each other by e-mail or web forum.

Of course, even better than typing messages to another person is talking right out loud. If your computer has a microphone and speakers, you can use IM or other systems to talk to people over the Net — even groups of people — with no toll charges. If you connect a digital video camera (or *webcam*) to your computer, your friends can even see you as you talk or type. It's not hard to do!

AIMing to Chat via Text

Instant messaging (IM) lets you type short messages that appear in a window on someone else's computer. It's faster than e-mail but slightly less intrusive than a phone call — whoever heard of people having their secretaries screen their IMs?

This chapter describes how to use the most popular IM system: AIM (the initials of AOL Instant Messenger; the initials AOL represent America Online). Google Chat, Windows Live Messenger, and Yahoo! Messenger work similarly, and have similar features. Facebook, described in Chapter 10, includes a chat feature. Skype, a voice-and-video-over-Internet program described in the section "Internet Phones and Voice Chat," later in this chapter, also includes IM chat.

AIM lets you type messages back and forth to other AIM users or to folks who use Facebook or Google Talk. You can also use its voice and video features to talk to and see your "chattees." You can use the stand-alone AIM program we describe here (version 7.5) or AIM Express, which runs in a web browser window (go to www.aim.com and click the AIM Express Chat Now button).

Instant message programs open a new window when one of your buddies sends you a message. If you have a program that blocks pop-up windows in your browser, IM windows aren't affected because pop-up blockers block only web browser pop-ups.

Taking AIM

To download and install the AIM program, visit www.aim.com and follow the directions. We recommend that you decline the various parasitical programs that arrive with AIM — just deselect their check boxes during installation. When you run AIM the first time, you see the window on the left side of the window, as shown in Figure 12-1.

After you install the program, you have to choose a username — which can be as long as 16 letters (be creative so that yours doesn't collide with one of the 40 million names already in use) — and a password. You also have to enter your e-mail address. AIM, refreshingly, wants no other personal information. The e-mail address you give has to be real; AIM sends a confirmation message to that address, and you must reply or else your screen name is deleted. Or, you can sign in with your Facebook account. (See Chapter 10 if you haven't heard of Facebook.)

Figure 12-1:
Choosing
an AIM
username,
signing in
to AIM, and
checking
out the AIM
window.

Normally, AIM runs in the background whenever you're online. If it isn't running, click the AIM icon on your desktop.

The first time you use AIM, you enter your AIM username (refer to the center of Figure 12-1). Type your screen name and password and click Sign In. If you want to use AIM every time you're online, select the Remember Me, Remember My Password, and Automatically Sign Me In check boxes before signing in. After you sign in, you see the AIM window (refer to the right side of Figure 12-1).

Where are my friends?

The first time you run AIM, it may display the Buddy List Builder window, asking whether to search your Facebook, Yahoo!, Gmail, and other address books to find friends who have AIM accounts. If you choose to try it, you have to enter the username and password for each account to give AIM access. Close the window when you're done.

If you use Facebook (described in Chapter 10), you can log in using your Facebook username and password and chat with any Facebook friends who happen to be online. Click the Login with Facebook button, enter your

Facebook username (usually your e-mail address) and password, and click Allow to give your permission for Facebook to share information with AIM. If AIM Lifestream asks for permission to access every single piece of information about you, we recommend that you click Don't Allow — how much does it need to know to enable chat?

Getting your buddies organized

When AIM opens, you see your *Buddy List;* that is, other AIM users you like to chat with (your friends). The window shows which of your many buddies is online now (everyone who isn't listed in the Offline category). What? None of your pals appears? You should add your friends' AIM screen names to your Buddy List.

Which instant message system should I use?

Unfortunately, not all instant message systems talk to one another. Because the goal of all these systems is to help you stay in touch with your friends, use whichever one they use. If you aren't sure who your friends are, AIM is a good bet because it is easy to set up and is widely used; it was originally the chat system for the AOL online service. AIM also enables you to chat with Facebook and Google Chat users. AIM, Google Chat, Windows Live Messenger, and Yahoo! Messenger have similar features because when one adds a feature, the others tend to follow suit. All are free; support text, voice, and video; and allow more than two people to chat. (We've held meetings on Yahoo! Messenger with six people on voice and two on video and everyone typing snappy comments at the same time.) Windows Live Messenger is preinstalled on recent versions of Windows, and it's easy to install if you don't have it.

The bottom line: Use whichever system your friends use. If you're message-mad or you

have friends on more than one system, you can run more than one messaging program at the same time. While we were writing this chapter, we had AIM, Windows Live Messenger, and Yahoo! Messenger all running at the same time. It was an awful lot of blinking and flashing, but it worked.

Better yet, use a program that speaks all three IM languages. We know of and like two (both are free): Pidgin, at `www.pidgin.im`, and Trillian, at `www.trillian.im`, simultaneously handle every IM system we've ever heard of. Trillian requires that you set up an account with it (separate from the accounts on the IM systems you're using) and tries to install a bunch of extra applications and toolbars when you install it; say No unless you're sure you want them. The Pro version has more features for $25. Pidgin is plain old-fashioned freeware — no ads, no registration, no begging. Adium, from `www.adiumx.com`, is the Mac version of Pidgin.

In the AIM window, choose Options⇨Add to Buddy List⇨Add Buddy or press Ctrl+D to display the New Buddy window. Enter an AIM username, a nickname to use for your friend or coworker, and (optionally) a cellphone number (preceded by 1 for U.S. numbers) and an e-mail address. (AIM can send IMs as text messages to cellphones.) Click the Buddy Group button to choose which group to put your new buddy in. AOL provides a few groups, but you can also make your own by choosing Options⇨Add to Buddy List⇨ Add Group. Click Save to add your friend as a buddy.

You can drag a buddy from one group to another in the Buddy List or get rid of a buddy (by clicking the buddy's name and then pressing Del).

Getting buddy-buddy online

To send a message to someone, double-click the buddy's name to open a message window, type the message, and click the Send button or press Enter. AIM pops up a window (shown in Figure 12-2) on the recipient's machine and plays a little song, and you and your buddy can type back and forth. When you're done, close the message window.

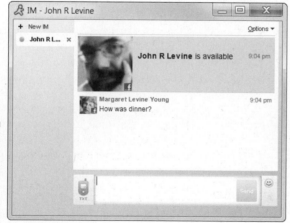

Figure 12-2: Chatting using AIM on your computer.

Buzz off

AIM evidently has a lot of ill-mannered users, because it has a system for warning and blocking users you don't like. If someone sends you an annoying message, you can choose Options⇨Block or Options⇨Report This User in the chat window.

What if someone IMs you when you aren't online? You can tell AIM to show you your missed messages by pressing F7 or choosing Options⇨Settings in the AIM window, which displays the Setting – Buddy List window. Click the Offline IM tab, select the settings you want, and click Save. AIM can save as many as 40 offline messages for as long as two weeks.

You can fine-tune whom you let send messages to you: Choose Options⇨ Settings and then click the Privacy tab. You can limit messages to people on your Buddy List, permit access to specific people, or block specific people. You can also add or delete people from your Block List. We recommend choosing Only Buddies on My Buddy List unless you like being contacted at inconvenient moments by total strangers, many of which are, in reality, software spambots.

The more the merrier — chatting with a group

AIM doesn't limit you to chatting with one person at a time. You can have several chat windows open at the same time and have a separate chat in each window. Keeping track of a bunch of conversations can make you crazy, though teenagers do it every day. AIM usually displays all your conversations in one chat window, with the names listed down the left side.

To start a group conversation, press Alt+C or choose Options⇨New Group Chat and type into a group chat window the screen names of people you want to invite. AIM opens a new tab in your chat window and sends invitations to your buddies; assuming that they click Accept, you're all in!

You can control whether your multiple chats appear in separate windows or as separate tabs in one window. In a chat window, choose Options⇨View⇨ Group IMs in One Window to switch between separate windows and tabs in one window.

AIM on your phone

You can tell AIM to forward messages to your cellphone by way of text message. Choose Options⇨Settings and then click the Mobile tab. Click Register a New Number to display the sign-up page in your web browser. AIM sends a text message to your phone with a code that you must type on the registration page to prove that the phone is truly yours. If you do this, be sure that your phone has a text plan that includes enough messages to cover the ones AIM sends, or else it can get mighty expensive.

If you have a smartphone (such as an iPhone, an Android model, or a BlackBerry) or an iPad, you can run AIM on it, too. Figure 12-3 shows what AIM looks like on an iPhone. Trillian and other multi-IM programs have smartphone versions, too.

Facebook has chat, too

👤 Chat (37) Facebook (the social networking site described in Chapter 10) has chat built into its website, so you can chat with any Facebook user who's online. Because Facebook users often are online just about 24/7 to fiddle with their pages and keep track of their friends, the chances of finding someone online for a chat are pretty good. In the lower-right corner of every Facebook web page is a little Chat icon showing the number of your friends who are online. Click it to see a list of potential chattees, pick a friend, and start typing. If someone chats with you, your Facebook page pops up a little chat window.

Some obvious rules of messaging conduct

Sending someone an instant message is the online equivalent of walking up to someone on the street and starting a conversation. If it's someone you know, it's one thing; if not, it's usually an intrusion.

Unless you have a good reason to expect that the other person will welcome your message, don't send instant messages to people you don't know who haven't invited you to do so. Don't say anything that you wouldn't say in an analogous situation on the street.

Most instant message programs allow you to send and receive files. Unsolicited files from people you don't know are always spam or viruses, or both. Most virus checkers don't monitor file transfers via IM programs.

The messages you send with AIM and other chat programs may appear to be ephemeral, but anyone in the conversation can easily store the messages. Most IM programs have a log feature that saves the series of messages in a text file, which may be embarrassing later. In AIM, you control your own logging by choosing Options⇨Settings and clicking the IM Logs tab.

Finally, if someone tells you to give a series of commands or to download and install a program, don't do it. And never tell anyone any of your passwords.

Instant messaging away from home

Most IM systems let you send and receive messages from a web browser, which is handy if you're at the library or a café that has public computers. The web version usually doesn't have all the goodies of the downloadable programs, but it's fine to exchange a few text messages.

For AIM, visit `www.aim.com` and click either the Chat Now button or the AIM Express button. A browser window pops up that looks a whole lot like regular AIM.

Figure 12-3:
Chatting using AIM on your smartphone.

Abbreviations and Smileys for Chat

Typing is much slower than talking, so when people IM (or participate in online chat, described later in this chapter), they tend to abbreviate wildly. Many chat abbreviations are the same as those used in e-mail. Because IM is live, however, some are unique. We also list some common *emoticons* (sometimes called *smileys*) — funky combinations of punctuation used to depict the emotional inflection of the sender. If at first you can't determine the meaning, try tilting your head to the left. Table 12-1 shows you a short list of chat abbreviations and emoticons.

Table 12-1	IM and Chat Shorthand		
Abbreviation	*What It Means*	*Abbreviation*	*What It Means*
AFK	Away from keyboard	RL	Real life (opposite of RP)
A/S/L	Age/sex/location (sample response: 35/f/LA)	ROTFL	Rolling on the floor laughing
BAK	Back at keyboard	RP	Role playing (acting out a character)
BBL	Be back later	TTFN	Ta-ta for now!
BRB	Be right back	WB	Welcome back
CYBER	A chat conversation of a prurient nature (short for *cybersex*)	WTG	Way to go!
FTF or F2F	Face to face	:) or :-)	Smiling
IC	In character (playing a role)	;)	Winking
IGGIE	To set the Ignore feature, as in "I've iggied Smart Mouth Sam"	{{{{bob}}}}	Hugs for Bob
IM	Instant message	:(or :-(	Frowning
J/K	Just kidding	:'(	Crying
LTNS	Long time no see	O:)	Angel
LOL	Laughing out loud	}:>	Devil
NP	No problem	:P	Sticking out tongue
OOC	Out of character (an RL aside during RP)	<----	Action marker that appears before a phrase indicating what you're doing (<----eating pizza, for example)
PM	Private message (same as IM)	*** or xox	Kisses
WTF?	What the heck?		

In addition to using the abbreviations in the table, chatters sometimes use simple shorthand abbreviations, as in `If u cn rd ths ur rdy 2 chat.`

Adding Voices and Faces

If you don't want to talk with or see people while you chat — that is, if you don't mind being limited to typing back and forth with your friends — skip this section. If you want the audiovisual goodies, read on. You can use a webcam with AIM and most other instant messaging programs.

Say what? Hooking up the sound

Almost every computer comes with speakers, which are connected to a *sound board* inside the computer. These speakers produce the various noises that your programs make. Most laptops have built-in microphones, and most desktop computers also have jacks for microphones, or a microphone built right into the monitor. (Check your computer manual or ask almost any teenager for help with this topic.)

If you don't have a microphone, you can get one that works with almost any computer. A mike should cost less than $20 at your local computer or office supply store. While you're there, also check the prices on computer headsets that have both headphones and a mike, because both you and the people you're talking to will sound much better over a headset than on the computer's built-in speakers. If you're thinking of getting a webcam (see the next section), many of them include microphones.

To test your mike and speakers on a Windows machine, run the Sound Recorder program; try recording yourself and playing it back:

1. **Choose Start➪All Programs➪Accessories➪Entertainment➪Sound Recorder or Start➪All Programs➪Accessories➪Sound Recorder.**

2. **Click the red Record button to start recording, and click the square Stop button to stop.**

   Talk or sing or make other noises between your Start and Stop clicks.

3. **Click the triangular Play button to hear what you just recorded.**

   Click Record again to add to the end of your recording. Choose File➪New to start over and throw away the sound you recorded.

4. **Choose File⇨Save to save it as a WAV (audio) file.**

   We like to make WAV recordings of our kids saying silly things and then e-mail them (the recordings, not the kids) to their grandparents.

You can adjust the volume of your microphone (for the sound coming into the computer) and your speakers or headphones (for the sound coming out) by choosing Start⇨All Programs⇨Accessories⇨Entertainment⇨Volume Control or clicking the Volume Control icon on the right side of the Windows taskbar. If a volume control for your microphone doesn't appear, choose Options⇨Properties, select the Microsoft check box so that a check mark appears, and click OK. Or, the audio system on your computer may come with its own controls.

If you can record yourself and hear the recording when you play it back, you're ready for Internet-based phone calls or chats!

If you want to test how voices from the Net sound on your computer, type the URL `http://net.gurus.org/ngc.wav` into your browser and see what happens. You may need to click an Open or Open with Default Application button after the sound downloads.

I see you!

If you want other people to be able to see you during online conversations, consider installing a *webcam*. This small digital video camera can connect to a computer. Some laptops, such as the MacBook, have built-in webcams above their screens; otherwise, you have to buy one. Webcams come in many sizes and shapes, and prices run from $30 to $300. More expensive webcams send higher-quality images at higher speeds and are supplied with better software. On the other hand, we've had great luck with a $36 webcam for chatting with friends and participating in videoconferences.

Most webcams connect to your computer's USB port, a little rectangular plug on the back of the computer. Some cameras connect to special video-capture cards, which you have to open your computer to install.

If you own a digital video camera for taking video of your family and friends, you may be able to connect it to your computer for use as a webcam. Check the manual that came with the camera.

Many webcam-related sites are, um, not, shall we say, family friendly. If you want to test your webcam with a total stranger, don't be surprised to see parts of the stranger that you wouldn't normally see.

Making noise and pictures with AIM

After you establish a conversation by using AIM, if both you and your friend have webcams, you can switch to voice or video (assuming that both parties have computers equipped with microphones and speakers and, for video, a camera). Choose Options⇨Start Audio Chat or Options⇨Start Video Chat. If your friend uses an IM program that does audio or video, and has a microphone and video camera, he sees a window asking whether he wants to make a direct connection with you. If your friend accepts the invitation, you see a message while AIM sets up the connection, and then your buddy's image appears!

You can choose Actions in the video window to control the size of the video image. You can chat using the microphone and speakers on your PC. Click Disconnect when you finish talking.

Internet Phones and Voice Chat

For about a decade, Internet phones were just around the corner. If you have a broadband Net connection, you're there — you have an Internet phone. No Internet phenomenon would be complete without an arcane abbreviation, so this one is VoIP, for Voice over Internet Protocol, pronounced either "v-o-i-p" or to sound like a dripping faucet.

Easy VoIP with Skype

The freeware VoIP service Skype is owned by eBay and located in Luxembourg, a tiny country in Europe whose main attraction is that it isn't anywhere else. You download and install Skype on your computer from www. skype.com, set up a free account, and start using the program to talk to other Skype users. You can use your computer's built-in speakers, camera, and microphone, a headset with headphones and a microphone, or a handset (which is like a phone handset) plugged into your computer, and/or a plug-in webcam. Skype voice quality over most broadband is quite good, much better than that of a normal phone. The video ranges from poor to good, depending on the speed of the computer at each end and the speed of the net connection between them. You can also buy Skype phones that work like regular cordless phones, except that calls are made by using Skype.

Using a regular phone for VoIP

If you want to use a regular phone for VoIP, setting up VoIP is moderately complicated. You visit a VoIP provider's website and complete the sign-up process, which includes giving your payment information and picking your phone number, which can be either where you live or anywhere you want people to be able to call you as a local call. Most VoIP companies can also *port* your existing phone number away from your old phone company so that you don't have to change your number. (If you later hate your VoIP company, you can port it back or to a different VoIP company.) The company then ships you a Terminal Adapter (TA), which you plug into your Internet connection. Then you plug a regular phone into the TA and you're ready to go.

Several VoIP companies sell combined routers (see Chapter 4 for information about what a router is) and VoIP terminal adapters at electronics stores. In that case, you set up your Internet connection with the router. Then you use your computer's web browser to go to the VoIP company's website to activate the terminal-adapter part of the router and plug a phone into the phone jack on the router, and you're ready to go. John uses Lingo, at www.lingo.com; Ooma, at www.ooma.com, looks good, too. See our website at http://net.gurus.org/phone for suggestions about VoIP companies.

If you have a cable modem, your cable company probably offers VoIP as part of a bundle with Internet and TV. If it does, it works better than independent VoIP providers, so it's worth a close look.

The nice thing about using a regular phone for VoIP is that it's *a phone*. When it rings, answer it. If you want to call someone, pick up the phone and dial. Most VoIP companies offer a full suite of phone features, such as voice mail, call forwarding, and caller ID, usually controlled from a web page rather than from the phone itself.

One not-so-nice thing about VoIP phones is that when your power goes out, your phone stops working, too. While we're on the subject, the same is true for cordless phones — any phone that plugs into a power outlet. Be sure that somewhere in your dwelling you have an old-fashioned corded phone that you can use when you are sitting in the dark and your cell phone battery has run out.

Skype isn't limited to talking to other Skype users. You can set up an account to which you add money — from a credit card or as a bonus included with certain computer headsets — and you can then call any normal phone in the world and pay by the minute. Rates are quite low, about 2 cents per minute for the United States, Canada, and Europe, and do not depend on where you're using Skype — only on where you're calling. John once called home using his laptop by way of a Wi-Fi connection in a hotel lobby in Argentina for 2 cents rather than the dollar a minute it would have cost from a pay phone. You can also use SkypeIn — a real phone number for your Skype phone so that people can call you — for a monthly fee.

Other Skype features

Skype lets you have conference calls of as many as five people and any combination of Skype users and SkypeOut calls to regular phones. It includes an IM feature for typing with your friends while talking to them (or even when you aren't talking to them). And, it has a chat feature with SkypeMe, in which you set up a profile, set your online status to SkypeMe, and invite people to call. Skype users live all over the world, so with luck you may make some new, faraway friends.

Around the Virtual Town Pump

Typing or talking to a few people is fun and interesting, but for good gossip, you need a group. Fortunately, the Internet offers limitless opportunities to find like-minded people and discuss anything you can imagine. Clubs, churches, and other groups use the Internet to hold meetings. Hobbyists and fans talk about an amazing variety of topics, from knitting to *American Idol* and everything in between. People with medical problems support each other and exchange tips. You get the idea — anything that people might want to talk about is now under intense discussion somewhere on the Net.

You can talk with groups of people on the Internet in lots of ways, including these:

- ✔ **E-mail mailing lists,** in which you exchange messages by e-mail.

- ✔ **Social networking sites,** such as Google+ and Facebook, described in Chapter 10.

- ✔ **Usenet newsgroups** (the original Internet discussion groups), which you read with a *newsreading* program. For a description of Usenet newsgroups and how to read them, see our website at http://net.gurus.org/usenet, or go to http://groups.google.com on the web and search for topics that interest you.

- ✔ **Web-based message boards,** where messages appear on a web page.

This section tells you how to participate in Internet-based discussions using e-mail mailing lists and web message boards. These systems are *instant,* like instant messaging: You post a message and, hours or days later, you receive a reply.

Mailing lists: Are you sure that this isn't junk mail?

An e-mail mailing list is quite different from a snail-mail mailing list. Yes, both distribute messages to the people on their lists, but the messages on most e-mail mailing lists contain discussions among subscribers rather than junk mail and catalogs.

Here's how an e-mail mailing list works. The list has its own, special e-mail address, and anything someone sends to that address is sent to all people on the list. Because these people in turn often respond to the messages, the result is a running conversation. For example, if the authors of this book hosted the *chocolate-lovers* discussion about the use and abuse of chocolate, and if the list-server program ran at `lists.gurus.org`, the list of the address would be `chocolate-lovers@lists.gurus.org`. (We run a bunch of lists, but not one about chocolate. Yet.)

Different lists have different styles. Some are relatively formal, hewing closely to the official topic of the list. Others tend to go flying off into outer space, topic-wise. You have to read them for a while to be able to tell which list works which way.

Mailing lists fall into three categories:

- **Discussion:** Every subscriber can post a message. These lists lead to freewheeling discussions and can include a certain number of off-topic messages.

- **Moderated:** A moderator reviews every message before it's distributed. The moderator can stop irrelevant, redundant, or clueless postings from wasting everyone's time.

- **Announcement-only:** Only the moderator posts messages. Announcement mailing lists are essentially online newsletters.

Who handles all this mail?

Something or somebody has to take on the job of keeping track of who's on the mailing list and distributing messages to all its subscribers. This job is *way* too boring for a human being to handle, so programs usually do the job. (A few lists are still run by human beings, and we pity them!) Most lists are run by *list servers* or *mailing list managers*. Popular list manager programs include LISTSERV, Lyris, MailMan, Majordomo, and many others, as well as web-based systems, such as Yahoo! Groups and Google Groups.

Talking to the human being in charge

Someone is in charge of every mailing list: the *list manager.* The list manager is in charge of helping people get on and off the list, answering questions about the list, and hosting the discussion. If you have a problem with a list, write a *nice* message to the list manager. Remember that most list managers are volunteers who sometimes eat, sleep, and work regular jobs as well as maintain mailing lists. If the reply takes longer than you want, be patient. *Don't* send cranky follow-ups — they just cheese off the list manager.

The list manager's address is usually the same as the list address with the addition of *owner-* at the beginning or *-request* just before the @ character. For example, the manager of the list

```
chocoloate-lovers@lists.gurus.org
```

would be

```
chocoloate-lovers-request@lists.gurus.org
```

Getting on and off lists

To find out how to subscribe to a list, or how to unsubscribe to a list, take a look at the instructions that (with luck) accompanied whatever information you received about the mailing list. With most lists, you can subscribe, unsubscribe, and change your subscription settings from the web — you go to a web page and fill out a form. Generally, you enter your e-mail address in a box on a web page and click either a Send or Subscribe button, and you're on the list. This strategy is often more convenient than sending a command by e-mail.

Before you subscribe, be sure that you see a way to get *off* the list (an option that some marketing-oriented outfits neglect to provide).

You should receive a chatty, machine-generated welcoming message telling you that you have joined the list, along with a description of some commands you can use to fiddle with your mailing list membership. Usually, this message includes a request to confirm that you received this message and that it was indeed you who wanted to subscribe. Follow the instructions by clicking a link or replying to this message or doing whatever else the instructions say to do. Confirmation helps lists ensure that they aren't mailing into the void and keeps people from sticking you on lists without your knowledge. If you don't provide this confirmation, you aren't added to the list.

Save the chatty, informative welcome message that tells you about all the commands you can use when you're dealing with the list. For one thing, the message tells you how to get *off* the mailing list if it isn't to your liking. We have in our mail program a folder named Mailing Lists, in which we store the welcome messages from all the mailing lists we join, so that we don't have to embarrass ourselves by asking for help with unsubscribing later.

To remove yourself from a list, you again visit the web page for the list and follow the unsubscription instructions. Do *not* send a *Please unsubscribe me* message, because it only wastes the other subscribers' time.

Stupid mailing list tricks

Most list servers know plenty of other non-essential commands, including commands to hold your mail for a while, commands to send you a daily message that includes all postings for the day, and commands to see a subscriber list. For the exact commands, which vary depending on the list server software, refer to the instructions you received when you subscribed to the list. (You saved the welcome message, didn't you?)

Sending messages to mailing lists

Okay, you're signed up on a mailing list. Now what? First, wait a week or so to see what sort of messages arrive from the list — that way, you can get an idea of what you should or should not send to it. When you think that you have seen enough to avoid embarrassing yourself, try sending something in. That's easy: You mail a message to the list address, which is the same as the name of the list — `chocolate-lovers@lists.gurus.org` or `dandruff-l @bluesuede.org` or whatever. Keep in mind that, because hundreds or thousands of people may be reading your pearls of wisdom, you shouldn't send anything until you have something to say, and try to spell things correctly. (You might think that this advice is obvious, but you would be sadly mistaken.) On popular lists, you may begin to get back responses within a few minutes of sending a message.

TIP

Urrp! Computers digest messages!

Some mailing lists are *digested*. No, they're not dripping with digital gastric juices — they're digested more in the sense of *Reader's Digest*. All the messages over a particular period (usually a day or two) are gathered into one big message with a table of contents added at the front. Many people find this method more convenient than receiving messages separately, because you can easily look at all messages on the topic at one time.

We prefer to receive our messages individually and to tell our e-mail program to sort our incoming messages into separate folders, one for each mailing list we subscribe to. Thunderbird, Windows Live Mail, and many other e-mail programs can sort your messages.

Boing!

Computer accounts are created and deleted often enough and e-mail addresses change often enough that a large list always contains, at any given moment, addresses that are no longer valid. If you send a message to the list, your message is forwarded to these invalid addresses — and a return message (reporting a bad address) is generated for each of them. Mailing list managers (both human and computer) normally try to deflect error messages to the list owner, who can do something about them, rather than to you. As often as not, however, a persistently dumb mail system sends one of these failure messages directly to you. Just ignore it because you can't do anything about it.

Sometimes, you may see the message "I'm away on vacation" or "Click here if you're not a spammer" in response to list messages you send. *Do not respond to these messages, either —* vacation and antispam programs shouldn't even be responding to list mail. Forward the messages to the list manager, though, so that she can suspend those recipients' subscriptions until they get their software under control.

Some mailing lists have rules about who is allowed to send messages, so just because you're on the list doesn't automatically mean that any messages you send appear on the list. Some lists are *moderated:* Any message you send in is sent to a human *moderator* who decides what goes to the list and what doesn't. Although this process may sound sort of fascist, moderation can make a list about 50 times more interesting than it would be otherwise because a good moderator can filter out the boring and irrelevant messages and keep the list on track. Indeed, the people who complain the loudest about moderator censorship are usually the ones whose messages most urgently need to be filtered out.

Another rule that sometimes causes trouble is that many lists allow messages to be sent only from people whose addresses appear on the list, to prevent the list from being overrun with spam. If your mailing address changes, you have to resubscribe or else you can't post anything.

The fine points of replying to list messages

Often, you receive an interesting message from a list and want to respond to it. When you send your answer, does it go *only* to the person who sent the original message or to the *entire list?* It depends on how the list manager set up the list. About half the list managers set up their lists so that replies are sent automatically to just the person who sent the original message, on the theory that your response is likely to be of interest to only the original author. The other half set up the lists so that replies are sent to the entire list, on the theory that the list is a running public discussion. In messages coming from the list, the mailing list software automatically sets the Reply-To header line to the address to which replies should be sent. (Which way to set it up is a topic that can provoke endless, impassioned debate, so don't ever suggest that they change it.)

Fortunately, you're in charge of this feature. When you start to create a reply, your mail program should show you the address to which it's replying. If you don't like the address it's using, change it. Check the To and Cc fields to make sure that you're sending your message where you want. Don't run the risk of sending to the entire list a message such as "I agree with you — aren't the rest of these people idiots?" if you intend it for only one person.

While you're fixing the recipient's address, you may also want to fix the Subject line. After a few rounds of replies to replies to replies, the topic of discussion often wanders away from the original topic. Change the subject to better describe what is truly under discussion, as a favor to the other folks trying to follow the discussion.

How to avoid looking like a dimwit

After you subscribe to a mailing list, don't send anything to it until you read it for a week. Trust us — the list has been getting along without your insights since it began, and it can get along without them for one more week.

You can determine which topics people really discuss and the tone of the list, for example. Waiting also gives you a fair idea about which topics people are tired of. The classic newcomer gaffe is to subscribe to a list and immediately send a message asking a dumb question that isn't germane to the topic and that was beaten to death three days earlier.

The number-two newcomer gaffe is to send a message directly to the list asking to subscribe or unsubscribe. This type of message should be sent to the list manager or list server program, *not* to the list itself, where all the other subscribers can see that you screwed up.

One more thing not to do when you subscribe to a mailing list: If you don't like what another person is posting (for example, a newbie is posting blank messages or "Unsubscribe me" messages or is ranting interminably about a topic), don't waste everyone's time by posting a response on the list. The only thing more stupid than a stupid posting is a response complaining about it. Instead, e-mail the person *privately* and ask him to stop, or e-mail the list manager and ask that person to intervene.

Posting to message boards

Mailing lists are useful if you want to receive messages by e-mail, but some people prefer to read messages on the web. These folks are in luck: A *message board* is a web-based discussion group that posts messages on a website. It's also known as a *discussion board, forum,* or *community.* Like mailing lists, some message boards are readable only by subscribers, some allow only subscribers to post, and some are *moderated* (that is, a moderator must approve messages before they appear on the message board). Other message boards are more similar to bulletin boards: Anyone can post at any time, and there's no continuity to the messages or feeling of community among the people who post.

Many websites include message boards. Some websites are dedicated to hosting message boards on lots of different topics. Some sites host message boards that can also send the messages to you by e-mail, so they work as message boards and mailing lists rolled into one.

Web-based discussion sites

Here are some of our favorite web-based discussion sites:

- ✔ **About.com, at** `www.about.com`: About.com hires semiprofessional experts in a wide variety of fields to host sites about each field. For example, the knitting site at `http://knitting.about.com` is run by a world-class knitter who posts articles and patterns and hosts one or more message boards about knitting. Find the Forums or My Forums link to join in. Figure 12-4 shows a discussion of knitting techniques.

- ✔ **Google Groups, at** `http://groups.google.com`: Google Groups started as a way for people to participate in Usenet newsgroups over the web. Then Google provided a way to set up new groups, too. You can search by topic for groups or messages of interest.

- ✔ **Yahoo! Groups, at** `http://groups.yahoo.com`: Yahoo! Groups includes message boards and file libraries, and you can read the messages either on the website or by e-mail — it's your choice when you join a group. Yahoo! Groups also features calendars for group events and real-time chats right on the website. To join, you must first sign up for a free Yahoo! ID, which also gets you a mailbox and free web space — what a deal! You can also create your own Yahoo! group by clicking links — either a public group for all to join or a private group for your club or family.

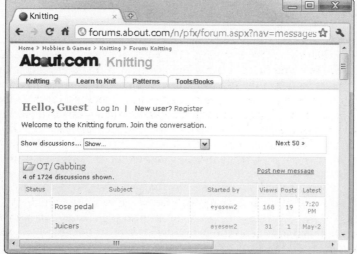

Figure 12-4:
About.
com hosts
sites about
hundreds
(thou-
sands?) of
topics, each
with a mes-
sage board.

Subscribing and participating

Most good message boards require you to register before you can subscribe, which means that you choose a username and password and possibly provide your e-mail address and then respond to a message sent to that address. Registration makes it harder for spam-posting robots to take over the message board.

To subscribe to a community on this type of website, just follow the instructions on the site. Some community websites let you read messages posted to their lists without subscribing — you can click links to display the messages in your web browser.

Finding interesting online communities

Tens of thousands of communities — in the form of mailing lists or message boards or hybrids of the two — reside on the Internet, but there's no central directory of them. This is partly because so many lists are intended only for specific groups of people, such as members of the board of directors of the First Parish Church of Podunk or students in Economics 101 at Tech State.

You can find some communities by searching the web (as we describe in Chapter 13) and including the word or phrase, mailing list, community, forum, or message board. Or, start at www.about.com, http://groups.google.com, or http://groups.yahoo.com and search for your topic.

You can set up your own mailing lists or message boards, too. It's free because the sites display ads on their web pages and may even tack on ads to the postings on the list. If you have an unusual hobby, job, interest, or ailment, you may want to create a list to discuss it. Or, set up a list for a committee or family group to use for online discussions.

Look Who's Chatting

If mailing lists and message boards are too slow — if you want to chat with strangers right now — you might want to try online chat, which is similar to CB radio. Online chat differs from IM chat because it's public and you usually don't know the other people in the discussion.

You begin chatting by entering an area of the Internet known as an electronic *chat room* (or *channel*). After you join a room, you can read onscreen what people are saying and then add your own comments by simply typing them and clicking Send. Although several people participating in the chat can type at the same time, every person's contribution is presented onscreen in the order it's received. Whatever people type appears in the general conversation window and is identified by screen name. On some chat systems, participants can select personal type fonts and colors for their comments.

If one of the people in a chat room seems to be someone you want to know better, you can ask to establish a *private room* or *direct connection,* which is a private conversation between you and the other person and not much different from instant messaging. And, of course, you might get this type of invitation from someone else. It isn't uncommon for someone in a chat room to be holding several direct conversations at the same time, although it's considered rude (not to mention confusing!) to overdo it.

You might also be asked to join a private chat room with several other people. We aren't quite sure just what goes on in those rooms because we've never been invited.

Where is everyone chatting?

Which groups of people you can chat with depends on which chat system you connect to. AOL (formerly America Online) sponsors zillions of chat rooms. You can sign up for a free AOL account to join in. Get *AOL For Dummies,* by John Kaufeld and Ted Leonsis (John Wiley & Sons, Inc.), for a full description of AOL chat rooms.

Many other websites include chat rooms, using a plug-in program that allows people to type at each other. Search the web for the word *chat* plus a topic that you want to talk to people about for a variety of chat venues.

Every chat room has a name; with luck, the name is an indication of what the chatters there are talking about or what they have in common. Some channels have names such as *lobby,* and the people there are probably just being sociable.

Who am I?

No matter which chat facility you use, every participant has a *screen name,* or *nickname,* often chosen to be unique, colorful, or clever and used as a mask. Chatters sometimes change their screen names. This anonymity makes a chat room a place where you need to be careful. On the other hand, one attraction of chatting is meeting new and interesting people. Many warm and wonderful friendships have evolved from a chance meeting in a chat room.

When you join a group and begin chatting, you see the screen names of the people who are already there and a window in which the current conversation often flies off the screen. If the group is friendly, somebody may even send you a welcome message.

As in real life, in a room full of strangers you're likely to encounter people you don't like much. Because it's possible to be fairly anonymous on the Internet, some people act boorish, vulgar, or crude. If you're new to chat, sooner or later you'll visit some disgusting places, although you'll find out how to avoid them and find rooms that have useful, friendly, and supportive conversations. Be extremely careful about letting children chat unsupervised (see Chapter 3). Even in chat rooms that are designed for young people and provide supervision, unwholesome goings-on can take place.

Starting to chat

Whatever chat service you use, the idea is the same: You read other people's messages and chime in with your own. In this section, we describe web-based chat because it's available to all Internet users without installing any extra programs.

Web-based chat sites have Java-based chat programs that your browser can download and run automatically. Other web chat sites require that you download a plug-in or an ActiveX control to add chat capability to your browser. See Chapter 7 for more information about these browser add-ons.

Most chat sites have directories or Search bars so that you can find a group talking about a topic of interest. We find that after you enter the chat room, 93 percent of chats are about nothing at all, or general flirting, so you may need to shop around. Also, you may make a number of tries before you find a chat room where people are actually chatting — sometimes, everyone appears to have wandered off.

Most web-based chat pages have a large window that displays the ongoing conversation, a smaller window that displays the screen names of the participants, and a text area where you type messages. After you type your message, press Enter or click Send and the message appears in the message window for you and everyone else in the chat room.

In some chat rooms, you can click a name in the list of participants to see more information about that person — perhaps a name, location, or picture. Some chat rooms have links or buttons that enable you to turn on voice capability so that you can talk into your computer's microphone and hear other people from the speakers. And, some have video buttons or links that can enable your webcam.

Type or talk?

The original chat rooms consisted entirely of people typing messages to each other. Newer chat systems include *voice chat* (which requires you to have a microphone and speakers on your computer) and even video (which requires a webcam if you want other people to be able to see you).

Getting used to chat culture

Your first time in a chat room can seem stupid or daunting or both. Here are some things you can do to survive your first encounters:

- Remember that when you enter a chat room, a conversation is probably already in progress. You don't know what went on before you arrived.

- Wait a minute or two to see a page full of exchanges so that you can understand some of the context before you start writing.

- Read messages for a while to figure out what's happening before sending a message to a chat group. (Reading without saying anything is known as *lurking*. When you finally venture to say something, you're *de-lurking*.) Lurking isn't necessarily a bad thing, but be aware that you might not always have the privacy you think you have.

- ✔ Some chat systems enable you to indicate people to ignore. Messages from these chatters no longer appear on your screen, although other members' replies to them appear. This strategy is usually the best way to deal with obnoxious chatters. You may also be able to set your chat program not to display the many system messages, which announce when people arrive or leave or are ejected forcefully from the chat room.

- ✔ Scroll up to see older messages if you have to, but remember that on most systems, after you scroll up, no new messages appear until you scroll back down.

Chatting etiquette isn't much different from e-mail etiquette, and common sense is your best guide. Here are some additional chatting tips:

- ✔ The first rule of chatting is not to hurt anyone. A real person with real feelings is at the other end of the computer-chat connection. Don't insult people and don't use foul language, and don't respond to people who do.

- ✔ The second rule is to be cautious. You really have no idea who the other people are. Remember, too, that people might be people hanging out in a chat room and quietly collecting information, and you might not notice them because they never say anything. (See Chapter 2.)

- ✔ Keep your messages short and to the point.

- ✔ Create a profile with selected information about yourself. Most chat systems have provisions for creating *profiles* (personal information) that other members can access.

Don't give out your last name, phone number, or address. Extra caution is necessary for kids: A kid should never enter her age, hometown, school, last name, phone number, or address. Although you don't have to tell everything about yourself in your profile, what you do say should be truthful. The one exception is role-playing chat, where everyone is acting out a fantasy character.

- ✔ If you want to talk to someone in private, send a message saying hi, who you are, and what you want.

- ✔ If the tone of conversation in one chat room offends or bores you, try another. As in real life, you run into lots of people in chat rooms that you *don't* want to meet — and you don't have to stay there.

As in society at large, online chat involves a certain amount of contact with strangers. Most encounters are with reasonable folks. For the rest, common sense dictates that you keep your wits about you — and your private information private. See Chapter 2 for some guidelines for staying safe while chatting with strangers.

Part IV
The Web Is Full of Cool Stuff

The 5th Wave   By Rich Tennant

"He should be all right now. I made him spend two and a half hours on a prisoners' chat line."

In this part . . .

No doubt about it, the web is the happenin' place. For many people, the World Wide Web is the Internet. We explain what the web is and how to get around, and we give you helpful tips about how to find truly interesting and useful stuff among the millions of clamoring web pages. We take a break to listen to lots of online music and watch online videos. Then, relaxed and refreshed, we tell you about web shopping and web banking so that you can confidently spend and save your money online, and find advice on travel or fine dining or just about anything else you want to do.

Chapter 13

Needles and Haystacks: Finding Almost Anything on the Net

"Okay, all this great stuff is out there on the Internet. How do I find it?" That's an excellent question — thanks for asking. Questions like that one are what make this country strong and vibrant. We salute you and say, "Keep asking questions!" Next question, please.

Oh, you want an *answer* to your question. Fortunately, quite a bit of stuff-finding stuff (that's a technical term) is on the web. More particularly, free services known as *search engines* and *directories* are available that cover most of the interesting material on the web. There's even a free encyclopedia, written by Internet users like you.

You can search in dozens or hundreds of different ways, depending on what you're looking for and how you prefer to search. Search can take some practice because billions of web pages are lurking out on the Net, most of which have nothing to do with the topic you're looking for. (John has remarked that his ideal restaurant has only one item on the menu, but it's exactly what he wants. The Internet is about as far from that ideal as you can possibly imagine.)

Search engine, directory — what's the difference?

When we talk about a *directory,* we mean a listing similar to an encyclopedia or a library's card catalog. (Well, similar to the computer system that *replaced* the card catalog.) A directory has named categories with entries assigned to them partly or entirely by human catalogers. You look up categories by finding one you want and seeing what it contains.

A s*earch engine,* on the other hand, periodically looks at every page it can find on the web, extracts keywords from them (all words except for *and* and *the* and the like), and makes a big list. (Yes, it takes a lot of computers. Google has several hundred thousand of them.) The search engine then tries to figure out which pages are most important, using factors such as how many other sites link to that page, and gives each page a score. You use the search engine by specifying some words that seem likely, and

it finds all entries that contain that word, ranking them by their score.

We think of the index in the back of the book as a hard-copy equivalent of a search engine; it has its advantages and disadvantages, as do directories, which are more like this book's table of contents. Directories are organized better, but search engines are easier to use and more comprehensive. Directories use consistent terminology, and search engines use whichever terms the underlying web pages use. Directories contain fewer useless pages, but search engines are updated more often.

Some overlap exists between search engines and directories — Yahoo! includes a directory and a search engine; Google, which is mainly a search engine, includes a version of the Open Directory Project (ODP) directory.

To provide a smidgen of structure to this discussion, we describe several different sorts of searches:

- **Built-in searches:** Topic searches that a browser does automatically, which we aren't always thrilled about it

- **Goods and services:** Stuff to buy or find out about, from mortgages to mouthwash

- **People:** Actual human beings whom you may want to contact, find out more about, or spy on

- **Topics:** Places, things, ideas, companies — anything you want to find out more about

To find topics, we use the various online search engines and directories, such as Google and Yahoo!. To find people, however, we use directories of people — those are (fortunately) different from directories of web pages. If you're wondering what we're talking about, read on!

Your Basic Search Strategy

When we look for topics on the Net, we always begin with a search engine, usually Google. (The word *google* has now been "verbed," much to the dismay of the Google trademark lawyers.)

You use all search engines in more or less the same way:

1. **Start your web browser, such as Chrome, Firefox, Internet Explorer, or Safari.**

   Flip to Chapter 6 if you don't know what a browser is.

2. **Go to your favorite search engine's home page.**

   You can try one of these URLs (web addresses): `www.bing.com`, `www.google.com`, or `www.yahoo.com`. We list the URLs of other search sites later in this section.

   Or, just click in the Search bar in the upper-right corner of your browser window, to the right of the Address bar. (In Chrome, it's the same box.)

3. **Type some likely keywords in the Search bar (either your browser's Search bar or the Search bar that appears on the search engine's home page) and press Enter.**

   After a delay (usually brief, but after all, the web *is* big), the search engine returns a page with some links to pages that it thinks match your keywords. The full list of links that match your keywords may be way too long to deal with — say, 300,000 of them — but the search engine tries to put them in a reasonable order and lets you look at them a screenful at a time.

4. **Adjust and repeat your search until you find something you like.**

   One trick is to pick keywords that relate to your topic from two or three different directions, such as *ethiopian restaurants dubuque* or *war women song*. Think of words that would be on a page containing the information you want. After some clicking around to get the hang of it, you find all sorts of good stuff.

5. **If the search engine is producing results too scattered to be useful and you can't think of any better keywords, try the Yahoo! Directory at** `dir.yahoo.com`.

   When you see a list of links to topic areas, click a topic area of interest. In the directory approach, you begin at a general topic and become more and more specific. Each page has links to pages that become increasingly specific until they link to actual pages that are likely to be of interest.

The lazy searcher's search page

You may feel a wee bit overwhelmed by all the search directories and search engines we discuss in this chapter. If it makes you feel any better, so do we.

To make a little sense of all this stuff, we made ourselves a search page that connects to all the directories and search engines we use — call it one-stop searching. You can use it, too. Give it a try at net.gurus.org/search.

In the not unlikely event that new search systems are created or some existing ones have moved or died, this page gives you our latest greatest list and lets you sign up for e-mailed updates whenever we change it.

Search, Ho!

Once upon a time in an Internet far, far away, lots of search engines and directories battled with each other to see which would be the favorite. Participants were AltaVista and Dogpile and lots of other sites you can find in earlier editions of this book. Well, it seems that the first pangalactic search war is pretty much over, with Google the victor — at least for now. However, Microsoft is fighting back with its Bing search engine. Visit net.gurus.org/search for all the exciting developments.

Google, our favorite search engine

Our favorite web search engine is Google. It has little (software) robots that spend their time merrily visiting web pages and reporting what they see. It makes a humongous index of which words occurred in which pages; when you search for a topic, it picks pages from the index that contain the words you asked for. Google uses a sophisticated ranking system, based on how many *other* websites refer to each page in the index. Usually, the Google ranking puts the best pages first.

Refining your search

Using Google or any other search engine is an exercise in remote-control mind reading. You have to guess words that will appear on the pages you're looking for. Sometimes it's easy — if you're looking for recipes for Key lime pie, *key lime pie* is a good set of search words because you know the name of what you're looking for. On the other hand, if you have forgotten that the capital of France is Paris, it's sometimes hard to tease a useful page out of a search engine because you don't know which words to look for. (If you try searching for *France capital,* some search engines show you information about capital gains taxation in France, or Fort de France, which is the capital of the French overseas département of Martinique. Many people must ask this question, because Google takes pity on you and tells you at the top: "Best guess for France capital is Paris.")

Now that we have you all discouraged, try some Google searches. Direct your browser to www.google.com. You see a screen like the one shown in Figure 13-1.

Figure 13-1:
Google,
classic
style. (It was
the anniver-
sary of the
first World's
Fair.)

Type some search terms and Google finds the pages that best match your terms. That's "*best* match," not "match" — if it can't match all the terms, it finds pages that match as well as possible. Google ignores words that occur too often to be usable as index terms, both the obvious (ones such as *and, the,* and *of*) and merely routine (terms such as *internet* and *mail*). These rules can sound somewhat discouraging, but in fact it's still not hard to get useful results from Google. You just have to think up good search terms. Try the recipe example by typing *key lime pie* and clicking the Search button. You see a response like the one shown in Figure 13-2.

The number-one reason a search doesn't find anything

Well, it may not be *your* number-one reason, but it's *our* number-one reason: A search word is spelled wrong or mistyped. John notes that his fingers insist on typing *Interent,* which doesn't find much — other than web pages from other people who can't spell or type. Google often catches spelling mistakes and helpfully suggests alternatives. We sometimes use a Google search to check the preferred spelling of words that haven't made it into the dictionary yet. (Thanks to our friend Jean Armour Polly for reminding us about this problem.)

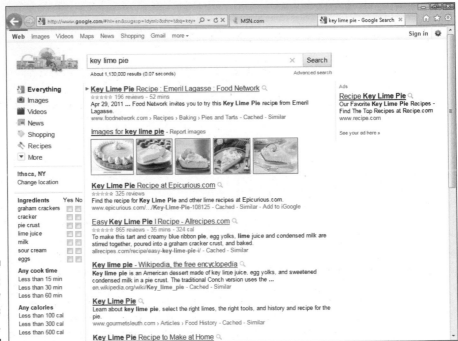

Figure 13-2:
Plenty
of pages
of pie.

Your results won't look exactly like Figure 13-2 because Google will have updated its database since this book was published. (These results have gotten a lot better since we started using this example in earlier editions of this book. Now it understands that you're probably looking for a recipe.) Most of the pages that Google found do, in fact, have something to do with Key lime pie — many have good recipes. Google says it found 1,130,000 matches (yow!), but in the interest of sanity it shows you about 100 of them, 10 at a time. Although that's still probably more than you want to look at, you should at least look at the next couple of screens of matches if the first screen doesn't have what you want. Because the list includes a lot of restaurants with Key lime pie on the menu and a hair salon named Key Lime Pie, you can simply narrow the search to only recipes by adding the keyword *recipe*. Search engines are dumb; you have to add the intelligence. At the bottom of the Google screen are page numbers; click Next to go to the next page.

The links in the right column and sometimes at the top of the results are *sponsored* links — that is, paid ads, ranked by how much the advertiser was willing to pay. Often they're worth clicking, but remember that they're ads.

The I'm Feeling Lucky button searches and takes you directly to the first link, which works, well, when you're lucky.

Even more Google options

Although Google looks very simple, it has plenty of other options that can be handy. You can

- ✔ **Get there from here.** Type a street address, and Google offers a link to a map. Type a person's name and a full or partial address, at least the state abbreviation, and Google gives you addresses and phone numbers. Type a phone number, and it often gives you the name and address. (Try typing *202-456-1414*). The information is all collected from public sources, but if you find this process a bit too creepy, look yourself up and if it finds you, it includes a link to a page where you can have your information removed.

- ✔ **Search Usenet for information.** *Usenet* is the giant collection of Internet *newsgroups* (online discussion groups) that has been around since before the web. Simply click the More link and then Groups above the Google Search bar. If a topic has been discussed in the past 30 years on Usenet (as it seems most topics have), this technique is the best way to find the messages about that topic. It's a useful place to find out how to fix computer problems — most likely, whatever question you have has already been asked and answered on Usenet, and Google has all of it. (John found material there that he wrote in 1981.) To browse around Usenet newsgroups, start at `groups.google.com`. For a description of Usenet, see `net.gurus.org/usenet`.

✔ **Search for images and videos as well as for text.** Often, Google shows some relevant images or videos in with its search results. You can click any of them, or to see more images or videos, just click the Image or Videos links on the left side of any Google results page. Google has no idea what each image or video is but looks at the surrounding text and the filename of the image or video and does a remarkably good job of guessing. If you search for a *key lime pie* image, you indeed see dozens of pictures of tasty pies, and a video search finds a lot of videos of pie-preparation. The SafeSearch feature omits pictures of naked people and the like. If you turn it off, you can find some impressively unsafe pictures.

✔ **Read the news.** Google News (click the News link or start at `news.google.com`) shows a summary of current online news culled automatically from thousands of sources all over the world. ***Warning:*** If you're interested in current events, you can easily waste 12 hours a day following links from here.

✔ **Limit your search to documents in a specific language.** There's no sense in finding pages in a language you can't read, although Google has a subsystem that can try, with mixed success, to translate pages from certain other languages. Click the Language Tools link to the right of the Search bar.

✔ **Do painless arithmetic.** Google is even a calculator. Type *2+2* and Google says `2 + 2 = 4`. It knows units, so if you type *4 feet 8.5 inches,* Google says `4 feet 8.5 inches = 1.4351 meters` and tells you why that's an interesting width. It can also convert currencies.

Handy search engine targeting tips

Google makes it easy to refine your search even more specifically to target the pages you want to find. After every search, your search terms appear in a box at the top of the page so that you can change them and try again. Here are some tips on how you may want to change your terms:

✔ If two or more words should appear together, put quotes around them, as in `"Elvis Presley"`. You can do that with the pie search ("key lime pie") because,

after all, that's the pie's name, although in this example, Google is clever enough to realize that it's a common phrase and pretends that you typed the quotes anyway.

✔ Use + and – to indicate words that must either appear or not appear, such as `+Elvis +Costello-Presley` if you're looking for Diana Krall's husband.

✔ Capitalization doesn't matter. We use all lowercase for our search terms.

Searching from your cellphone

Google isn't limited to the Internet; you can use it from any phone that can send and receive text messages. Google has a special five-digit phone number — 46645 (GOOGL) — that you can text from any phone that can send and receive text messages. Here's how:

1. **Compose a text message to the phone number 46645 (GOOGL).**

2. **In the text of the message, type a Google search command.**

   Here are some search commands you can use:

   • For driving directions, type the two addresses separated by *to*. For example, type *1600 Pennsylvania Avenue, Washington DC to 1 Fifth Avenue, New York, NY*.

   • For nearby restaurants, type the name or type of restaurant followed by the city and state or the zip code. For example, type *pizza Middlebury VT*.

   • For movie times, type the name of the movie followed by the city and state or zip code.

   • For help with other commands you can use, type *help*.

3. **Send the message.**

   Within a few minutes, you receive a text message back from Google with the results of your search.

See Google SMS, at `sms.google.com`, for more information. If your phone has a web browser, you can use Google from it too, the same way you visit any other web page.

Bing!

Microsoft never cedes any part of the computer business without a struggle to the death, and web search is no exception. After many false starts over many years, its Bing search engine, shown in Figure 13-3, shows promise. Its basic operation is a lot like Google: You type some search terms and it finds you some web pages. If you would rather see images or videos, look at the clickable Images and Videos links at the top of the page (unless Microsoft moves them), just like Google. If you want maps and satellite images, use the Maps link, just like the one at Google. If you're looking for news stories, well, you get the idea, even though Bing is reputed to mean Bing Is Not Google. If imitation is the sincerest form of flattery, Google must be feeling extremely flattered.

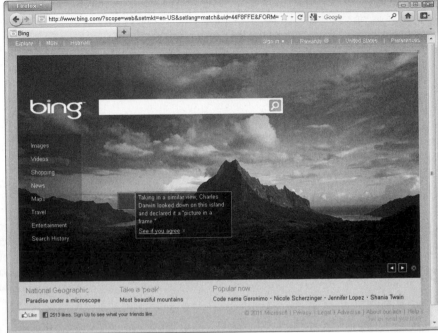

Figure 13-3:
Bing, ready
to go, with
a bonus
geography
lesson.

Google does more than search

Here are a bunch of other services that Google offers. (As far as we can tell, all these services are part of the Google Grand Plan for Global Domination, but the services are free and good, so we use them.)

You can find files fast on your own computer. Google offers Google Desktop, a program you can download to your PC that lets you do Google-like searches (while viewing Google-like ads) of the contents of your PC's hard drive. We find Google Desktop particularly useful for finding old files and e-mail messages that we're convinced are somewhere on our computers. Download it from `desktop.google.com`.

You can see a map of almost anywhere. At Google Maps, you type an address and see a map of the area or a satellite photo of the same

area or both superimposed. Try it at `maps.google.com`. Or, if you're tired of hearing about Google all the time, try MapQuest, at `www.mapquest.com`, another excellent map site, or Yahoo! Local Maps at `maps.yahoo.com`. Even cooler is Google Earth (at `earth.google.com`), which displays 3D maps and images.

You can create and store word processing documents and spreadsheets. Why buy Microsoft Word or Microsoft Excel or WordPerfect when Google Docs & Spreadsheets can do the job? Visit `docs.google.com`, create a free Google account, and go to it. All you need is your browser. Neither the word processor nor the spreadsheet program is as powerful as PC-based programs such as Word and Excel, but for basic documents, they do the job and they're getting better. One of the nicest features is that you can share your documents and spreadsheets with your co-workers and friends so that they can see and edit the documents, too. See the section in Chapter 17 about sharing documents and calendars for more information.

You can send and receive e-mail. We tell you about Google Mail (Gmail) in Chapter 8.

You can organize and display your digital photos. Google offers the Picasa program (at `picasa.google.com`), which helps you organize your photos, provides a photo editor, and enables you to upload them to your own photo website.

Google adds more features almost every week. To see what it's offering, start at `www.google.com`, click More, and choose Even More from the menu that appears.

Bing isn't exactly the same as Google. In most cases, in its results, it suggests related searches you might want to try. The video search runs previews of the videos it found if you mouse over any of them, which is kind of cute. Its satellite images are different from Google's, so you might see a clearer view in one than in the other. Overall, we don't find any overwhelming reason to prefer Bing, but it's worth a look.

One significant difference in Bing is that Microsoft has made it easy to embed Bing searches into other websites, including a split of the money from any ads in the search results, so you can expect to find Bing lurking in lots of other places on the web.

Browsing with Directories

Sometimes a web search just doesn't find what you're looking for. Coming up with the right search terms can be tricky if no specific word or phrase sums up what you want to know. This is the moment to try a web directory. If you know in general but not in detail what you're looking for, clicking up and down through directory pages is a good way to narrow your search and find pages of interest.

Yahoo! for directories

Yahoo! (yes, you normally see it with an exclamation point, but we don't like to yell) is one of the oldest directories — and still a good one. You can search for entries or click from category to category until you find something you like. Start at `dir.yahoo.com`. (At least the page name doesn't use an exclamation point.) As with all web pages, the exact design may have changed by the time you read this section. A whole bunch of categories and subcategories are listed on the left; click any of them to see another page that has even more subcategories and links to actual web pages. You can click a link to a page if you see one you like, or click a sub-subcategory, and so on. Figure 13-4 shows the Yahoo! Directory page for Recreation & Sports.

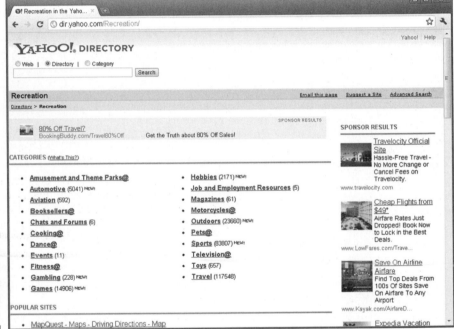

Figure 13-4:
Yahoo!
shows you
how to
have fun.

Early on, you could easily submit a web page to Yahoo! by simply entering a page description and web address of the page into the Submissions page and waiting a week or so for the editors to look at the new page. Submitting pages is now so popular that normal submissions take a *long* time (months) before anyone on staff looks at them, unless you pay them $299 per year for the "express" service. You can draw your own conclusions about how the fee affects what information gets into Yahoo! (and what doesn't).

Yahoo! also has a search engine, but it's actually Bing underneath.

The 404 blues

More often than we want to admit, when you click a link from a search results page, you see — rather than the promised page — a message such as 404 Not Found. What did you do wrong? Nothing. Web pages come and go and move around with great velocity, and the various web search engines were designed as delivery vehicles (not garbage trucks), so they do a lousy job of cleaning out links to old, dead pages that have gone away.

At least the search engines are a bit better in this regard than the manual directories. That's because search engines have software robots (called *spiders* because they roam the web) that revisit all indexed pages every once in a while and note whether they still exist. Even so, many lonely months can pass between robot visits, and a great deal can happen to a page in the meantime. Google *caches* (stores) a copy of most pages it visits, so even if the original has gone away, you can click the Cache link at the end of a Google index entry to see a copy of the page as it was when Google last looked at it.

Here are some other ways to chase down a tantalizing link that has wandered off into nowhere:

✔ The Internet Archive operates a nifty service, the Wayback Machine, that can retrieve older versions of websites. Enter your broken link in its Search bar at www.archive.org. (Yes, this site owns a lot of computers too.)

✔ Sometimes websites try to tidy up a bit and move their files around in the process. If the broken link is a long one — say, www.frobliedoop.org/glompty-dompty/snrok/amazingtip.html — try its shorter versions: www.frobliedoop.org/glompty-dompty/snrok or www.frobliedoop.org/glompty-dompty or even www.frobliedoop.org to find clues to where they put that tip. Also try a Google search on just the filename, such as amazingtip.html. You might find a copy at another website.

✔ Finally, we should mention that websites sometimes shut down, because of either equipment failure or periodic maintenance. (Late nights, Sunday mornings, and major holidays are favorite times for the latter.) Your 404 link just might magically work tomorrow.

Bad links are all just part of life on the online frontier — the high-tech equivalent of riding your horse along the trail in the Old West and noticing that there sure are a lot of bleached-white cattle skulls lying around.

For facts, try Wikipedia first

Wikipedia, at en.wikipedia.org, is an encyclopedia you can use for free over the Internet. The site looks like Figure 13-5. *Wiki* means fast in Hawaiian (actually, *wikiwiki* does, best known before the Internet as the name of the interterminal bus at the Honolulu airport), and Wikipedia has earned its name.

The Wikipedia project, which started in 2001, has grown to more than 3 million articles in English, covering almost every conceivable topic, from the Battle of Dunkirk to *For Dummies* books. Yes, it even has a Key lime pie article, where you read this: "Key lime pie is made with canned sweetened condensed milk, since fresh milk was not a common commodity in the Florida Keys before modern refrigerated distribution methods." Also, since 2006, it has been the Florida state pie.

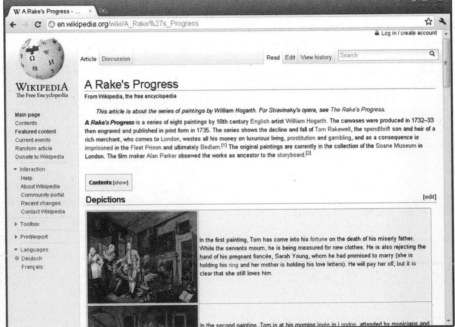

Figure 13-5:
Anyone can edit the Wikipedia online encyclopedia.

If you're looking for the scoop on most topics, Wikipedia is a helpful place to start. You can search for article titles or article text. Words in the article body that are highlighted in blue link to other articles in Wikipedia. Many articles also have links to external websites that have more information on the topic. Articles are created and edited by a volunteer team of more than 300,000 active contributors. Wikipedias exist in dozens of other languages as well. (Adding the en characters at the beginning of its web address gets you the English version. Check out is.wikipedia.org if you've ever wondered what the Icelandic language looks like.)

Who pays for all this stuff?

You may be wondering who pays for all these wonderful search systems. Advertising supports all except two of them. On every page of most search systems, you see lots and lots of ads. It used to be that ad revenue was skimpy — hence the dot-com bust of 2000 — but then the search sites discovered an important secret: When you enter keywords, you're telling the search site something about your interests at the moment. This information turns out to be *extremely* valuable to advertisers. An automobile company might pay a lot to have its ad near the top of the results page when you search for *automobile dealer Kansas.* Some sites (notably, Google) auction off prime ad placement. Google marks these ads as `sponsored` links. Usually, they're on the right side of the results page, but sometimes they're on top with a colored background. (Surprise — this type costs more.) Other search sites may not be as scrupulous. Advertisers pay Google when you click their links.

Wikipedia works on the open source model. The vast majority of contributors are unpaid volunteers, but the substantial bills for running the site are paid for by grants and donations. If you use Wikipedia much, you should kick in a few bucks.

Anyone can edit most Wikipedia articles whenever they want. This concept might seem to be a prescription for chaos, but most articles are watched over by interested volunteers, and inappropriate edits are quickly reversed, so the overall quality remains remarkably high.

If the idea of editing encyclopedia articles on your favorite subjects sounds appealing, talk to your family first. Wikipedia can be extremely addictive.

Articles are supposed to reflect a neutral point of view (NPOV, in Wikispeak), but a few topics — such as abortion, creationism, and Middle East politics — are continually debated. Wikipedia isn't as authoritative as conventional works, like *Encyclopædia Britannica,* but its articles are usually up to date and to the point, with side issues dealt with by links to other articles. One particularly cool Wikipedia feature is its collection of comprehensive lists, `en.wikipedia.org/wiki/Category:Lists`, on all sorts of arcane subjects. One of our favorites is the list of countries with electric mains power plugs, voltages, and frequencies; type *mains power systems* in the Search bar to find it.

If you do a Google search on a topic, a Wikipedia article is likely to show up as one of the links Google returns. That link might be a good place to start reading.

The Usual Suspects: Other Useful Search Sites

After you surf around Yahoo!, Google, and Bing for a while, you may want to check out the competition. Here are some sites that provide specialized types of searches:

✔ **DuckDuckGo:** This quirky search engine (at duckduckgo.com or ddg.gg) promises not to collect personal information, as all the other search engines do, but does a respectable job of searching anyway. It fetches results from a wide range of other sources (with permission) ranging from Bing to the Pokemon Encyclopedia.

✔ **About.com:** This directory (at www.about.com) has several hundred semiprofessional "guides" who manage the topic areas. The guides vary from okay to very good (Margy knows a couple of very good ones), so if you're looking for in-depth information on a topic, check About.com to see what the guide has to say. The site was purchased by the *New York Times* in 2005.

✔ **Ask.com:** Originally named Ask Jeeves, this site's (at www.ask.com) original gimmick was that you could ask your question in English and it'd try to answer it. When you're typing text into a little box, it turns out to be easier to type some keywords than a long polite sentence, but the underlying search engine is worth a try. It was purchased by the media conglomerate IAC in 2005.

✔ **Aardvark:** This so-called social search engine (found at vark.com) asks live people in your list of friends or friends of friends to find answers to questions. The quality of the answers naturally reflects the quality of your friends, but it can be fun. Owned by Google, but run separately.

The ten-minute challenge

Our friend Doug Hacker (his real name) claims to be able to find the answer to any factual query on the Net in less than ten minutes. We challenged him to find a quote we vaguely knew from the liner notes of a Duke Ellington album whose title we couldn't remember. He had the complete quote in about an hour but spent less than five minutes himself actually searching. How? He found a mailing list about Duke Ellington, subscribed, and asked the question. Several members replied in short order. The more time you spend finding your way around the Net, the more you know where to go for the information you need.

Finding People

Finding people on the Internet is surprisingly easy. It's so easy that, indeed, sometimes it's creepy. Two overlapping categories of people-finders are available: those that look for people's e-mail and web addresses and those that look for people's phone numbers and street addresses.

Looking for e-mail addresses

The process of finding e-mail and web addresses is hit-and-miss. Because no online equivalent to the telephone company's official phone book has ever existed, your best bet is to type into Google a person's name and a few other identifying words (such as the town where the person lives and the company where the person works) to see whether any of the matches it finds includes an address. Finding addresses by searching used to be pretty easy, but in recent years, as spammers have taken to scraping off the web every address they can find, a lot of websites now *munge* (obscure) or delete e-mail addresses.

You can search online all you want, but there's no substitute for calling someone up and asking, "What's your e-mail address?"

Googling for people

Type someone's name and address at Google (for the address, type at least the state abbreviation, but more is better), and it shows you matches from phone book listings.

If you're wondering whether someone has a website, use Bing or Google to search for only the person's name. If you're wondering whether you're famous, use Bing or Google to search for your own name to see how many people mention you or link to your web pages. (If you do it more than once, you're *egosurfing*.) If you receive e-mail from someone you don't know, search for the e-mail address — unless the message was spam, the address is bound to appear on a web page somewhere.

Using other people-search sites

Here are some other sites that search for people:

✔ **Canada 411:** Canada 411 (`canada411.ca`) is a complete Canadian telephone book, sponsored by the major Canadian telephone companies. *Aussi disponible en français,* eh? For several years, the listings for Alberta and Saskatchewan were missing, leading to concern that the two provinces were too boring to bother with, but they're all there now, proving that they're just as gnarly as everyone else.

✔ **WhoWhere:** WhoWhere (`whowhere.lycos.com`) is an e-mail address directory. Although search engines usually give better results, some people are listed in WhoWhere who aren't listed in other places.

✔ **Yahoo! People Search:** You can search for addresses and phone numbers and e-mail addresses at `people.yahoo.com`. If you don't like your own listing, you can add, update, or delete it.

✔ **Yellow pages directories:** Quite a few "yellow pages" business directories, both national and local, are on the web, at `www.superpages.com`, `www.yp.com`, and `www.infousa.com`. The directories in this list are some of the national ones. InfoUSA even offers credit reports and other unpleasantly intrusive information.

We're from Your Browser, and We're Here to Help You

Every search engine wants to be your best friend, which, no doubt by coincidence, will increase its market share. (Who? Us? Opinionated?) To cement this friendship, browser makers go to great effort to arrange things so that when you type some search words, the search happens on its own search engine rather than on anyone else's.

Internet Explorer, Firefox, and Safari all have the Search bar to the right of the Address bar, as shown in Figure 13-6.

Figure 13-6: Shortcut Search bars in Internet Explorer, Firefox, and Safari.

If you type a word or phrase in the Search bar, your browser opens your preferred search engine and displays the results of a search for whatever you typed. Or, if you type on the Address bar an entry that doesn't look like an address, it pretends that you typed it on the Search bar and searches anyway. (Google Chrome has only one box where you type something, and it decides what you want.) How convenient is that! You can specify which search engine you want this feature to use:

- **Firefox:** Choose a search engine from its short list by clicking the Search Engine icon to the right of the Address bar (and to the left of the Search bar). Click the icon and choose a different site. Or, choose Manage Search Engines to display a list of search engines that Firefox knows about and add your favorites.

- **Google Chrome:** Click the Customize (little wrench) icon to the right of the Address bar, select Options, click the Basics tab if it isn't already selected, and set Default Search to your favorite search site. Click the Manage button if you want to choose a site that isn't on their list.

- **Internet Explorer:** Choose Tools⇨Internet Options, click the General tab if it isn't already selected, and click the Settings button in the Search section.

- **Safari:** Click the little magnifying glass in the Search bar, where the menu offers a choice between Google and Yahoo!.

Too Many Toolbars

Every search engine vendor offers a *toolbar* that you can add to your browser. The *toolbar* is a bar above your browser's main window with the Search bar and some other stuff on it, such as links to relevant websites and sometimes browser tools such as pop-up blockers. Back when browsers were young and had no Search bars or built-in pop-up blockers, the toolbars were somewhat useful. These days, they're mostly a way to force another search-engine-specific Search bar into your browser, taking up space on your screen that would otherwise be available to look at web pages (refer to Figure 13-7).

Getting the goods on goods and services

All commercial directories and search engines now offer shopping information to help get your credit card closer to the web faster. Search results from Google and Bing have a Shopping link at the top, which opens a page full of links to items at online stores. You can find stuff for sale from all over, offering every conceivable item (and some inconceivable items). We tell you all the do's, don'ts, and how-to's in Chapter 15.

We generally recommend that you decline any invitations to install browser toolbars, because their value is negligible. If a specific toolbar has a specific feature you want that isn't otherwise available in your browser, such as the page rank display on the Google toolbar, it doesn't hurt to install it, other than losing that half-inch of screen real estate.

Figure 13-7:
Toolbar mania: Don't let this happen to you.

To get rid of unwanted toolbars in Internet Explorer, right-click in a blank part of any menu or toolbar to open a menu where you can deselect the ones you don't want. To get rid of toolbars in Firefox, choose Tools⇨Add-Ons (which shows all add-ons, including the toolbars), click the one you don't want, and then click the Uninstall button that appears.

Making a Custom Start Page

Many sites want you to use them as your *start page* (the page that your browser loads when it starts up, as described in Chapter 7). To encourage you to do so, these sites enable you to customize them to show all kinds of useful information just for you.

Stumbling upon something interesting

John doesn't like it, but Margy enjoys using StumbleUpon (www.stumbleupon.com) to find websites. Rather than allow you to specify what you're looking for, StumbleUpon tries to guess which web pages you might find interesting and shows one to you. You can click a button to say whether you like the site and then click the Stumble button to see another web page. StumbleUpon adjusts its guesses based on what you say you like.

For example, if you create a free Google account, you can have a fancy, custom iGoogle page rather than the boring, plain one that most folks use. Click the Sign In link in the upper-right corner of the Google page and create an account if you don't already have one (by clicking the Create an Account Now link). After you're logged in, go to igoogle.com if you don't see instructions for making a personalized home page. Your page can include a clock, a calendar, a weather report, news headlines, and other features.

Yahoo! provides similar features. (They predate Google's by several years.) From my.yahoo.com, sign in and click Add Content to choose items to put on your My Yahoo! page, which can contain news headlines, stock prices, sports scores, Facebook updates, and other news. John likes My Yahoo! enough that he has made it his home page.

Chapter 14

Music and Video on the Web

A thousand years ago, when we wrote the first edition of *The Internet For Dummies,* Internet content consisted almost entirely of text. (It was 1993, but it sure *feels* like a thousand years ago.) You could download a few archives of pictures, and there was this weird thing, the World Wide Web, that could mix together pictures and text on the same page, but for the most part, it consisted of text: People's connections were so slow, downloading pictures took so long, and computer screens were so fuzzy that we stuck to text. The pictures you could download were single images, such as cartoons and snapshots. Audio was nearly unheard of (so to speak), and video files were so bulky that even if you could find a clip and wait a week for it to download, it wouldn't fit on your computer's hard drive. By the late 1990s, Internet connections had sped up enough and screens had improved enough that pictures were normal fare — and audio was entering the mainstream enough that we put a sample voice message on our website, in case any of our readers had sound cards. (It's still there, at net.gurus.org/ngc.wav.)

Things have advanced a little since then. Ordinary users now have Net connections that run at several million bits per second — faster than the main backbones of the early 1990s — and the capacity of computer hard drives has become enormous beyond imagining. Passing around audio and video over the Net has become practical and widespread. In fact, the amounts of available audio and video are now so vast that you could spend your entire life looking at online commercials without ever finding anything worth watching. This chapter tries to bring a little order to the vast wasteland of online media.

To avoid writing *audio and/or video* a hundred more times in this chapter, henceforth we use the concise (albeit imprecise) term *media* to refer to them.

Seven Ways to Get Media and One Way Not To

You can get your media fix in approximately ten zillion different programs and formats. Fortunately, they fall into a modest number of categories: free, streaming, rented, purchased, shared, and outright stolen.

Receive it as a gift

The simplest approach is to download media offered for free and then play it. Visit www.nasa.gov/multimedia, where NASA has lots of free little movies on topics ranging from dust storms on Mars to how a roller coaster ride feels like taking off in the space shuttle. You can also find independent movies and videos from producers more interested in letting people see their work than in charging for it. Visit epitonic.com for an eclectic collection of music by artists, some well known and some obscure, released so that people can listen to it and make their own mixes.

Borrow it

Even on a broadband connection, downloading a whole media clip can take a while. Rather than download first and play later, *streaming* media downloads as it plays, thereby re-creating (in a complex digital manner) the way that radio and TV have worked since the 1920s. As with TV and radio, after it's streamed, it's gone — and if you want to play it again, you have to stream it again. Streaming audio can work over a dialup connection, but streaming video needs a broadband connection.

Most streaming media is provided *on demand:* You click a link and they send you whatever it is, sort of like a jukebox. Alternatively, sometimes streaming media is a single program to which you can listen in and hear what's playing at any moment. Not surprisingly, it's named *Internet radio,* and in many cases the audio stream is an actual radio program, such as our local public radio stations at wrvo.fm in upstate New York and www.vpr.net (click Listen Live) in Vermont. We say more about Internet radio later in this chapter.

Rent it

A great deal of music isn't available for free, but it's available for cheap. Services such as Real Networks Rhapsody (`www.real.com/rhapsody`) offer monthly subscriptions that let you listen to large libraries of recorded music. Napster (`www.napster.com`) charges about $5 per month for unlimited streaming music and five MP3 downloads each month that you can play on your MP3 player or cellphone. You pay a fixed monthly fee, and then you can click songs from a catalog to play them and to make and share playlists of your favorites.

These rental services have enormous catalogs of music, and each one claims to be the largest. They really *are* large: While checking out Rhapsody, we were finally able to do a side-by-side comparison of Desi Arnaz's muscular late-1940s version of *Babalu* and his mentor Xavier Cugat's more elegant 1941 recording. (You'll just have to decide for yourself which one you like better.) However, when you stop paying rent, your music vanishes. Remember — you never owned it.

You can find video rental websites too — not just for renting a DVD but also for downloading the video over the Internet and watching it on your computer. For example, Netflix, at `www.netflix.com`, is known for its DVD-rental-by-mail service, but you can also download videos on demand. Not all its DVDs are available for download, but for the ones that are, you see a Play button on the website. Blockbuster, at `www.blockbuster.com`, lets you rent or buy downloaded movies. Note that the Blockbuster player, which you have to download and install to watch their videos, works only with Internet Explorer, not with Firefox, Safari, or Chrome.

Buy it

Apple iTunes makes buying music and video easy. Go to `www.apple.com/itunes` to listen to the first little bit of any song in its catalog. If you like it, you can buy your own, permanent copy (for 99 cents) that you can copy to your iPod, play on your computer, or burn on a CD. You don't have to be a Mac user to use iTunes; you can play the tunes by using the Windows version of the iTunes program. (See the section "Organizing your music with iTunes," later in this chapter.) It's no surprise that people buy in droves, making iTunes the biggest online music store. Likewise, many more websites sell music either from a web-based store or as an add-on to a rental service, most for about the same price as at iTunes.

Apple makes it easy to listen to and watch your iTunes music and videos on an iPhone, iPod, or iPad. If you have an Android or other smartphone or tablet, programs are also available for transferring your music and videos to your phone.

Amazon.com (www.amazon.com), the world's largest bookstore, also sells downloadable tunes in MP3 format.

Already own it

You probably own a whole lot of digital music in the form of music CDs. Copying your music CDs to your computer is known as *ripping,* and it's easy to do. Windows Media Player, iTunes, and other music programs can copy all tracks from a CD and put the songs into your music library so that you can play them from your computer (without the CD) or copy them to your MP3 player. See "Copying music from your own CDs," later in this chapter.

Share it

The original version of Napster was the first well-known music exchange service, allowing members to download MP3 music files from each other for free. The system was the first large-scale *peer-to-peer* (P2P) information exchange, where people exchange files with each other rather than download them from a central library. Eventually, the big record labels sued and shut it down because most of the material that people exchanged was in flagrant violation of the music's copyright. Napster was later reincarnated as a site for music rental and free online music streaming — but no free downloading.

The popular file-sharing system BitTorrent (www.bittorrent.com) has thus far been able to fly under the legal radar, unlike LimeWire (www.limewire.com), which was shut down by a court order. They resemble an earlier Napster — a network from which you can download music for free, a certain amount of which is provided against the wishes of the owners of said music. While you're downloading music from other people's computers, they are in turn downloading music from you, so they can significantly slow down your computer and your Internet connection. The music industry insists that these folks are morally reprehensible, but people use BitTorrent in particular to share large amounts of entirely legal and legitimate material along with the dodgy stuff. We suggest that you stay away from it — as legal music gets cheaper and cheaper, why break the law to save a few bucks?

Downloads for the post-literate

Not all downloadable audio files contain music. A thriving market exists for what used to be called "talking books." You can download books and magazines and just about anything else you might otherwise read, as well as radio programs you might have missed. Although listening to downloaded books on your computer works fine — and it can be an essential tool for the visually impaired — it's kind of pointless if you can read the paper book faster than you can listen to it (and kick back on the patio while you're at it). But if you drive to work or go jogging, a talking book on CD in the car player (or copied to the MP3 player or iPod on your belt) is just the ticket.

The largest source of talking books is Amazon's Audible.com (www.audible.com). You can buy individual books for book-like prices or subscribe and listen to one or two books a month cheaper than you can by paying individually. Either way, the books you buy are yours to keep.

They provide a reasonably nice program that you can download and install to keep track of the files for the books you bought and then burn them to CDs (*lots* of CDs — about 15 for a full-length book). Audible has also made deals with many other media programs, so you can find an Audible plug-in for iTunes that lets you copy your books to an iPod, as well as a plug-in for Windows Media Player for all the MP3 devices it handles, and so forth.

Audible usually offers a trial subscription with a couple of free books, and its catalog includes public-interest stuff (such as presidential inaugural speeches) available for free if you want to try it out. *Warning:* John tried it out and ended up inventing errands that involved driving to faraway stores so that he could listen to the last CD of *The DaVinci Code*. On the other hand, Margy's husband survived a long commute thanks to his Audible subscription.

Subscribe to it

You can subscribe to audio programs over the Internet. A *podcast* is an audio file distributed over the Net for listening to on an iPod or another type of MP3 player or any computer with speakers. Many radio shows are available as podcasts; go to www.npr.org to find many of them. Lots of organizations and people make podcasts, too. See the section "Subscribing to podcasts with iTunes," later in this chapter, for instructions.

Steal it — um, no

Plenty of pirated stuff is still on the Net, and probably always will be. We expect that our readers, because they're of good moral character, wouldn't want to look for it, but if you do, you have to do so without our help.

What Are You Listening With?

The two most popular programs used for playing web-based online media are Windows Media Player and Apple iTunes. The first two include separate player programs and plug-ins for web browsers so that web pages can embed little windows that show movies or play music. You eventually have to install all three if you want to handle all the links you click. All three work pretty well.

iTunes

`www.apple.com/itunes`

Apple iTunes, shown in Figure 14-1, has become insanely popular because you have to use it if you have an iPhone or iPod. In addition to playing and organizing music, iTunes is the way to load music from your computer onto the iPod or iPhone. You may have heard of it as a music store and a way to organize music, but iTunes can play all sorts of media, including videos. iTunes supports streaming video as well as audio in most popular formats.

Ripping CDs to your computer and keeping your music organized in iTunes are described later in this chapter.

Figure 14-1:
You can use iTunes to buy music, rip and burn CDs, organize songs into playlists, subscribe to podcasts, and maybe even wash the dishes.

Windows Media Player

www.microsoft.com/windows/windowsmedia

Microsoft has its own streaming audio and video formats, and it bundles a player for them with Windows. The Windows Media Player program, shown in Figure 14-2, can play files in Advanced Systems Format (with the extension .asf or .asx), in addition to most other formats. More recent versions added useful new features, so if you don't have Media Player version 11 or later, it's worth your time to visit Windows Update or the Media Player site to download it. (Media Player itself may nag you to upgrade, if you have an older version.)

Figure 14-2:
Organizing your music with Windows Media Player.

Click the Music and Videos links on the left side of the Media Player window to see which audio and video files you have. Click Media Guide to browse links to popular music. When you put an audio CD into your computer's CD drive, it displays the list of tracks on the CD and you can click Rip CD to *rip* (copy) tracks from the CD to your hard drive and to your Windows Media Player library. You can also burn music CDs by clicking the Burn tab.

Okay, How about Some Music?

Two hot activities on the Internet are downloading and exchanging music files with your friends in the MP3 file format. MP3 stands for *MP*EG level *3* (acronyms within acronyms — how technoid) and is simply the soundtrack format used with MPEG movies. Because this format is widely available and does a good job of compressing music to a reasonable size for downloading, it has been adopted by music lovers on the Net. As you may already have guessed, MP3 players (similar to the iPod and little, less-expensive devices from Sandisk and Rio) can play MP3 files, too, which is the main reason for their popularity. Many cellphones can play MP3 files, too.

You can play MP3 files by using many different programs, including iTunes and Windows Media Player. This section explains how to use iTunes to organize music, subscribe to podcasts, make playlists, and listen to radio stations over the Internet because all the programs are fairly similar. If you use Windows Media Player, you get the general idea.

Naturally, Microsoft has the competing file format WMA, with the extension .wma. iTunes can also handle WMA files.

Copying music from your own CDs

You already own tons of music on those racks of CDs that will soon be obsolete. You can rip (copy) the tracks from an audio CD by using iTunes. When you put an audio CD into your computer's CD drive, iTunes asks whether you want to import the tracks into your iTunes library. Click Yes to begin copying. iTunes looks up the CD using an online database so that you can see the titles of the tracks and even the album artwork.

When you rip music from CDs, you can specify which format to store the files in. We use the MP3 format because the files are smaller than some other formats and because every music player can handle MP3s. In iTunes, choose Edit➪Preferences, click the General tab if it isn't already selected, click the Import Settings button, click the Import Using option, set it to MP3 Encoder, and click OK twice. You can also choose the quality, where you trade off file size against sound quality.

Organizing your music with iTunes

Apple iTunes (www.apple.com/itunes) lets you buy legal, downloaded songs for a reasonable price, from 69 cents apiece and up, based on popularity. Both Mac and Windows users can buy and play songs from iTunes by downloading the free iTunes program, which is excellent for keeping your songs organized even if you don't have an iPod or buy from the iTunes store. Click iTunes Store to browse the store — iTunes turns into a web browser to enable you to click around to find audio and video files.

Making playlists

In iTunes, you can organize your music into playlists, which are your own, customized albums. One playlist can be music you like to listen to while washing the dishes, and another playlist might be for your fabulous oldies collection. Or, each user of your computer can have her own playlists. You can have as many playlists as you like. (Margy has one playlist of the baritone parts she needs to learn for her women's barbershop group, Maiden Vermont, and another playlist of instrumental jazz, 1960s rock, and Hindu chanting to listen to while working.)

You create a new playlist by choosing File⇨New Playlist or by pressing Ctrl+N. You can name the playlist whatever you want and then drag in music from your library. Dragging a song from the library to a playlist doesn't remove it from the library or copy the file — you can put the same song into multiple playlists, and all the while it continues to be stored in your general iTunes library just once.

Subscribing to Podcasts

Podcasts are audio magazines that deliver MP3 files of talk or music directly to your computer (see the section "Subscribe to it," earlier in this chapter). The word is a combination of i*Pod* and broad*cast,* but you don't need an iPod to listen to them — any computer or MP3 player will do. Radio programs, companies, musicians, comedians, and just plain people produce podcasts about a huge variety of different subjects, everything from "The Twilight Saga" to the stock market.

Video podcasts are the same idea, but you receive video rather than audio files.

Subscribing to podcasts on the web

Several websites provide directories of podcasts, including Podcast.com and PodcastAlley.com. They enable you to find podcasts by topic, subscribe to them, and listen to them from the website.

Or, go to the website of the program you want to subscribe to. National Public Radio at www.npr.org originates dozens of podcasts.

Subscribing to podcasts with iTunes

To subscribe to a podcast, click the iTunes Store link in iTunes and then click the Podcasts link. When you find a podcast that looks interesting, you can click an episode to listen to it on the spot or click the Subscribe button to receive all future episodes automatically. Most podcasts are free, and iTunes downloads the latest episodes every time you start the program.

Playing Music and Podcasts

If you want to listen to music or podcasts while you're sitting in front of your computer, you're all set — fire up iTunes or Windows Media Player and listen. But we hear that some people actually have lives and want to listen to music in other places.

You can buy a portable MP3 player — an iPod, a cheaper alternative from another manufacturer, or a phone that includes an MP3 player — and take thousands of MP3 cuts to listen to while you jog, travel, or just hang out. It's similar to a Walkman, but you don't need tapes or CDs. You hook your MP3 player to your computer whenever you want to download new tunes. These players can hold *weeks* of music and podcasts. The most popular is the ubiquitous Apple iPod, but other players are cheaper and work fine. Only iPods can play M4P (copy-protected) music — and only files to which you own a license. Or, check whether your phone can play MP3s.

More threats and promises

Folks ripping their favorite tunes from CDs and e-mailing them to their 50 closest friends comprise a hideous threat to the recording industry, not to mention that they're violating copyright law. (The previous hideous threats, for readers old enough to remember, were cassette tapes and home VCRs, which totally destroyed the music and movie industries. What — they didn't? Uh, well, *this* time it's different because, um, just because it is.) The industry's efforts to shut down websites that offer ripped songs for free downloading has been moderately successful, but private e-mail is hard to stop.

The recording industry came up with the Secure Digital Music Initiative, a music file format of its own. The SDMI was intended to let you download but not share music. It flopped, partly because it had technical defects quickly analyzed and reported by enterprising college professors and students and partly because nobody wanted crippleware music. The recording industry has been filing lawsuits against the most visible music sharers, on the peculiar theory that if it threatens and sues its customers, their attitudes will improve and they will buy more stuff. Maybe someday the industry will figure out, as Apple did, that if it sells decent music at reasonable prices and lets customers listen to it the way they want to, people will pay for it.

There's CDs, and then there's CDs

Although all CDs look the same, they don't all play the same. Normal audio CDs contain a maximum of about 74 minutes of music and work on every CD player ever made. When you burn a CD-R (the kind of CD you can write to only once), you're making a normal audio CD. Because blank CD-Rs are cheap (about 20 cents apiece if you buy them in quantity), the main disadvantage of this approach is that you end up with large stacks of CDs.

MP3 files are much smaller than audio CD files, so if you burn a CD full of MP3s, you can put about ten hours of music on each disc. DVD players and many recent CD players, including the one in your car, can play MP3 CDs. If you're not sure whether your player can handle MP3 CDs, just make one on your computer and try it in your player. It doesn't hurt your player, although you might see some odd error messages. Although rewritable CD-RWs don't work in normal CD players, players that can handle MP3 CDs can usually handle CD-RWs. Again, if you're not sure, try it; it doesn't hurt anything if it doesn't work.

Listening to Internet Radio

If you like to listen to music while you work, check out real radio stations or Internet-only radio stations. Most radio stations now *stream* their talk and music on the Internet in addition to broadcasting it over the air. Go to a radio station's website and click the Listen Now or similarly named link — for example, we're listening to a show about backyard chickens at `wbur.org` as we write this section. Many radio stations have MP3 players built into their websites.

Tuning in to a station

Like real radio stations, Internet-only stations offer a mix of music and talk and sometimes commercials. Unlike real (broadcast) radio stations, they're extremely cheap to set up, so lots and lots of people do — providing lots of quirky little niche stations run by people all over the world. You listen to them in a streaming program, usually iTunes or Windows Media. Most are available for free, some require a subscription, and some have a subscription option to make the ads go away.

If you use iTunes, click the Radio link in iTunes to get started. You see a menu of different types of stations, and after choosing one, you can peruse stations from across the country at your leisure for free. Double-click a station to listen to it.

To get started, here are some directories of Internet radio stations:

- `music.yahoo.com` — Visit Yahoo! Music and click the Radio button.
- `shoutcast.com` — SHOUTcast Radio Directory gives you a choice of using its own SHOUTcast Radio Mini Player or your existing player.
- `www.live365.com` — Live 365 Internet Radio streams several thousand stations with every possible kind of music.

Either way (broadcast radio or Internet-only radio), you can listen to talk and music from all over the United States — or the world.

Making your own station

Every radio station — Internet or broadcast — chooses a range of styles of music to play. Why should you be limited to the musical tastes of existing radio stations? Instead, you can create your own musical mix, including music you don't even own!

Enter Pandora Radio, at `www.pandora.com` (shown in Figure 14-3). As its website states, it's a new kind of radio station, one that plays only music you like. Type the names of a musician or group or the name of a song, and Pandora finds, in its huge musical database, music that's similar to what you specify. You can't play the exact song you want, but you can play similar music, displaying information about the artist and album. When Pandora guesses wrong about what it thinks you like, you can click the thumbs-down icon to kill the song. When it guesses right, click the thumbs-up icon to tell it to play more songs like that one.

Figure 14-3:
Make your own radio station at Pandora.

You can name your "radio station" and have several stations for different kinds of music — maybe one for working and another for paying bills. You can also share your radio station with other people so that they can listen to the mix you have created.

Jango (at `www.jango.com`) and last.fm (at `last.fm` — no *.com*) work like Pandora. Many of these sites also have apps for iPhones, Android OS phone, and other smartphones and tablet computers.

Watching Movies on the Web

Now that most people have fast Internet connections, watching video over the Net has become possible and popular. You can watch short videos at YouTube, television shows, or entire movies or upload your own videos for others to watch.

Older web browsers, like Firefox before version 3.5, can't play videos — you need to get a player program. You also need a reasonably fast computer to display movies in anything close to real time. Flash, the most widely used player, plugs into your web browser (download it for free from `get.adobe.com/flashplayer`). iTunes and Windows Media Player also handle movies (and are described earlier in this chapter). Neither the iPhone, iPod touch, nor iPad (as of 2011) supports Flash, the technology that web browsers use to display video, so not all these options will work on these devices.

The YouTube thing

Probably the largest Internet video phenomenon is YouTube (`www.youtube.com`). It's a site like Google (which owns YouTube), but rather than an Internet search engine for information at large, it's only for videos. On YouTube you can find everything from *Saturday Night Live* clips to previews for upcoming movies to strange homemade Lego flicks. According to the *New York Times,* people post more than 100 million videos on YouTube every *day* — 48 hours of video uploaded every minute, with over 3 billion video views every day. Unfortunately, Google is losing an amazing amount of money on YouTube every day because few advertisers want their ads displayed alongside such a weird and unpredictable collection of videos.

In the Search bar, you can type a word or phrase related to the video you're looking for and YouTube displays a list of links of possible videos, as shown in Figure 14-4. Click the image or title to play the video. Video-playing software is embedded in the website, so you need nothing but an Internet connection to watch videos on YouTube. (See the later sidebar "Too many video file formats.") If you see a video you like a lot and want to share with your 50 closest friends, you can click the Share link below the video to e-mail a link, post a tweet on Twitter (see Chapter 11), or write it on your Facebook wall, as described in Chapter 10.

Figure 14-4:
Millions of weird and occasionally wonderful videos are available on YouTube.

Other YouTube-like websites include Vimeo (`www.vimeo.com`), Metacafe (`www.metacafe.com`), and Bing Videos (`bing.com/videos`). Justin.tv (`www.justin.tv` — no *.com*) shows live video — stuff that's happening right now. The Online Video Guide (`www.ovguide.com`) can help you find TV and movies on the web.

If you have an iPhone, iPod touch, or iPad, you can't display YouTube in its web browser. Instead, these devices come with a YouTube app preinstalled.

Putting the You in YouTube

You can upload a video to YouTube as long as it's on your computer, you own the copyright (YouTube deletes stolen videos), it's neither defamatory nor pornographic, and it's no longer than ten minutes. To upload, follow these steps:

1. **Create a free YouTube account by clicking the Create Account link in the upper-right corner of any YouTube page.**

   Or, sign in to your existing account. If you have a Google account, use it.

2. **Click the Upload button.**

   Or, click the Post a Video Response link below an existing video.

3. **Select the video file on your computer and follow the instructions.**

   You can choose whether to make the video public or private, name the video, and specify which category it's in. YouTube uploads your video and converts it to the Flash format for streaming. Uploading can take a while (ten minutes or more) depending on the speed of your Internet connection.

After your video is on YouTube, you can share it with your friends.

If a video is public on YouTube, it's really, really public. Think twice about including personally identifying information about yourself or your kids unless the video is something you're truly proud of. After you upload a file, you can click your account name in the upper-right corner of the web page, choose My Videos, click the Edit button below a video, and change the Broadcasting and Sharing Options from Public to Unlisted (anyone with the link can view) or Private (only people you choose can view).

Watching movies

You can stream movies from the web, although usually not for free (at least, not legally). If you have a Netflix account to receive DVDs by mail, you can stream videos from its website (at www.netflix.com) without paying anything extra. Netflix has a huge inventory of DVDs, and many of them are also available for streaming. On the website, you add movies to your queue if you want to watch them later or receive the DVD by mail. Or, click the Watch Instantly tab to find a movie and watch it now.

Too many video file formats

The original standard digital-movie format is Moving Picture Experts Group (MPEG). MPEG was designed by a committee down the hall from the JPEG committee that defined file formats for scanned photos and (practically unprecedented in the history of computer standards efforts) was designed based on earlier work. MPEG files have the extension .mpeg or .mpg.

Microsoft, responding to the challenge of emerging standards that it didn't control, created its own formats. Audio/Visual Interleave (AVI) format is for nonstreaming video, with the extension .avi. Advanced Streaming Format (with the extension .asf or .asx) is for both streaming audio and video data. Their latest entry is Silverlight, which is a lot like Flash, only different. It's available on Windows and Macs. The mostly compatible open source package, Moonlight, is available for Linux.

All these formats are being replaced by Flash because it's what YouTube uses — files that end with .flv and a few variations. The Flash player (a free download from get.adobe.com/flashplayer) plugs into your web browser and plays streaming video in several qualities, including one that's similar to HD television. Unfortunately, Apples hates Flash and doesn't allow it to work on the iPhone, iPod touch, or iPad (at least, not as of mid-2011).

Blockbuster, whose lunch Netflix was eating when Netflix began its DVD rental business, retaliated with an online service at www.blockbuster.com that is quite similar to Netflix.

Amazon.com offers a Video On Demand service, which enables you to stream movies for a fee. You can save movies for later after you pay for them or watch previously purchased videos again. Choose the Movies Music & Games department and then click Amazon Instant Video.

Watching TV

Missed your favorite television show? Didn't record it on your TiVo? You might be able to catch it on Hulu, at www.hulu.com. It's supported by ABC, Fox, NBC, and others, so it shows entire episodes, not ten-minute clips, and copyrighted shows aren't liable to be deleted, as they are on YouTube. YouTube has responded with YouTube Shows, at www.youtube.com/shows, which is different from the regular YouTube site; like Hulu, it has commercial video, with no amateur uploads.

Blip.tv (at blip.tv — no *.com* at the end) hosts shows you may never have heard of because they're made by independent creators. Link TV (at www.linktv.org) shows educational programs from around the world.

Netflix has television shows as well as movies, so if you have a Netflix account, you can stream TV, too.

Sharing media around the home and dorm

Microsoft Windows 7 has a feature that lets you set up all your computers, at least the ones running Windows 7, as a *HomeGroup* that can easily share resources on all your computers and other networked devices. Open Windows Media Player, switch to the Library page, and click Stream⇨Turn On Media Streaming. If your computer isn't already in a HomeGroup, it undergoes the process to join an existing group and set one up. After you do that, the Library page shows an icon for the libraries of everyone else, on your computer and others, who has turned on media streaming, and you can play their stuff just like you can play your own. You're also supposed to be able to play from your computer onto networked players and other devices; if your Windows 7 computer can see them on the network, it sets up icons so that you can access them.

You also have the option to allow streaming to the Internet, which we do *not* recommend because, unless you set up your system file protections very carefully, you can allow random strangers on the Net into your computer. We expect the most enthusiastic use of network media streaming will be in "homes" that are college dormitories, where everyone in the dorm is already on the same network, so now they can all share each other's music at the click of a mouse.

Chapter 15

More Shopping, Less Dropping

*W*e've gone shopping on the Internet, and we've gone shopping in the *souq* in Marrakech. The experiences were surprisingly similar except that the *souq* smelled more interesting and probably had more live snakes. The Internet is the world's biggest bazaar, with stores that carry everything from books to blouses, from DVDs to prescription drugs, from mutual funds to musical instruments, and from plane tickets to, uh, specialized personal products. (Don't read too much into that one.) Shopping online is convenient — no parking or standing in line — and you can compare prices easily. But is online shopping safe? Well, we've bought all kinds of products online, and we're still alive to tell the tale. (We got a nice rug in the *souq*, too.)

Shopping Online: Pros and Cons

Here are some reasons for shopping on the Net:

- ✔ Online stores are convenient and open all night, and they don't mind if you aren't wearing shoes or if you window-shop for a week before you buy something.

- ✔ Prices are often lower online, and you can compare prices at several online establishments in a matter of minutes. Even if you eventually make your purchase in a brick-and-mortar store, the information you find online can save you money. Shipping and handling is usually the same as you pay for mail order (although some sites offer free shipping for large orders), and you don't have to drive or park.

- Online stores can sometimes offer a better selection. They usually ship from a central warehouse rather than keep stock on the shelf at dozens of branches. If you're looking for an item that's hard to find — for example, a part for that vintage toaster oven you're repairing — the web can save you weeks of searching.

- Sometimes, stuff just isn't available locally, and buying online can save you a trip. (The authors of this book live in small rural towns. Trumansburg, New York, is a wonderful place, but if you want to buy a new toaster, you're out of luck. And Margy couldn't find a harmonium anywhere in the Champlain Valley.)

- Some online stores offer smartphone apps. When someone tells Margy about an interesting book, she's likely to order it on the spot, using an online bookseller's iPhone app.

- Unlike malls, online stores don't have Muzak. (A few websites play background music, but we don't linger on those sites.)

On the other hand, here are some reasons that you shouldn't buy everything on the Net:

- You can't physically look at or try on stuff before you buy it, and in most cases, you have to wait for it to be shipped to you. (We haven't had much luck buying pants online, f'rinstance.)

- Your local stores deserve support so that they'll be there when you need something right now or need their help in picking something out.

- You can't flirt with the staff at a web store or find out the latest town gossip.

The Credit Card Question

How do you pay for products you buy online? Usually, you pay by credit card, the same way you pay for anything else. Isn't it incredibly, awfully dangerous to give out your credit card number online, though? Well, no.

When you use "plastic" at a restaurant, you give your physical card with your physical signature to the server, who takes it to the back room, does who-knows-what with it, and then brings it back. Compared with that, the risk of sending your number to an online store is pretty small. A friend of ours used to run a restaurant and later an online store and assures us that there's no comparison: The online store had none of the credit card problems that the restaurant did.

Many books (including earlier editions of this one) make a big deal about whether a website has a security certificate, which means that it shows a little lock in the corner of the web browser window. The lock is nice to have, but the problem it solves — bad guys snooping on the connection some-where between your PC and the seller's web site — isn't a likely one unless you're using a public wireless network connection. We think you should worry more about whether a store selling something is run well enough that it ships you the item you bought. Recent security breaches that revealed credit card numbers to crooks came about when those crooks broke into a store's database, not snooped on your Internet connection.

Credit cards and debit cards look the same and spend the same, but credit cards bill you at the end of the month whereas debit cards take the money right out of your bank account. In the United States, consumer protection laws are much stronger for credit cards. The important difference is that in case of a disputed transaction, *you* have the money if you used a credit card but *they* have it if you used a debit card. Use a credit card to get the better protection, and then pay the bill at the end of the month so that you don't owe interest.

If, after this harangue, you still don't want to send your credit card number over the Internet, most online stores are happy to have you call in your card number over the phone (although, likely as not, an operator halfway around the globe then enters your credit card number by using the Internet). If you're one of those fiscally responsible holdouts who doesn't "do plastic," send a check or money order.

Take a credit card number — any number

One of the more clever innovations in online banking is *virtual* credit cards. If you want to place an online credit card order with a mer-chant you don't entirely trust, first visit your bank's website and tell the bank how much the order will cost, and, on the spot, it may be able to concoct a brand-new card number. Then you return to the merchant's site and order with that card number rather than with your regu-lar number. As soon as the merchant places the charge, your bank links the new number to the merchant, so even if the merchant leaks the number, it's no good to anyone else. The number's credit limit is the amount you set when you created it, so if the merchant tries to overcharge you, the bank says no. You can also create virtual numbers that are good for a set number of charges, for example, for subscrip-tions that require regular payments.

Different banks use different names for this service. Citibank and Discover call it *virtual numbers*. Ask your bank whether it offers this service.

John found that virtual numbers also work for phone orders and mail orders and any other type of charge where you don't use your physi-cal card. Because he's paranoid, he uses vir-tual numbers for everything from his electric bill to his college alumni association. *Don't* use them for buying plane tickets or reserving hotel rooms, though, because you often have to show a real card with the number at the check-in desk.

Cookie alert

You may have heard horrible stories about the cookies that websites reputedly use to spy on you, steal your data, ravage your computer, inject cellulite into your hips while you sleep, and otherwise make your life miserable. After extensive investigation, we have found that most cookies aren't bad; when you're shopping online, they're quite helpful. (See Chapter 2 for more on cookies.)

A *cookie* is no more than a little chunk of text that a website sends to a PC with a request (not a command) to send the cookie back during future visits to the same website. The cookie is stored on your computer in the form of a tiny snippet of text. That's all it is. For online shopping carts, cookies let the web server track the items you have selected but not yet bought, even if you log out and turn off your computer in the interim. Stores can also use cookies to keep track of the last time you visited and what you bought, but they can keep that data on their own computers, so what's the big deal? (If you don't want websites to store cookies on your computer, you can prevent them; see how in Chapter 7.)

Paying at the Store

Buying stuff at an online store isn't much different from buying it at a regular store. Most stores hope you will buy several items at a time, so they use *shopping carts* instead. As you click your way around a site, you can toss items into your cart, adding and removing them as you want, by clicking a button labeled something like Add Item or Buy Now. When you have the items you want, you visit the virtual checkout line and buy the items in your cart, at which point you tell them where to send your items and how you're paying. Until you visit the checkout, you can always take the items out of your cart if you decide that you don't want them, and at online stores they don't become shopworn, no matter how often you do that.

Figure 15-1 shows the shopping cart at an online book store we like, with two items in it. When you click the Secure Checkout button, the next page asks for the rest of your order details.

Some stores even have the online equivalents of layaway plans and gift registries. For example, some web shopping sites let you add items to a wish list that you can share with your friends so that you or someone else can buy the item for you later. Some sites offer gift certificates, too, for shopping online.

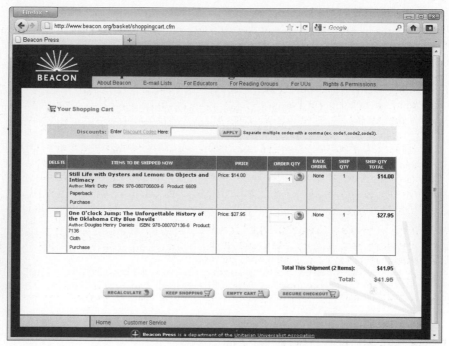

Figure 15-1:
Have you
finished
your holiday
shopping?

How Little Do You Want to Pay?

You want to pay as little as possible, of course. About 15 minutes after the second online store appeared, someone realized that you could look at the stores to find who charges how much for which item and then report back on your own website. Price comparison sites work well *if* you can exactly identify the products you want to buy. For books, consumer electronics, computers, and computer parts, it's always worth a look. But if you're looking for khaki pants, no two pairs are the same, and most of us would rather pay an extra ten bucks to avoid a pair that makes us look like a spandex-wrapped potato.

Comparison sites now work two ways. One is to visit store sites and *scrape* (copy) the prices. The other is to make a deal with interested stores and let them upload their prices directly, typically in return for a commission when users click through. Both methods work okay, but we have occasionally seen comparison sites showing different prices from the ones you see if you visit the store site directly. Here are a few of our favorites:

- ✔ **Google Product Search** (`www.google.com/prdhp`) is the latest incarnation of the Google price comparison site that was originally named Froogle. Stores upload prices, but Google doesn't charge them. (The search pages have ads on the right.) The searching is helpful, but the inventory is spotty.

- ✔ **ISBN.NU** (`isbn.nu`) checks prices for new books at a dozen online stores and tells you which one has the best price. The site scrapes the prices and then uses the stores' affiliate programs to get paid.

- ✔ **MySimon** (`www.mysimon.com`) compares prices from a wide variety of online stores, finding its information about high-tech products from CNET and about nontechnical products from Shopping.com.

- ✔ **Nextag** (`www.nextag.com`) also covers a wide range of products, but we would decline their offer to help you shop for online degrees.

- ✔ **Pricegrabber** (`www.pricegrabber.com`) has good coverage of everything from musical instruments to computer parts.

- ✔ **Red Laser** (`redlaser.com`) is an iPhone and Android app that enables you to scan a barcode while you're standing in a store. The app then displays a list of online stores that sell it, with prices.

Up, Up, and Away

We buy lots of airline tickets online. Although the online travel sites aren't as good as the very best human travel agents, the sites are now better than most agents and vastly better than bad travel agents. Even if you have a good agent, online sites let you look around to see your options before you get on the phone. Some airlines offer on their own websites some cheap fares that aren't available any other way. The airlines know that it costs them much less to let the web do the work, and they pay you (in the form of a hefty discount) to use the web.

The theory of airline tickets

Three giant airline computer systems in the United States — Sabre, Galileo/Worldspan (two formerly separate systems that are merging), and Amadeus — handle nearly all airline reservations in the United States. (A site such as this is known as a *CRS*, or a computer reservations systems, or a *GDS*, for global distribution system.) Although every airline has a "home" GDS, the systems are all interlinked so that you can, with few exceptions, buy tickets for any airline from any GDS. Some low-price, start-up airlines are available by way of GDS, and others — notably, Southwest — don't participate in any of these systems but have instead their own websites, where you can check flights and buy tickets.

In theory, all these systems show the same data; in practice, however, they get a little out of sync with each other. If you're looking for seats on a sold-out flight, an airline's home system is most likely to have that last, elusive seat. If you're looking for the lowest fare to somewhere, check all four systems (using different travel websites) because a fare that's marked as sold out on one system often mysteriously reappears on another system. Also check Orbitz (www.orbitz.com/), which has direct-connect access to many airlines, bypassing GDS altogether.

Some fare categories are visible only to travel agents and don't appear on any websites, particularly if you aren't staying over a weekend, so check with a good agent before buying if you're taking a short trip during the week. On the other hand, many airlines offer some special deals that are *only* on their web sites and that agents often don't know about. Confused? You should be. We were.

The confusion is even worse if you want to fly internationally. Official fares to most countries are set by way of the IATA cartel, so computer systems usually list IATA fares for only international flights. If you need to buy tickets sooner than a month ahead, you can often find entirely legal *consolidator tickets* for considerably less than the official price, so an online or offline agent is extremely useful for finding the best price. International airlines also have some impressive online offers, most notably from Cathay Pacific, which usually has a pass that includes a ticket from the United States to Hong Kong and then unlimited travel all over Asia.

Here's our distilled wisdom about buying tickets online:

- ✔ **Check online systems.** See which flights are available and the range of prices. Check sites that use different GDSs. (We list some sites at the end of this section.)

- ✔ **After you find a likely airline, check that airline's site.** Look for special, web-only deals. If a low-fare airline flies the route, be sure to check that one, too.

- ✔ **Check prices on flights serving all nearby airports.** An extra 45 minutes of driving time can save you hundreds of dollars.

- ✔ **For a trip more complicated than a simple round trip, check with a travel agent.** You can check by phone, e-mail, or the agent's website to see whether he can beat the online price, and buy your tickets from the agent unless the online deal is better.

- ✔ **For international tickets, check for consolidator tickets.** Do everything in this list and check both online and with your agent, particularly if you don't qualify for the lowest published fare. For complex international trips, such as around the world, agents can usually find routes and prices that the automated systems can't.

- ✔ **Don't overbid.** If you bid on airline tickets at a travel auction website, make sure that you already know the price at which you can buy the ticket.

Before looking at online agents, check out ITA Software (www.itasoftware.com). This company produces the fare search engine used by Orbitz and many airline sites. ITA's own site has a version that just searches and doesn't try to sell you any tickets, with more search options than most of its clients offer. They've been bought by Google, so by the time you read this chapter, their searches may well be integrated into Google searches.

If you hate flying or would rather take the train, Amtrak and VIA Rail Canada offer online reservations (www.amtrak.com and www.viarail.ca). If you're visiting Europe, a Eurailpass at www.raileurope.com can make sense if you plan to take a whole lot of trains. Check schedules and fares for most European railways at the German railways site at www.db.de (click the small English link near the right center).

Major airline ticket sites, other than individual airlines, include

- **Expedia:** The Microsoft entry into the travel biz (www.expedia.com) is now a part of the Interactive media empire.

- **Hotwire:** This multi-airline site (www.hotwire.com) offers discounted leftover tickets and rental cars and hotels.

- **Orbitz:** Orbitz (www.orbitz.com) is the high-tech entry into the travel biz, with most airlines' weekly web specials.

- **Travelocity:** Travelocity (www.travelocity.com) is the Sabre entry into the travel biz. Yahoo! Travel and the AOL travel section are both Travelocity underneath.

Fare-comparison sites abound, including Kayak (www.kayak.com), Mobissimo (www.mobissimo.com), and FareCompare (www.farecompare.com). We don't find any of them comprehensive enough to depend on, but they're worth a look if you want to try to find that elusive last cheap seat.

More about online airlines

Because the online airline situation changes weekly, anything more we print here would be out of date before you read it. One author of this book is an air travel nerd in his spare time; to see his current list of online airline websites, web specials, and online travel agents, visit airinfo.travel.

Even More Places to Shop

Here are a few other places for you to shop on the web. We have even bought stuff from most of them.

Auctions and used stuff

You can participate in online auctions of everything from computers and computer parts to antiques to vacation packages. Online auctions resemble any other kind of auction in at least one respect: If you know what you're looking for and know what it's worth, you can find some outstanding values; if you don't, you can easily overpay for junk. When someone swiped our car phone handset, we found an exact replacement phone at eBay for $31, rather than the $150 the manufacturer charged for just the handset.

Many auctions — notably, eBay (as shown in Figure 15-2) — also allow you to list your own stuff for sale, which can be a way to get rid of some of your household clutter a little more discreetly than in a yard sale. The PayPal service (www.paypal.com), now owned by eBay, lets you accept credit card payment from the highest bidder by e-mail. (See Chapter 16 for more information about PayPal.)

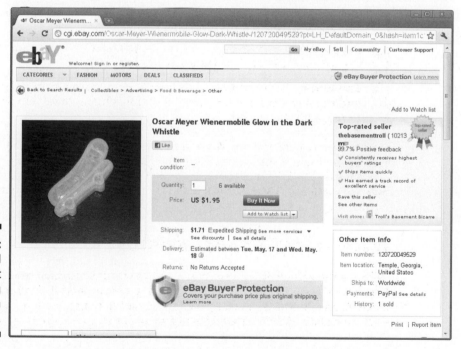

Figure 15-2: You can find just about anything for sale on eBay.

Online auction sites include

✔ **eBay:** eBay (www.ebay.com) is the most popular auction site on the web, and people flock there to sell all sorts of stuff, from baby clothes and toys to computer parts to cars to the occasional tropical island. You can sell stuff, too, by registering as a seller. eBay charges a small commission for auctions, which the seller pays. Searching the completed auctions at eBay is also a terrific way to find out how much an item is worth — you can see what people end up paying for items. If you're thinking of selling that rare Beanie Baby, search the completed auctions for the bad news that it's worth slightly less than it was when it was new.

✔ **Half.com:** This division of eBay (www.half.com) is more like a consignment shop than an auction. Sellers list used items they want to sell at a fixed price, such as books (including textbooks), CDs, movies, video games, electronic equipment, and trading cards. eBay maintains that it'll merge this site into its main eBay site, but it never does.

✔ **Priceline.com:** Priceline.com (www.priceline.com) sells airline tickets, hotel rooms, rental cars, and a grab bag of other items. Mostly like anyone else, you tell it what you want and it tells you the price. It still has its famous reverse auction where you can specify a price for what you want and Priceline then accepts or rejects it.

Don't fall for these online scams

Online commerce, like any other commerce, has a few bad apples. Here are some rotten spots to avoid, particularly on eBay and Craigslist, where you're often buying or selling from individuals, not established companies. Our key piece of advice is that every site has a normal way to do business, and anything out of the ordinary is a red flag. On eBay, the normal way to pay is by using Paypal. Unless you happen to buy from a seller close enough that you can pick up the goods and look at them before you pay, don't pay any other way. On Craigslist, the normal way to buy stuff is for the buyer and seller to meet in person to look at the goods and pay.

The nonresident landlord: A Craigslist ad shows a fabulous apartment at a low price. When you write to the landlord, he explains that he had to move to a faraway city for a new job, he still needs to sublet his old apartment, and he's too far away to come back, so just send him the paperwork and the deposit. Uh, no, unless you never want to see your deposit again. The apartments are usually real, ads copied from real ads, but the "landlord" is not.

The large cashier's check: You sell something on eBay for $100. The buyer explains that he has a $1,000 cashier's check that he'll send you, deposit it, wait a few days for it to clear, and you can just wire back $850 and keep an extra $50 for your trouble. What could go wrong? A forged check can take a week or more to bounce, by which time you're out the $850 and the scammer is long gone. A similar oil rig scam targets restaurants; see dirtcandynyc.com/?p=82.

The too-good-to-be-true deal: An eBay seller or a website offers an iPhone for $20 or a similarly fabulous deal. Your $20 may be real, but the iPhone isn't. Now and then you can get a great deal on eBay from a seller who underprices an auction on an obscure item, but we all know what an iPhone costs, and it isn't $20.

Craigslist

Craigslist (craigslist.org), Figure 15-3, is the website that your local newspaper hates the most, because it's just like the classified ads, only free. It has subsites for cities large and small all over the world, where you can find everything from a used car to a new apartment, job, or boyfriend. Unlike eBay, Craigslist listings are supposed to be local, so the two parties (we'd say buyer and seller, but some of the ads are for personals) can meet in person to complete the deal. Nearly all ads are free; they only charge for real estate ads in a few large cities, which brings in enough money to pay for everything else.

Figure 15-3: Buy and sell locally with Craigslist.

We've had good luck buying and selling appliances, cars, and even an elderly Sunfish sailboat on Craigslist. They do a good job of policing bogus ads, but see the earlier section "Don't fall for these online scams" to know what to watch out for.

Books, music, and more

You can't flip through the books in an online bookstore as easily as you can in person (although Amazon.com comes close by offering a selection of pages from many books). However, if you know what you want, you can find good deals.

Here are some top sites:

- **AbeBooks:** This site, formerly Advanced Book Exchange, offers the combined catalogs of thousands of secondhand booksellers at www. abebooks.com. You pay the same price as you would in a used-book shop (plus shipping, of course), and you save hours of searching. Whether you're looking for a favorite book from your childhood or a rare, first-edition *For Dummies* book, this site is worth visiting.

- **AddALL:** AddALL (www.addall.com) is another good used-book site offering titles from thousands of used-book stores as well as a price comparison service for new books.

- **Amazon.com:** Amazon, one of the great online-commerce success stories (at www.amazon.com), sprang up from nothing — if you call several million dollars of seed money nothing — to become one of the Net's biggest online stores. Amazon.com has an enormous catalog of books and CDs and a growing variety of other junk, much of which can get to you in a few days. It also has an affiliates program in which other websites can refer you to their favorite books for sale at Amazon, creating sort of a virtual virtual-bookstore. Amazon sells most books at less than list price, and in most cases also has used copies from independent sellers. It also has used books, DVDs, and just about everything else from pogo sticks to underwear.

- **Barnes and Noble:** Barnes & Noble (www.bn.com) is the biggest bookstore chain in the United States, and its online bookstore is big, complete, and well done. You can even return online purchases at any of its stores. It also has a large selection of music.

- **J&R Music World:** The online presence of one of New York's largest music stores (www.jr.com) has a huge selection of music CDs. You can also buy a stereo to listen to your new CDs and a refrigerator to keep appropriate beverages at hand.

- **Powell's Books:** The largest independent (nonchain) bookstore in the United States has a correspondingly large website (www.powellbooks. com) offering new and used books. We like its e-mail newsletter with new and rediscovered books and author interviews.

Clothes

This section points out a few familiar clothing merchants with online stores. Directories such as Yahoo! (at `dir.yahoo.com`) have hundreds of other stores, both familiar and obscure:

- **Eddie Bauer:** This site (`www.eddiebauer.com`) has way more stuff than is available in its stores. (John gave up on the stores about the third time they said, "Oh, you have to order that from the website.")

- **The Gap:** This site (`www.gap.com`) has the same stuff you find in its stores, but for people of unusual vertical or horizontal dimension, it also has jeans in sizes the stores don't stock, as well as links to Banana Republic and Old Navy, its upscale and downscale divisions.

- **Lands' End:** Most of this catalog is online (`www.landsend.com`), and you can order anything you find in any of its individual printed catalogs along with online-only discounted overstocks. It also has plenty of the folksy blather that encourages you to think of the company in terms of a few folks in the cornfields of Wisconsin rather than a corporate mail-order colossus belonging to Sears Roebuck. (It's both.)

- **REI:** This large sports-equipment and outdoor-wear co-op is headquartered in Seattle. Members receive a small rebate on purchases. The whole catalog is online (`www.rei.com`), and you can find occasional online specials and discounts.

An online shopper's checklist

Here are some questions to keep in mind when you're shopping online. Astute shoppers will notice that these questions are the same ones to keep in mind wherever you're shopping:

- Are the descriptions clear enough to know what you're ordering?

- Are the prices competitive, with other online stores *and* with mail-order and regular retail?

- Does the store have the products in stock, or does it offer a firm shipping date?

- Does the store have a good reputation?

- Does the store have a clearly written privacy policy that limits what it can do with the data it collects from you?

- Can you ask questions about your order?

- How can you return unsatisfactory goods?

Computers

When you're shopping for computer hardware online, be sure that the vendor you're considering offers both a good return policy (in case the computer doesn't work when it arrives) and a long warranty.

Here are a few well-known vendors:

- ✔ **Apple Computer:** The Apple site (`store.apple.com`) has lots of information about Macintosh computers, and now it offers online purchasing of the iPad, iPod, and iPhone, too.

- ✔ **Best Buy:** This site (`www.bestbuy.com`) is the online version of the ubiquitous big-box store. Orders can be shipped, or you can pick them up at your local store.

- ✔ **CDW:** CDW (`www.cdw.com`) has a good selection of hardware and software, and we've found it to be reliable.

- ✔ **Dell Computers:** This site (`www.dell.com`) has an extensive catalog with online ordering and custom computer system configurations.

- ✔ **PC Connection and Mac Connection:** For computer hardware, software, and accessories, PC Connection and Mac Connection (`www.pc connection.com` and `www.macconnection.com`) are two of the oldest and most reliable online computer retailers. And, you can specify overnight delivery within the continental United States even if you order as late as 2 a.m.!

Food

To show the range of edibles available online, here are some of our favorite places to point, click, and chow down:

- ✔ **Bobolink Dairy:** A recovering software nerd and his family in rural New Jersey make and sell their own cheese — a rich, gooey, French-style cheese. Its URL (`www.cowsoutside.com`) refers to cows out in the pasture rather than tied up in the barn.

- ✔ **Cabot Creamery:** This site (`www.cabotcheese.coop`) sells some of the best cheddar in Vermont. (Don't tell anyone that a lot of the milk comes from New York.)

- ✔ **Gaspar's:** If you weren't aware that Portuguese garlic sausage is one of the four basic food groups, Gaspar's site (`www.linguica.com`) will fix that problem. Oddly, online orders incur steep shipping charges, but phone or fax orders are shipped free, so we print and fax the order form. Also check out the competition at `www.amarals.com` and `www.chourico.com`.

✔ **Gimme Coffee:** This site (www.gimmecoffee.com) features highly opinionated coffee from the wilds of upstate New York. Gimme Coffee has online orders and lots of advice on what to do with your coffee after it arrives; follow the Gimme Locations link to find pictures of the place John goes when he's in need of literary inspiration, also known as *caffeine.*

✔ **The Kitchen Link:** Search this site (www.kitchenlink.com) for the perfect recipe and then shop for the ingredients.

✔ **Peapod:** Peapod (www.peapod.com) lets you shop for groceries online and then delivers them to your home. You have to live in an area that the parent grocery chains serve — the northeast and the Chicago area. If you live somewhere else, Netgrocer (www.netgrocer.com) delivers nonperishables by rather pricey overnight express, and it delivers perishables in a limited area near its New Jersey headquarters.

More Opinions Than You Ever Imagined

With all the products available to buy on the web, how can you decide what to get? Fortunately, you aren't on your own. Lots and lots of websites offer you advice on everything from cruise ships to restaurants to used cars. Many of these sites are part of *Web 2.0*, a jargonful way to say that most of what's on the website was contributed by the users. This concept has two helpful benefits: You get the combined experience of all those users, and the website gets all that stuff for free. In many cases, sites show a combination of professional reviews and user comments, which would be Web 1½. Here are some review sites we've found useful.

Travel and food

Travel guidebooks have been around since Baedeker in the 1820s, and restaurant guides have been around at least since Michelin in 1900. Now the guidebooks have moved online, so you can check out their advice and then let their publishers know if you disagree:

✔ **Yelp:** As shown in Figure 15-4, Yelp (yelp.com) is the most comprehensive city guide around, with geographically organized reviews of everything from car dealers to restaurants to botanical gardens. It's a good spot to look for places to eat.

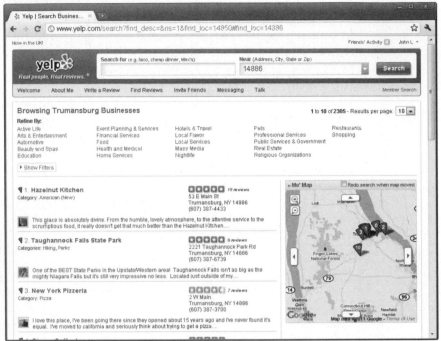

Figure 15-4:
Yelp
reviews
just about
everything.

✔ **TripAdvisor:** As its name suggests, TripAdvisor (tripadvisor.com) is a site for travelers. Type a place name, and it tells you where to stay, what to see, and perhaps how to get there. The site is aimed more at people visiting an area, as opposed to Yelp, which is more for people who live there. The company has an empire of related travel websites including seatguru.com (where to sit on a plane) and flipkey.com (vacation house rentals).

✔ **Zagat:** Zagat (zagat.com) made the leap from printed guides to online quite successfully. Everything in the printed guides is on the website, and web reviews are now the main material for the printed guides. Basic information is available for free, and access to full reviews requires a subscription. If you contribute reviews, the site often comps subscriptions or sends you the next printed guide. This site has recently been sold to Google, which says it plans to integrate Zagat's reviews into its local searches.

✔ **Opentable:** The largest site for making restaurant reservations, Opentable (opentable.com) also has reviews from both their own users and Zagat. We use it to quickly find out who has a table and at what time tonight. If you already know which restaurant you want to visit, call directly rather than use Opentable, saving the restaurant the fee it has to pay for the reservation.

✔ **Via Michelin:** The famous Michelin guides (viamichelin.com) made the transition to online as well. It has restaurant reviews for much of Europe, New York, Chicago, and San Francisco and hotel and sightseeing guides for nearly everywhere. Reviews show both their professional reviews and user comments.

Vroom, vroom

A car is one of the biggest purchases most of us make. Now you can do your research so that by the time you reach the dealer, you probably know more about the car you want to buy than the salesman does. Let these sites help you:

✔ **Edmunds:** This site (edmunds.com) is where we start looking for a car. It has reviews of new and used cars (both professional and user contributed), listings of vehicles for sale, and typical sale prices so that you have a good idea of how much you should pay.

✔ **Cars.com:** Remember back when you looked for a car in the classified ads in the paper instead of pointing and clicking? The papers have realized that the ads aren't coming back to the paper, so five large newspaper chains jointly run Cars.com. Its original purpose was to be the online version of the classifieds so that the papers could compete with online markets such as Craigslist. Now the site has expanded to become a full-service car info site. If you want to buy or sell a used car, be sure to check the suggested Kelly price on Cars.com and the Edmunds price, because they're often quite different.

✔ **Dealerrater:** This site (dealerrater.com) just has ratings of car dealers, for both sales and service. The dealers take their ratings quite seriously, so it's worth letting the world know when you have a particularly good or bad experience.

For that even bigger purchase, a place to live, Yelp has reviews of real estate agents and apartments.

Are these reviews real?

If anyone can write a review, what keeps ethically challenged businesses from writing fake favorable reviews for themselves and unfavorable reviews of their competitors? Nothing, unfortunately. All legitimate review sites try to police their reviews (look at the page of conditions at Dealerrater, saying thatif you or a relative work in the car business, you absolutely, totally, cannot review anything, so go away and don't even think about it), but some fake reviews show up, particularly on TripAdvisor. Most of the people writing fake reviews aren't good at it, so if you see a place with five favorable reviews and one that hated it, or vice versa, it might be a fake. It's also possible that the place is inconsistent, but after you read reviews for a while, you can easily tell.

Also, quite a lot of "review" sites are completely fake. Any site, other than Bank Rate (www.bankrate.com), purporting to compare credit cards is a fake trying to sell you whichever card it reviews favorably. Again, it isn't hard to tell; if you stumble across a review site you've never heard of and it generously offers to sell you whatever item has the most stars, now you know why.

Questions and Answers

Several sites match people with questions and people with answers. Ask anything, and as likely as not you'll get answers. Often the answers are even correct. (This problem is a chronic one in Web 2.0.) All of them organize questions by topic, so you can browse existing answered and unanswered questions and write your own questions and answers. The usual suspects include

- ✔ **Answers.com:** The largest Q-and-A site (www.answers.com) has a huge range of topics. The questions range from middle schoolers who want you to do their homework ("What was the cold war?") to complex questions about science and finance. The system does a good job of guessing when a new question is the same as an old one and links them.

- ✔ **Quora:** The latest entry in the Q and A biz, Quora (www.quora.com) appeals to a more business-oriented and professional audience. Rather than put questions into categories, they tag questions with keywords so that you can look for questions about Bank and New Jersey or the like.

- ✔ **Yahoo! Answers:** This site (answers.yahoo.com) is similar to Answers.com but has a younger crowd.

Chapter 16

Banking, Bill Paying, and Investing Online

*O*nce upon a time, money was substantial stuff that glinted in the sun and clinked when you dropped it on the table. Investments were engraved certificates that you kept in your safe-deposit box if they worked out, or used as bathroom wallpaper if they didn't. Well, that was then. Now, money and investments are mere electronic blips scampering from computer to computer, and if you do any banking or investing, one of the computers they scamper through might as well be yours.

You can do just about any banking online that doesn't require physically handling pieces of paper, which means everything except depositing checks and withdrawing cash. For these tasks, you have to use an ATM or, if you're truly retro, physically visit a bank branch and talk to a human being. But we help you avoid the last option as much as possible.

Going to the Bank without Ever Leaving Home

Nearly every bank in the United States now offers online banking. They don't do it to be cool; they do it because online banking is vastly cheaper for them than ATMs or tellers. Because both you and your bank have a strong interest in making sure that the person messing around online with your accounts is *you*, the sign-up process is usually a bit complicated — the bank either calls you to verify that you signed up or mails you a paper letter specifying your password. After you're signed up, you visit the bank's website and log in with your new username or number and password. Every bank's website is different, but they all show you an account statement along the lines of the one from John's bank, shown in Figure 16-1.

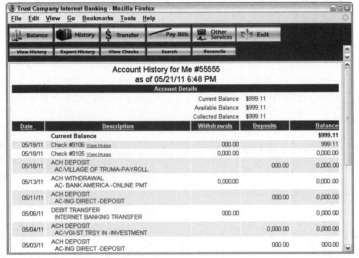

Figure 16-1:
A week of bank stuff, give or take a few details.

As you can see, deposits and withdrawals look like they do on printed statements you receive in the mail. If you click the View Image link next to a check number, it shows you a picture of the canceled check. The Automated Clearing House, or ACH, lines are described in the nearby sidebar "ACH! It's better than a check!"

If you use an accounting program such as Quicken or Microsoft Money, banks invariably offer a way to download your account info into your program. Look for a link labeled Download or Export. In Figure 16-1, it's the small Export History button, near the upper-left corner.

Details differ, but beyond the capability to check your statement, all banks offer roughly the same services, including transfers and bill-paying.

ACH! It's better than a check!

For the past 150 years or so, the usual way to move money from one person's account at a bank to a second person's account at another bank has been for the first person to write a check and give it to the second person, who takes it to her bank and deposits it. (At least, that's the system in the United States — in Europe, the first person writes out a bank transfer and gives it to his bank to set up the payment.) Now that we're in the computer age, we have a high-tech replacement for this process: ACH transfers.

Automated Clearing House, or *ACH*, transfers can do anything a check can do. Rather than print payroll checks, companies can use ACH to deposit money directly into employees' bank accounts. The U.S. government uses ACH to make Social Security payments. You can use ACH to pay bills or to move money between accounts at different banks. For most purposes, ACH transactions are better than paper checks because they're faster and more reliable.

To identify the account to use for an ACH transfer, you need to provide the *routing number,* which identifies the bank, and the account number at that bank. The easiest way to find the routing number for your own checking account is to look at the line of funny-looking numbers printed along the bottom of one of your checks. The routing number consists of nine digits, usually printed at the left end of the line. The account number also appears on that line, and a check number (which ACH doesn't use) may appear, too. Savings accounts also work for ACH transfers; to find the routing number, look at a check from the same bank or call the bank and ask.

You may be wondering, "Can anyone who knows my account number suck money from my account by using ACH?" Well, yes. But when you receive your statement, you can challenge any bogus ACH transaction just as you can challenge a forged check and get your money back. In practice, ACH is safe and reliable, and we use it for our own accounts all the time.

Transferring money between bank accounts

If you have more than one account at a bank, a checking and savings account, some CDs, or a mortgage, you can usually move money from one account to another. In the account shown in Figure 16-1, the line that says *Internet Banking Transfer* indicates that money has been transferred from the checking account to a mortgage account, to make the monthly mortgage payment. To get a better idea of how this transaction works, here are the steps for transferring money from a checking account to a mortgage account (again, specific steps vary among banks):

1. **Click the Transfer button (or whatever your bank's website calls it).**

2. **Enter the amount you want to transfer in the box labeled Amount (or similar wording).**

3. **Select the account that the transferred money is coming from, generally from a list of possible From accounts.**

4. **Select the account number the transferred money is going to, generally from a list of possible To accounts.**

5. **Click the button labeled Transfer or Do It (or similar wording) — it's done.**

It's that easy. Most banks handle transfers within the bank the same day; at John's bank, you can enter a transfer as late as 7 p.m., which is handy when you remember at dinnertime that the mortgage is due today.

Many banks also let you make transfers to and from accounts at *other* banks, using ACH. To set up transfers, you provide the other bank's routing code and account number. Depending on the bank, you may be required to provide a voided check from that account, verify that the account name is the same as your account name, or make a couple of tiny deposits into the account and answer correctly when they ask you for the amounts. After you set up a transfer, it resembles a transfer within your own bank: You specify the accounts and the amount and then click. You can also transfer money between your bank and your mutual fund or brokerage account. In Figure 16-1, for example, the ACH deposits from ING Direct are from another bank, and the ACH deposit from VGI-ST TRSY is from a Vanguard mutual fund.

Transfers to other banks have two important differences: time and price. Even though the transfer is handled entirely electronically, the money takes anywhere from two days to a week to show up at the other end, depending on the other bank. The time it takes for any particular bank is consistent, so if the transaction took three days the last time, expect it to take three days the next time. If you must have the money available so that you can write checks on it, allow a week and keep an eye on your balances until you've made enough transfers to know how long they take.

The price for transfers varies from zero to two bucks, with no consistency among banks. A transfer can be started from either the sending *(push)* or receiving *(pull)* end; often, Bank A charges you a dollar if you tell it to *send* money to Bank B, but if (instead) you tell Bank B to *receive* exactly the same amount of money from Bank A, it's free. All else being equal, pushing gets the money there faster.

You can use PayPal to move money from just about any bank account to any other bank account for free. It's a handy way to make online transfers (and we describe it later in this chapter).

Paying bills online

Writing checks is *so* 20th century. Now you can pay most of your bills online. In many cases, you can arrange for automatic payments from your bank account for routine monthly bills. (In Figure 16-1, *Bank America* refers to the MasterCard bill.) We've arranged automatic payments for credit card, electric and gas, and mobile phone bills — a typical mix. Most banks offer a *bill-pay* service, using one of a handful of specialized companies in this field. Some banks provide bill-pay for free, some charge, and some provide it for free as part of a package. Even if your bank doesn't offer bill-pay, utility and credit card companies often can arrange for you to pay their bills automatically from your checking account.

When the bank pays the bill, it sends an ACH transfer if it recognizes the payee (generally larger companies); otherwise, it mails a paper check. If the bank pays by ACH, the payment is usually received the next day; otherwise it's mailed the next day — and the mail takes however long it takes.

Each of these companies has its own procedure. We use a credit card example to show how this process usually works. Figure 16-2 shows the online payment page at American Express. When logged in to its website, you set up payments by entering your bank account's routing code and account number, which ACH needs. (See the preceding sidebar, "ACH! It's better than a check!") After the payment info is set up, you visit the website and specify how much you want to pay and when, and the bill is then paid from your bank account. Usually, you get credit the same day, which is a big help to avoid paying credit card interest when you remember at the last minute that the bill is due. Some cards, including American Express, also offer the option to pay every month automatically on the due date — just the thing for thrifty card users who pay off their bills every month.

Figure 16-3 shows the bill payment service from John's bank. To set it up, you pick the companies to pay and then enter your account number and the name and address of the company to pay, if the bank doesn't already have it on file. Some bill-pay systems offer the option of *electronic presentment,* in which you see your bill on the web rather than receive it by paper mail. You also tell the system which bank account you want to pay the bills from. Then, to pay your bills each month, you just visit the bank's website and enter the amounts to pay and the date. The bank automatically moves the money out of your account on the date for each payment. Some banks offer recurring payments so that you can tell them to pay the same amounts every month.

Figure 16-2:
Pay the
credit card
bill with one
click.

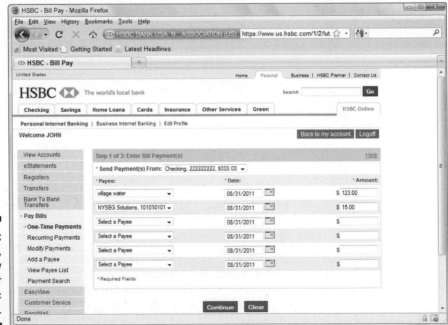

Figure 16-3:
Point, click,
and pay
the water
and electric
bills.

Taking advantage of other online bank services

Because doing business over the web is much cheaper than doing it in person, banks are putting all sorts of other services online. Visit your bank's website to see what it offers. Among some of the services we've seen offered are

- Loan applications
- New accounts
- Retirement accounts
- Checkbook-balancing calculators

Checking out a few recommended banks

These days, any bank you pass while driving down the street offers online banking, but some specialist banks do everything online. Although it's possible to do all your banking online, we prefer to have our main account at a local bank, where we can drop by and argue with the staff, and to use an online bank for a high-interest savings account that you can't get at a local bank.

To give you a flavor of what's available, here are two banks we use and recommend:

- **HSBC Direct** (www.us.hsbc.com): A British bank that is, by some measures, the largest bank in the world
- **ING Direct** (www.ingdirect.com): A large Dutch bank also with subsidiaries all over the world (not as large as HSBC, but still big)

Both have U.S. subsidiaries that offer online accounts with better interest rates than most competitors and no minimum balances. HSBC has a lot of physical offices, but for the high-interest online account, you have to sign up online. ING has an office in Wilmington, Delaware, that we walked past one time, but we saw no reason to go in.

To open an account at either bank, you fill out a form on its website, including the ACH info about your existing checking account to link to your new HSBC or ING account. After it's set up, you can move money back and forth between the accounts as needed. (Money you put into your ING account has to stay there for a week before you can get it back. The HSBC account limits you to six withdrawals per month. Accounts at other banks have similar rules.) Both also offer checkless checking accounts, certificates of deposit, mortgages, home equity loans, and retirement accounts. HSBC, a full-service bank, offers everything else a bank offers, all available online if you want it.

We've used both these banks quite happily, but we give the nod to HSBC because it pays slightly more interest and gives you an ATM card you can use for withdrawals anywhere and for deposits at HSBC branches. If you travel a lot, you pay no withdrawal fee at any HSBC machine anywhere in the world.

 To squeeze the last bit of interest out of your money, visit `www.bankrate.com` where you can find a listing of banks paying the highest rates on online savings accounts or certificates of deposit. Search for *MMA* (money market account) for an online savings account.

Trying out combo banking

If you have an account with a stockbroker, such as the ones we list later in this chapter, it generally offers a check-writing option, which makes it act like a checking account, usually at low cost. If you don't have a local bank you like, this option can be a good one.

How safe are these banks, anyway?

When you open a bank account in person, you visit the bank and then look around to see that the bank looks like a bank, with tellers, people in suits, and a vault, which is good — or, you see a couple of people in a Winnebago with card tables and some money in cooler chests, which is bad. When you visit a bank's website, it's hard to tell a good one from a bad one. But it's not hard to do a little research.

Every real bank in the United States is a member of the Federal Deposit Insurance Corporation (FDIC). The FDIC has a nice-looking website at `www.fdic.gov` that has, among other things, detailed reports on every member bank. On the home page, click the Deposit Insurance link near the upper-left corner, and then click Bank Find, at the top of the list. On that page, you can search by name or location. For example,

to check out ING Bank, enter its full name (*ING bank, fsb,* as it says on its home page), select Delaware as the state, and search. (For this particular bank, an alternative route to the same information is to click the FDIC icon on the bank's home page.) Either way, you see a reassuring page indicating that yes, it's insured. For more information, click Financial Information to see the bank's latest balance sheets. In this case, it says that the bank has $87 billion in assets and $8.8 billion in capital. Sounds like a bank to us.

Credit unions (joining one isn't a bad idea if you're eligible) are insured by the National Credit Union Association at `www.ncua.gov`. You can search for the name of your credit union to check its status.

Dealing with Credit Cards

Just about every credit card in the country offers online access for the same reason that bank accounts do — online transactions are a lot cheaper for them than calls to the toll-free number.

Online credit card services start with applying for the card. Search your fave search engine for credit cards and you find a phantasmagoria of offers. They change daily, but you can look for various goodies — no annual fee, bonuses and rebates, and low interest rates. Most sites that appear to compare cards are in fact selling one bank's cards, so treat their claims of unique and superior features with skepticism.

After you have your card, typical online conveniences include these:

✔ Check your balance and recent transactions.

✔ Pay your bill from your checking account.

✔ Apply for a credit line increase.

✔ Ask for copies of sales slips for charges you don't recognize, or challenge ones you think are bogus.

✔ Download account information into Quicken and other personal finance programs.

✔ Manage rebate and bonus programs related to the cards.

Different credit-card-issuing banks have somewhat different versions of these services, but comparing them without getting the credit card first is difficult. For example, some banks let you set up automatic payments to pay each bill in full on the due date, getting the maximum use of your money without paying interest. At others, you have to visit their websites every month to schedule the month's payment. Some have single-use card numbers, some don't. We would make a list of features, but it would be out of date before it was printed, so visit some bank websites to see what they're offering. (We compared two different banks in the tenth edition of this book, but then they merged, keeping the worst features of each one. Sigh.)

Pay Your Pals with PayPal

Credit cards are easy to use — if you're *spending* money. Until recently, it has been all but impossible for individuals (rather than companies) to receive payments by credit card. Even small businesses found it expensive and time consuming to accept credit card payments. PayPal (www.paypal.com) has changed all that, and it also provides an easy way to move money among accounts at different banks.

PayPal is a boon to individuals who buy and sell at auction sites such as eBay (which owns PayPal), but it has many other uses, too. PayPal helps you start a small business on the web: Small organizations can use PayPal to collect payments for events such as dinners and amateur theater, nonprofits can accept donations, and it's just about the only way to make payments to individuals in other countries without paying a service charge larger than the amount you're paying.

If you plan to accept PayPal for your business, be sure to heed PayPal's warnings regarding shipping *only to verified buyer addresses*. Be sure to comply carefully with all the fine print to protect yourself against fraud. Most first-time sellers learn the hard way that it's they who pay the cost of fraud — and even the cost of their customers' innocent errors. The PayPal fraud rate is lower than that of most credit card fraud, but it's a case of *merchant beware* — know your customer and take appropriate steps to safeguard your transactions.

To use PayPal, you set up an account, which is quite easy. It wants your name, mailing address, phone number, and e-mail address. The basic personal account is all you need unless you plan to sell a whole lot of stuff on eBay. (If your plans change, you can upgrade your account.) PayPal encourages you to provide it with your bank account number so that when you pay somebody, PayPal can take the money directly. That way, they don't have to pay the credit card companies, and you can move any money you receive into your account with minimum hassle. You can and probably should also link a credit card if you have one.

When you first tell PayPal to link your account to a bank account, PayPal verifies your bank account number by making two random deposits of less than a dollar. You then have to tell it the amount of the deposits to complete your registration. You can link several bank accounts to your PayPal account and then move money out of one account and into PayPal, wait a few days for the transaction to be complete, and then move the money out of PayPal and into a different account — all for free. If you live in the United States, you can link only U.S. bank accounts; if you live anywhere else, you can link both U.S. accounts and accounts in your own country.

After you open an account, you can send money to anyone who can receive e-mail. If that person doesn't already have a PayPal account, she opens one when "cashing" your e-mail. The money you send can come from the balance in your PayPal account or from a bank account or credit card that you link to your PayPal account. After you have money in your account, you can use it to pay other people, move it to your linked bank account, or spend it with a debit card linked to your PayPal account. Check the list of fees carefully. Payments marked *Personal* and made without using a credit card are generally free. Everything else has about a 3 percent fee. Every time you set up a payment, PayPal deducts it from your balance, if any, and then from your linked bank account. If you want to pay with your credit card instead, usually a good idea for eBay and other commercial payments, you have to click a little Change link and change it before completing the payment.

PayPal is usually the easiest and cheapest way to send moderate (less than $1,000) amounts of money to people in other countries. It charges a few percent to change money from one currency to another, but compared to the alternatives, such as foreign currency checks or Western Union, it's a bargain.

Criminals send out spam claiming to be from PayPal and claiming that you "must" provide them with your account number and password right away to clear up an account problem. Don't fall for it. PayPal will *never* ask you for your password or account information in an e-mail message — or anywhere other than on its website. If you receive a message that seems to be from PayPal and are unsure whether it's real, don't click on any links in the message — instead, manually type **www.paypal.com** into your web browser and log in. If anything's wrong, the website tells you.

Investing Your Money Online

If you invest in mutual funds or the stock market (something that's difficult to avoid these days unless you anticipate dying at an early age), you can find a remarkable range of resources online. An enormous amount of stock information is also available, providing Net users with research resources as good as professional analysts had before the advent of online investing.

The most important thing to remember about *all* online financial resources is that everyone has an ax to grind — and wants to get paid somehow. In most cases, the situation is straightforward; for example, a mutual fund manager wants you to invest with her funds, and a stockbroker wants you to buy and sell stocks with him. Some other sites are less obvious: Some are supported by advertising, and others push certain special kinds of investments. Just consider the source (and any vested interests they may have in mind) when you're considering that source's advice.

Mutual funds

Mutual funds are definitely the investment of the baby boomer generation. The world now has more mutual funds than it has stocks for the funds to buy. (Kind of makes you wonder, doesn't it?) Most fund managers have at least descriptions of the funds and prospectuses online, and many now provide online access so that you can check your account, move money from one fund to another within a fund group, and buy and sell funds — all with the money coming from and going to your bank account by way of ACH.

Well-known fund groups include

- **American Century:** A broad group of funds at www.americancentury.com

- **Fidelity Investments:** The 500-pound gorilla of mutual funds; specializes in actively managed funds at www.fidelity.com

- **Vanguard Group:** The other 500-pound gorilla; specializes in low-cost and index funds at www.vanguard.com

The online brokers listed in the following section also let you buy and sell mutual funds, although it almost always costs less if you deal directly with the fund manager.

Stockbrokers

Most well-known, full-service brokerage firms have jumped onto the web, along with a new generation of low-cost online brokers that offer remarkably cheap stock trading. A trade that may cost $100 with a full-service firm can cost as little as $8 with a low-cost broker. The main difference is that the cheap firms don't offer investment advice and don't assign you to a specific broker. For people who do their own research and don't want advice from a broker, the low-cost firms work well. For people who need some advice, the partial- or full-service firms often offer lower-cost trades online, and they let you get a complete view of your account whenever you want. The number of extra services the brokerages offer (such as retirement accounts, dividend reinvestment, and automatic transfers to and from your checking account) varies widely.

Online brokers include

- **Charles Schwab:** The original discount broker (www.schwab.com) offers somewhat more investment help than E-Trade and TD Ameritrade, but at a slightly higher price. Kathleen Sindell, the author of *Investing Online For Dummies,* 5th Edition (John Wiley & Sons, Inc.), recommended this site to us.

- **E-Trade:** This low-cost, no-advice broker (www.etrade.com) also offers bank accounts, credit cards, boat loans, and just about every other financial service known to humankind.

- **Scottrade:** Another low-cost, no-advice broker, Scottrade (www.scottrade.com) also has offices with live brokers, for people who want extra help at extra cost.

- **TD Ameritrade:** The low-cost, limited-advice broker (www.tdameritrade.com) is affiliated with Toronto-Dominion Bank, one of the largest Canadian banks. It has good online research tools.

Most fund groups, including the ones in the preceding list, have brokerage departments — which can be a good choice if you want to hold both individual stocks and funds.

Portfolio tracking

Several services let you track your portfolio online. You enter the number of shares of every fund and stock you own, and the service can tell you — at any time — exactly how much they're worth and how much money you lost today. Some of them send, by e-mail, a daily portfolio report, if requested. These reports are handy if you have mutual funds from more than one group or both funds and stocks. All tracking services are either supported by advertising or run by a brokerage that hopes to gain your trading business:

- ✔ **Google Finance:** This tracking service (www.google.com/finance) offers multiple portfolios with a minimalist Google style. Google is, at the moment, the only site that offers real-time, as opposed to 20-minute delayed, stock quotes for people who think they can beat the market.

- ✔ **MSN Money:** This service (money.msn.com) also has portfolios and lots of information, although we find it cumbersome to set up and more of a pain to use than My Yahoo!. To use all its features, you have to use Internet Explorer.

- ✔ **My Yahoo!:** Enter multiple portfolios and customize your screens with related company and general news reports at my.yahoo.com. You can also see lots of company and industry news, including some access to sites that otherwise require paid subscriptions. It's advertiser supported, comprehensive, and easy to use.

- ✔ **Smart Money:** This online part (www.smartmoney.com) of the *Wall Street Journal* lets you track portfolios and read news stories. Although the site wants you to subscribe to the magazines, the free portfolio tracker isn't bad. Click the Register link to get started, and remember that you don't have to sign up for its e-mail newsletters if you don't want to.

Budgeting Tools

Sites to help spend, pay, and invest your money are useful, assuming that you have money to spend, pay, and invest. Toward that end, some websites help you make and follow a budget. They link to your bank and credit card accounts so that they can track the money coming in and out and let you know how reality compares to your budget. We've found some significant bugs in the ones we've tried that made them misreport our financial situation, so check their numbers before you trust them. However, if your finances are simple (and all in one currency), these sites can be useful for categorizing your spending and comparing it to your budget.

Mint (`www.mint.com`), the site that many people use, tracks your budget against your bank accounts, with occasional offers from their sponsors. It's strong in budgeting tools, suggestions about how your budget compares with its other million users, warnings of upcoming bills, and lots of pretty charts and graphs. They're a subsidiary of Intuit, makers of popular finance package Quicken, but you don't need Quicken in order to use the Mint site.

Part V
Putting Your Own Stuff on the Net

The 5th Wave   By Rich Tennant

"Ooo-wait! That's perfect for the clinic's home page. Just stretch it out a little further... little more..."

In this part . . .

The Internet is different from other computer networks because it's flat — every computer is, in principle, equal to every other. So you have no excuse for being a virtual couch potato who only looks at other people's stuff — you can publish your own. We look at different ways you can make or contribute to websites, such as photo gallery sites, video sharing sites, and particularly blogs, which are online diaries for everyone to read.

Chapter 17

Making a Splash Online

In This Chapter

▶ Putting material on the web

▶ Showing off your family photos online

▶ Posting documents and calendars online for viewing and editing by other people

▶ Making your own website from scratch

▶ Creating an online store or just selling random stuff

*B*ack at the dawn of the World Wide Web (in 1989), the plan was that people all over the world would communicate among themselves — a virtual rustic global village. That isn't exactly how it turned out, with giant megamalls like Amazon.com making the Net a distinctly nonrustic experience. But after you've used the Internet and browsed the web for a while, you'll probably think of putting your own material on the web. Hey, you've got interesting things to say, probably more interesting than a lot of websites you've surfed past!

Yes, it's time to stop just browsing the web and start putting yourself out there in various ways. This chapter walks you through a bunch of ways to post information on the web and explains how to start with ones that are easy.

Ways to Go Public on the Web

You can post information on the Internet in lots of different ways. Some require more start-up effort than others. Here's an overview of the best methods for putting your own information online:

✔ **Join a social network:** Websites such as Facebook, LinkedIn, and MySpace started as glorified personal ads and have expanded to include photos, video, e-mail, blogs, polls — you name it. See Chapter 10.

✔ **Create photo galleries:** Many sites enable you to create an online gallery of photos or other pictures. Make your gallery public or share it with only friends and family. See the later section "Say 'Cheese!'"

 ✔ **Share videos:** If you have home videos, animated movies, or other digital video you created or edited using software on your PC or Mac, you can post it on a number of video sites. See Chapter 14.

 ✔ **Share documents, spreadsheets, and calendars:** Post word processing documents or spreadsheets that select personnel can view or edit, and create calendars that others can see and change. See the section "Sharing Documents and Calendars," later in this chapter.

 ✔ **Write a weblog (blog):** Create an online diary or journal with chronological entries. Chapter 18 describes how to read blogs and write your own blog.

 ✔ **Use Twitter to let your friends know what you're up to:** Twitter is a little, tiny blog where you post short messages *(tweets)* and read other people's messages. See Chapter 11.

 ✔ **Build a handcrafted website:** You can use Google Sites, Homestead, Weebly, or a web page editor to create a website with pages of your choosing. See the section "Making Your Own Website," later in this chapter, to find out how.

 ✔ **Sell stuff:** Sell goods or services in an online storefront or auction. See the section "Setting Up an Online Shop," at the end of this chapter.

Say "Cheese!"

We love sharing our family photos with other people, and the web makes it easy. Also, sharing over the web saves you the cost of making extra prints of your snapshots, and it's quick. Several websites enable you to upload your digital pictures to the sites and share the pictures with your friends and family. These free photo-sharing sites make their money by selling prints — after your family sees that gorgeous shot of little Daisy finger-painting with pudding, they'll *have* to have a copy for the fridge!

Of course, the most popular way to share pictures is on Facebook.

You can try one of these photo-sharing sites:

 ✔ **Flickr** (part of Yahoo!) at `flickr.com` is probably the biggest photo-sharing site. Upload pictures from your computer, e-mail them, or send them from your phone — videos, too. Flickr gives you the choice of making photos public to all Flickr users, accessible only to specific groups of people, or completely private.

 ✔ **Picasa** (from Google) at `picasa.google.com` combines a free photo-organizing program with a web-based picture-sharing site, at `picasa web.google.com`.

 ✔ **Photobucket** (owned by Fox) at `photobucket.com` hosts both pictures and video.

✔ **Snapfish** at www.snapfish.com lets you set up online photo albums using either photos you upload or rolls of film you mail in to the site. You can share the albums and order prints.

After you create an account at one of these sites, you can upload photos into online photo albums by filling out forms on the website. Then you can share your albums with your friends. If you want, you can make your photos on these sites invisible to the general public — only to the people with whom you share the album.

You (and your friends) can also order prints of your uploaded photos — that's how these sites make their money. The prices for prints are reasonable, and we find these systems convenient. You can print your photos as calendars, cards, books, and even postage stamps.

Another way to share photos is to include them on a blog, as described in Chapter 18. Blogs are useful if you want to use your photos to illustrate a narrative, such as the story of your trip to Spain.

Organizing Your Photos, Too

Several programs help you organize the pictures on your computer as well as upload and share them online. Picasa is the Google photo management program, which you can download from www.picasa.com or picasa.google. com. The program finds the photos on your computer (identifying them by their filename extensions) and helps you organize, caption, and edit them. You can then upload the photos or albums to the website for sharing with your friends and family. Figure 17-1 shows the Picasa photo sharing website.

Figure 17-1: Picasa helps organize your photos and upload them to its website for sharing.

Picture formats

Pictures come in dozens of formats. Fortunately, only three picture formats are in common use on the web: GIF, JPEG, and PNG. Many lengthy — er, *free* and *frank* — discussions have occurred on the Internet concerning the relative merits of these formats. John, who is an Official Graphics Format Expert, by virtue of having persuaded two otherwise reputable publishers to publish his books on the topic, suggests that photographs work better in JPEG format, whereas clip art, icons, and cartoons are better in GIF or PNG. If you're in doubt, JPEG files are smaller, and they download faster. PNG is a superior, new replacement for GIF, and its only disadvantage is that people with very old browsers (Netscape 3.0 and older, for example) can't easily view PNG files.

If you have a picture in any other format, such as BMP or PCX, you must convert it to GIF, JPEG, or PNG before you can use it on the web. Windows comes with Paint, which you can run by choosing Start⇨All Programs⇨Accessories⇨Paint. Or, check out Tucows, at `tucows.com/windows` or Download.com at `www.download.com` for graphics programs that can convert file formats. For the Mac, consider GraphicConverter at `www.lemkesoft.de`; click the American flag for the English version of the site.

Sharing Documents and Calendars

Have you ever wished that you could share a spreadsheet or word processing document with other people, and maybe even let them make changes? Suppose that you're the commissioner of a fantasy football league and you want to share a spreadsheet of players and their statistics with the other players. Yeah, you can e-mail a spreadsheet to everyone, but what if you make updates? Instead, you can upload the spreadsheet to a document-sharing site and share it with the other players.

Or, a document or spreadsheet might be just for you, but you may need to be able to edit it from more than one computer. Our kids use a document sharing site to work on their school papers both at home and at school — it's much easier than copying their files to a thumb drive or disk, which they'd probably forget on the kitchen counter, right next to their lunch.

Several document sharing sites let you use the web as your word processing, spreadsheet, or presentation program, storing your files online. You can see, edit, and print your documents, spreadsheets, and presentations from any computer that's on the Internet. In fact, these sites are so good that some people use them for all their documents and spreadsheets, even if they have word processing and spreadsheet programs on their computers.

Creating a Google Docs document

The most popular document sharing site is Google Docs, at `docs.google.com`. It doesn't support every advanced feature of Microsoft Word and Excel, but it handles all the basics. Figure 17-2 shows a Google word processing document. The toolbar just above the document provides formatting options, much like a "real" word processor, and the menu bar (File, Edit, View, and so on) provides other features. You can print your spreadsheet, presentation, or document or export it to your computer as a normal document file.

Figure 17-2:
A group
of people
can view
and edit
a Google
Doc, unless
they're too
hungry to
concen-
trate.

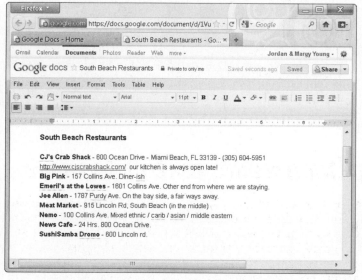

To get started with Google Docs, follow these steps:

1. **Sign in at `docs.google.com` with your Google account username and password.**

   Or, if you're already signed in at another Google site, click Documents on the list of Google services at the top of the screen. Either way, you see the Google Docs screen, with a list of the documents and spreadsheets you can view or edit.

2. **To upload a word processing document, presentation, or spreadsheet from your computer, click Upload, click Browse, and select the file or folder to import. Then click Upload File.**

   Google Docs uploads the file and creates a new document, presentation, or spreadsheet you can edit and share.

3. **To create a new document, presentation, or spreadsheet from scratch (rather than upload it), choose Create New⇨Document, Create New⇨ Presentation, or Create New⇨Spreadsheet.**

   Hey, the Create New menu has a bunch of other options, too (maybe more since we wrote this chapter), such as Presentation, which enables you to create a PowerPoint-style set of slides.

   Google creates a new element of the type you chose and displays it on the screen, with the appropriate menu bar and icons for editing.

4. **If you created the file from scratch, give it a name. Choose File⇨ Rename from the menu bar in Google Docs (not the menu bar at the top of your browser window) and type a name.**

5. **Type information in the document, presentation, or spreadsheet as usual.**

   If you made a spreadsheet, click in a cell and then type in it. To edit a cell, double-click it or click it and press F2.

6. **When Google Docs asks whether to start autosaving your information, click Start Autosaving.**

   Google saves your data in the *cloud* — in one of the innumerable web servers that Google maintains and that you never have to see or worry about. Your changes are saved every few minutes, so you're unlikely to lose your work.

Sharing the wealth

After you have a document or spreadsheet (or presentation) in Google Docs, you can share it with other people. Click the Share button and cut-and-paste or type e-mail addresses into the Add People box. Click Can Edit if you want to allow them to make changes to your document or spreadsheet, or click Can View if they can look but not touch. Enter the text of the e-mail message that Google Docs will send to invite them to look at your document or spreadsheet, and click Share.

Your invitees receive a message explaining how to access the information you're sharing.

You can also give people a web address they can use to view the document or spreadsheet (no editing). Click Share, click the Change link, and choose Anyone with the Link to see a rather long URL that you can e-mail or IM to people so that they can take a look.

Making and sharing an online calendar

A handy kind of information you can share is an online calendar. Maybe your club, church, theater, or another organization holds public events. Or, maybe it has a schedule of meetings to share with a small group of people. Either way, you can make an online calendar, enter events or meetings on it, and make it available for viewing or editing.

Google Calendars, at `calendar.google.com`, enables you to make one or more calendars, share them with other people, and make them public. You can display more than one calendar, overlaid in different colors, so that you can see your own events alongside your friends' or co-workers' events. Microsoft has a similar service at `calendar.live.com`.

Margy's family has a Google calendar for tracking family events. On the computer in her kitchen, family members refer to the online calendar rather than to the traditional, coffee-stained, paper wall calendar. They sync their family Google calendar with the calendars on their smartphones or other devices, such as the iPhone, iPod touch, and Android Captivate. (Okay, we *are* geeks, but having a shared family calendar with us all the time sure is convenient! John, on the other hand, thinks that a Google calendar is no substitute for a paper calendar with pictures of Japanese anime cartoons.)

Looking beyond Google Docs

Google Docs isn't the only online document sharing site. Zoho (`www.zoho.com`) offers free accounts (you can even log in using your Google account name) that you can use to create and share several types of files:

- ✔ **Zoho Writer** has more formatting options than Google Docs.
- ✔ **Zoho Sheet** provides online spreadsheets.
- ✔ **Zoho Show** makes slide show presentations.

Holy cow — it's a complete Microsoft Office-like set of programs, all for free!

Not surprisingly, Microsoft has decided to play this game, too. If you go to Microsoft Office Live, at `www.officelive.com`, you can create (surprise!) documents, presentations, and spreadsheets by uploading them to your Office Web Apps account. To get started, sign in with your Windows Live account, such as your Hotmail account (or make one for free).

Making Your Own Website

At the beginning of this chapter, we list a bunch of ways you can put information on the web. These ways are terrific, just terrific — we love them all — but they may not be enough for you. What if you want more? What if you need a website with a bunch of pages, with titles you choose, about topics you choose, and maybe even with your own domain name? Okay, you're ready for the next step.

Page creators abound

You have (as usual) several ways to create a website, beyond using Facebook, photo sharing sites, and blogs. The simplest is to use a *page creator site*. At these sites, you can design the look of your site, create a home page for the site, and create as many other pages as you want. Different pages can have different layouts. You don't have to learn to use HTML, the formatting language used by all web pages; see the later sidebar "Why you don't care (much) about HTML."

Page creator sites offer a variety of features, so look carefully before choosing one:

- **Cost:** The site may be free or may incur a monthly charge. Free sites often display ads over which you have little control.

- **Customization:** Some page creator sites allow more customization of the design than others. Some let you see the HTML (web page code) that makes up your pages and tweak it so that your pages look just right. Others don't allow it.

- **Subdomain:** Your site can be a *subdomain* of the page creator site, where your web address is the main site's address with www replaced by a name you choose.

- **Design:** Page creator sites offer lots of standard designs. See whether any sites have a design you like.

- **Special features:** Some sites let you include message boards, guest books, blogs, calendars, photo galleries, and video on your site. Some help you sell items on your site, with connections to PayPal for checkout.

- **Size:** The amount of information you can store on your website varies, along with the maximum number of pages.

Here are some page creator sites we know about:

- ✔ **Google Sites,** at `sites.google.com`, is a free page creator site run by (who else?) Google. It isn't hugely flexible, but it's easy to use.

- ✔ **Homestead,** at `www.homestead.com`, is for small businesses and lets you start from more than 2,000 business templates.

- ✔ **Jigsy,** at `www.jigsy.com`, is free for one small, personal website, but charges a modest fee for a larger or commercial site. You can include Twitter messages, Google maps, and other fancy components on your pages.

- ✔ **uCoz,** at `www.ucoz.com`, hosts websites for free and lets you include photos, videos, photo albums, polls, guest books, and forms that e-mail you the information that people fill in. It's one of the most popular sites in Russia.

- ✔ **Weebly,** at `www.weebly.com`, has a nice drag-and-drop system for setting up your site — and no ads.

- ✔ **Webs,** at `www.webs.com`, has lots of design templates and can host photos, videos, blogs, and message forums.

- ✔ **Yola,** at `www.yola.com`, is another well-regarded page creator site.

All these sites make creating your own website incredibly easy — for free. You can add pages, add text and pictures to the pages, and create links in the text. Most page creator sites provide a bunch of other items you can add to your pages, such as a calendar, a weather report, a Google map, a blog, an MP3 music player, and videos. For example, you can include a map to your church's or club's meeting location.

What do you say?

Creating a web page is easy. Choosing what to put on your page, however, is harder. What is the page for? What kind of person do you want to see it? Is it for you and your family and friends and potential friends across the world, or are you advertising your business online?

Consider which information you want the entire world to know, because a website is potentially visible to absolutely anyone, including that guy who has hated you ever since fifth grade. If your page is a personal page, don't include your home address or phone number unless you want random people who see the page potentially calling you up. If it's a business page, include your address, phone number, and any other information that potential customers might want.

Why you don't care (much) about HTML

Just so you know what *HTML* is, in case someone asks, it stands for *HyperText Markup Language,* the language used for formatting web pages. Web pages are made up of text and pictures that are stuck together and formatted with HTML codes. In ye olden days of the past millennium (1999), you had to write the HTML yourself. Fortunately, you have waited until now to start creating a web page: Clever page-creator websites and programs are available that let you create your pages by writing the HTML codes for you automatically.

If you want to write a lot of web pages, you should eventually master some HTML. Although

complex, interactive pages require a fair amount of programming, the basics aren't all that complicated. The HTML for **complicated** is `<b>complicated</b>` (that's `<b>` for bold type). In case you decide that you want to be in the web-page creation business, entire books have been written about how to do it. We recommend *HTML, XHTML & CSS For Dummies,* 7th Edition, written by Ed Tittel and Jeff Noble (John Wiley & Sons, Inc.) for the basics, and *Web Design in a Nutshell,* 3rd Edition, written by Jennifer Niederst (O'Reilly Media) for more advanced information.

If you put your e-mail address on your website, you can expect lots more spam because spammers *scrape* websites: Their programs visit websites looking for text with at-signs (@) in it. You can deter these programs somewhat by inserting a space on either side of the @ (as in `internet13 @ gurus.org`) or replacing it with the word *at* (as in `internet13 at gurus. org`), although these programs may get wise to this trick.

Setting Up an Online Shop

Selling stuff on the Internet used to take hundreds of thousands of dollars' worth of software and programming talent. A number of sites now let you create web stores for modest fees. Here are a few:

- ✔ **Amazon.com Marketplace,** at `sellercentral.amazon.com`, is easy to set up. Sign in with an Amazon.com account (the same account you use if you buy books or other items on the site), click Your Account, and click Your Seller Account to find out how to set up a seller account. Or, search Amazon.com for the item you want to sell and click the Sell Yours Here button. The site even processes credit card sales for you, eliminating what was once a horrible pain in the neck.

- ✔ **eBay.com Stores,** at `pages.ebay.com/sellercentral`, enables you to sell items in auctions (for which eBay is famous) or at fixed prices (using the Buy It Now option). Your store can have its own name and logo, and items in your store show up when people search eBay for merchandise.

- ✔ **Craigslist,** at www.craiglist.com, is a huge online classified ads site. You can list almost anything for sale. The site has separate sections for every major city and every U.S. state; if your browser displays the wrong site, click links in the righthand column to find the site for your area.

- ✔ **Etsy,** at www.etsy.com, lets you sell crafts, including clothing, jewelry, ceramics, and anything else you can make by hand.

- ✔ **Yahoo,** at smallbusiness.yahoo.com, lets you create a storefront for a monthly fee.

To set up a store, you sign up for a free account at the website and then click the link to create the store. You provide information about the items you sell, including descriptions, prices, and shipping costs. On eBay, you're usually paid by PayPal; on Craigslist, buyer and seller usually meet in person and pay in cash or with a local check; for everyone else, the site typically accepts credit cards and deposits your share to your own bank account.

If you don't want to set up a whole store, you can still sell individual items either on consignment at sites such as www.half.com or at auction at sites such as www.ebay.com. eBay owns Half.com, so when you set up an account to buy or sell items on one, you're ready to buy or sell on the other, too.

To sell an item on Half.com (or any other consignment site), first find the item you want to sell. Half specializes in books, movies, and music, and it has almost everything in print in its database. When you find your item, click the Sell My Copy link, specify the condition of the item, add a description, and state your asking price. When you click the List Item link, your listing goes into the Half.com database and appears on the site within an hour. When you sell your item — which can be minutes, hours, or months later — Half.com keeps a commission.

Selling an item on eBay is similar for books, CDs, and DVDs, but for other items it can be a little more complicated. You write a description for the item and take or scan a digital picture of it. Start at www.ebay.com, click the Sell tab or link, and follow the directions. Auctions can last as long as seven days, or you can set up a fixed-price offer with no end date. eBay charges you a listing fee, although if your item doesn't sell, you can usually relist it (try again, perhaps with a lower starting price) for free. Click Customer Support in the upper-right corner of any eBay page, and then click Selling & Seller Fees for instructions and hints for selling.

Chapter 18

Blogging: The World
Reads Your Diary

∙∙

In This Chapter
▶ Reading other people's blogs, or online diaries

▶ Subscribing to a blog so that you know when it has a new posting

▶ Making your own blog

▶ Posting to your blog

∙∙

Diaries are as old as writing. (We made up that statement, but it may well be true. Perhaps you can do some Internet research and let us know whether it is.) However, diaries that every single person on the entire Internet can read are a more recent invention. Not many people have always dreamed of publishing their diaries, but lots of people want to write regular columns where they can express their opinion, tell stories, or post pictures. Blogs have made that expression possible, easy, and free.

If you're not an enthusiastic and voluminous writer and you want to post tiny articles or journal entries, Twitter was invented for you. This chapter explains how blogs work, including microblogs (the technical term for what Twitter is).

What's in a Blog?

A *weblog,* usually abbreviated as *blog,* is a public online diary where someone posts more or less regular updates. A blog uses software that lets you easily post entries by using your web browser — no additional software is needed. You can even post updates by e-mail or from your cellphone.

Most blogs are updated frequently by one author and contain short, dated entries, as in a diary, with the newest ones at the top. Other blogs are more complex, with multiple topics or pictures as well as or instead of words, but they retain the idea of relatively short entries, updated relatively often. Figure 18-1 shows the political blog of a friend of ours, Doug Muder, who posts once a week at `weeklysift.com`.

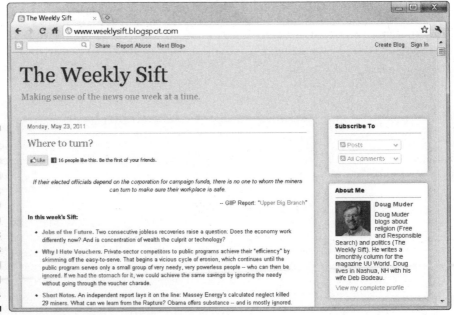

Figure 18-1:
A blog is sort of an online diary, and its value depends on whether its author has anything interesting to say.

The best blogs offer cutting-edge journalism and commentary and brilliant, witty, sparkling writing, whereas the worst disprove the old cliché that a million monkeys at a million typewriters would eventually produce the works of Shakespeare. If you search Google (`google.com`) for the word *blog* or *weblog* and some topic words that are of interest to you, you'll invariably find someone blogging away at it. But keep reading to find out better ways to discover and organize the blogs you read.

As blogs have become more popular, many websites have added blogs to post news, gossip, or behind-the-scenes stories. Every *New York Times* columnist (at `www.nytimes.com`) has a blog — go to `nytimes.com/blogs` to see a list. Some sites show the latest blog posting or two in a prominent spot, and you can click a link to see older posts.

Some popular blogs

A few blogs have become quite successful, and some have even been sold to mainstream media outlets. Here are a few popular blogs:

- Boing Boing, at `www.boingboing.net`, for eclectic technogossip

- Business insider, at `www.businessinsider.com`

- Engadget, at `www.engadget.com`, for news about cool gadgets

- FailBlog, at `www.failblog.org`, with videos of epic failures (a favorite of teenagers everywhere)

- *The Huffington Post,* at `www.huffingtonpost.com`, which expanded to become an online newspaper and was bought by *AOL*

- Mashable, at `www.mashable.com`, with news about technology, media, and web culture

- TMZ, at `www.tmz.com`, for celebrity gossip

- Wonkette, at `www.wonkette.com`, for Washington, DC, political gossip

How to read a blog

Reading a blog is easy because blogs are just web pages. Point your browser at the home page of the one you're interested in and read it. (Bet you thought it would be more complicated than that.) If you want to see more information about a particular story, click the link in the story.

Reading one blog is like eating only one potato chip, which never happens. When you find one blog, it usually has links to other blogs. If you search for one blog on a particular topic, you find a dozen blogs on that subject, and before you know it, you're mired deep in the swamps of Blogistan, with far too many interesting blogs to keep track of.

Because blogs change frequently (at least they're supposed to), you might want to bookmark your favorite ones in your browser so that you can find them again. As you find more blogs, you soon find your bookmark folder and your brain exploding, from trying to keep track of them. The sidebar "Some popular blogs" lists a few blogs, many of which garner millions of monthly visitors.

Subscribing to blogs

Luckily, you can subscribe to blogs so that you don't have to remember to return to each blog website to read the latest postings. When you subscribe to a blog, the new entries arrive on your computer automatically, so you don't have to check the blog website. You can find two kinds of blog subscriptions: RSS and e-mail.

RSS blog subscriptions

An RSS feed is one way to subscribe to a blog and receive new postings automagically. (*RSS* stands for Really Simple Syndication.) An *RSS feed* is a special web address (URL) that usually ends with .rss. When you're reading a blog in your browser, look for a Subscribe link or RSS link, which should display information about the site's RSS feed. Some blogs use a URL at feedburner.google.com for their feeds.

The system you use to read your RSS subscriptions is an *aggregator,* although almost no one uses the term. Look for web-based *aggregators,* or websites that track and show you all your favorite blogs. You can go to Google Reader (reader.google.com), log in with your free Google ID, and read your blog subscriptions there. If you use iGoogle (at igoogle.com or google.com/ ig) or My Yahoo! (my.yahoo.com) to create your own web start page, you can add your subscriptions to the page.

E-mail blog subscriptions

We use a system that alerts us to new information — it's called e-mail. Rather than bother with RSS feeds and aggregator sites, we'd rather just get an e-mail message when our favorite blogs have a new posting. Many, but not all, blogs enable you to subscribe to receive e-mail notifications. If yours don't, you can go to FeedMyInbox (www.feedmyinbox.com) and sign up to receive e-mail notifications for as many as five blogs for free. You cut and paste the RSS feed address and your e-mail address, and you're all set.

Writing Your Own Blog

After you're comfortable reading other people's blogs, how about starting your own? People read blogs for their brilliant, witty, sparkling content. Sparkling is hard, and sparkling regularly is exhausting. If you start your own blog, try blogging for a while on your own before telling all your friends about it. Otherwise they may say, "It was okay at the beginning, but now, big yawn."

Many blogging sites accept text, photos, and even video as part of your blog. You don't have to decide in advance what kind of material you'll include. If you lead an interesting life and want a way to let your friends and family know what's up, a blog may be perfect for you.

Can I make big buck$ with my blog?

Probably not. The alleged path to blog riches is that you start a blog, fill it with fabulous writing, and add some ads down the side, and then millions of people flock to your blog and click the ads, making your share of the advertising income enough to buy a tropical island where you retire.

A few famous blogs have succeeded with this plan, such as those listed in the earlier sidebar "Some popular blogs," but you can probably count them on your fingers, and running each one is a full-time job. We've experimented with ads on some of our bloggish websites, such as John's airline information site at `http://airinfo.travel` and his blog about Internet and e-mail policy, at `http://jl.ly`, and we've never seen more than a few dollars a day, which means that our tropical island will be limited to about four square inches.

You can put up a blog with ads for free at Blogger (`www.blogger.com`), so you have nothing to lose other than your time and perhaps your self-esteem. Don't quit your day job quite yet.

Finding a place for your blog

Many big blog sites let you blog away without having to install anything. These sites offer a basic usable blog for free. Some also have extra-cost add-ons that they hope you'll use. For reasons that will shortly become apparent if you read this entire section, we suggest that most of our users try Blogger.

The following few sections describe some popular blog-hosting sites.

Blogger

Also known as Blogspot, Blogger (`www.blogger.com`) is part of the Google empire. After you create an account, you can add and edit blog entries at the website, customize it in any of a zillion ways, and publish your blog. Blog entries can include photos and videos. You can even post text and pictures from your mobile phone.

Blogger is remarkably uninterested in asking for your money. As far as we can figure out, its reason for existence is mostly to be a place for people to display Google ads. That's fine — it's a nice site, and the ads are entirely optional.

LiveJournal

The cliché LiveJournal user is a college student who needs to provide too much information to her 100,000 closest friends on topics ranging from taste in music to short-term party plans to personal political philosophy. If this sounds like you, LiveJournal (`www.livejournal.com`) is the place to be. Blog entries can include photos, video, and other cool stuff.

The top five reasons not to start your own blog

Blog entries are usually short, so in that spirit, we offer you a short list:

5. You work on your blog when you should be working on your day job, annoying your co-workers and boss, and you spend hours reading *other* blogs, looking for topics to comment on or borrow.

4. Every conversation or experience becomes a potential blog entry rather than part of your life (also known as novelist's syndrome).

3. You try to have strange conversations and experiences in order to have something to blog (bad novelist's syndrome).

2. Everything, no matter how trivial, takes on a deep bloggable meaning. ("Did you ever notice all the different ways that rain streaks the dirt on the side of a city bus?")

1. You realize that you have nothing to say.

We practice what we preach here. None of us has a personal blog, just work-related ones.

WordPress

WordPress (www.wordpress.com) can provide you with a customizable blog for free. Because its software is widely used, lots of plug-ins allow you to mix photos from Flickr, posts from Twitter, and other kinds of information directly into your blog. You can also create nonjournal pages, such as an About Me page.

Xanga

Xanga (www.xanga.com) is a lot like LiveJournal except that the average user seems to be about five years younger. Unlike the other two sites, Xanga shows its ads on your blog unless you buy a premium account. Xanga also includes some social networking features, along the lines of Facebook and MySpace.

When you create a blog at one of these sites, you choose a name for the blog and this name plus the site name becomes the web address of your blog. For example, if you name your blog Weekly Sift at Blogspot.com, the address of the blog is http://weeklysift.blogspot.com.

Going postal

When you're ready to post to your article, diary entry, story, or rant, you have a number of options:

✔ **Use your web browser.** Go to the blog's website in your browser and click the Create Post or New Post link. Type your article, or cut and paste it from your word processor. Most blog sites allow you to preview your posting before publishing for the world to see.

- ✔ **Use your smartphone.** You can install an app on your iPhone or Android or other type of smartphone that enables you to post on your blog. For example, the BlogPress app for the iPhone lets you post to blogs at Blogger, WordPress, LiveJournal, and other blogging sites.

- ✔ **Mail it in.** At certain blog sites in this list, you can e-mail articles to a special address. In Blogger, you click Settings and then Email to set up the address.

- ✔ **Text it in.** Some blog sites — notably, Twitter (see Chapter 11) — let you send them text messages that are then posted to your blog. You can either set up the blog from your phone or register your phone to post messages on a blog you already created. Go to `http://go.blogger.com` if you use Blogger.

For more ways to blog, get *Blogging For Dummies,* by Susannah Gardner and Shane Birley (John Wiley & Sons, Inc.).

Illustrating your blog

Text is so 20th century. (Actually, it's more 15th century, but who's counting?) If you find text constraining, just about every blog site, including the ones we describe in the preceding section, lets you include pictures as part of your blog, often uploaded directly from your mobile phone.

For example, when you're creating a new post on Blogger, you can add a picture or video to your post. You upload it and there it is, in your blog!

Gack — it's a trackback

Bloggers frequently comment on each other. Sometimes the comments are nice, and sometimes they're not so nice, but they're certainly, uh, involved. Most blogs let visitors leave comments, but the serious discussions are often between two or more blogs, with each one containing comments on the other blog. Anyone reading the blog with comments can see the reference to the original blog, but there's no way for someone reading the original to know where to look for comments. That's where *trackbacks* come in.

Let's say that one blogger — call him John (not his real name) — posts a provocative entry in his blog. Then a second blogger, Margy (not her real name either) posts "For an utterly priceless example of disenchronia, check out this entry in John's blog" with a link to John's blog. If John's blog software is set up to handle trackbacks, Margy's blog system can tell John's blog about the new link so that John's blog adds a trackback note with a link to the comment, thereby making the connection two-way.

The original vision of hypertext, of which the web is a quick-and-dirty, hacked-up version, made all links two-way. Trackbacks bring the real-life web closer to what it was originally supposed to be.

Blogging in song

If you're a storyteller or musician, or you just have a lot to say, you can post your digital recording on the web as a *podcast,* which is an audio blog. You can upload any audio file you created yourself, containing music, speech, or any sounds you like, and other people can subscribe to it, just like on a blog. Chapter 14 describes how to find and subscribe to podcasts.

One way to set up a podcast is to make a blog and post audio files on it. Several websites will host your podcast for free or for a small monthly fee. Here are two:

- ✔ **PodBean,** at www.podbean.com, is free for personal podcasting, for the first 100MB of audio files. To store more files, you need to pay a modest monthly fee.

- ✔ **Liberated Syndication,** at www.libsyn.com, offers accounts starting at $5 per month.

After you have a podcast, be sure to submit it to the iTunes Store so that people who use iTunes can easily subscribe: Run the free iTunes program (which is useful even if you don't own an i-Anything), click iTunes Store, click Podcasts, and click Submit a Podcast. (See Chapter 14 to find out how to use iTunes.)

For details on creating and maintaining a podcast, read *Podcasting For Dummies,* by Tee Morris, Chuck Tomasi, and Evo Terra (John Wiley & Sons, Inc.).

Part VI
The Part of Tens

The 5th Wave   By Rich Tennant

"Honey! Our web browser got out last night and dumped the trash all over Mr. Belcher's home page."

In this part . . .

We have lots of interesting odds and ends we want to tell you about, so (to provide the illusion of organization) we grouped them into lists. By the strangest coincidence, every list consists of exactly ten facts. (Note to the literal-minded: You may have to cut off or glue on some fingers to make your version of ten match up with ours. Perhaps it would be easier to simply take our word for it.)

Chapter 19

Ten Problems and Ten Solutions

*G*osh, using the Internet is exciting. But sometimes things get so fouled up that you want to push your computer out the window and go back to the communication methods our ancestors used, like newspapers, telephones, and smoke signals.

Don't give up just yet. This chapter offers up some common problems that many Internet users encounter, as well as some solutions to those problems.

My PC Takes Forever to Boot Up, and Pop-Up Ads Took Over the Screen

Slow start-up, sluggish operation, and annoying pop-ups all suggest that your computer is infested with *malware,* sneaky programs that do bad things to your computer, including spyware (which arrives by way of your web browser), viruses (which arrive by e-mail), and worms (which arrive all by themselves). A full-scale war is being waged in cyberspace for control of the world's PCs, and your computer is likely a casualty. Chapter 2 describes both types of malware, and Chapter 4 suggests strongly that you install virus-checker and antispyware programs. Make sure that you have downloaded the latest improvements to your Windows operating system, and ensure that your virus checker and your spyware removers are up to date. And, if you still use Internet Explorer to browse the web, consider trying a different browser, such as Firefox, Chrome, or Safari.

We like these antispyware programs, all three of which we use:

- ✔ Ad-Aware, from Lavasoft, at `www.lavasoftusa.com` (free for basic version)

- ✔ Microsoft Windows Defender, at `www.microsoft.com/windows/products/winfamily/defender` (free, already included in Windows 7 and Vista)

- ✔ Spybot Search & Destroy, from `www.safer-networking.org` (shareware)

For all three programs, download, install, and run them, and be sure to download updates regularly.

The nuclear option

If you have installed and run antivirus and antispyware programs and you still have problems, it may be too late for Band-Aid remedies. Your computer may be so thoroughly infested that you have no choice but to blow everything away and start over.

Before you reinstall Windows, you *must* install a firewall to protect your computer. Most distributed versions of Windows are so insecure that you simply cannot install the program and all its security updates before you're reinfected with viruses and worms. (Installing and updating Windows and your application programs take a couple of hours. Infection takes perhaps ten seconds.) The routers we mention in Chapter 5 that let you connect several computers to your Internet connection include adequate firewalls that are quite cheap. Even if you have only one computer, the $30 you spend for a router is well worth it.

Before you reinstall Windows, be sure to make a copy of all your files. If you haven't been backing up regularly, make two copies, just to be safe. Back up at least one copy to more reliable CD-Rs or DVD-Rs rather than to rewritable media. Make sure that you have the installation CD or DVDs and all registration codes, license codes, and key codes for all applications you use.

Before reinstalling Windows, you may want to get a copy of *Windows 7 For Dummies* (written by Andy Rathbone and published by John Wiley & Sons, Inc.), *Windows XP Home Edition: The Complete Reference,* or *Windows Vista: The Complete Reference.* (The latter two books were written by John and Margy and published by Osborne/McGraw-Hill.) These books contain more details about how to reinstall Windows than we have room for here. You need the original CDs that came with your computer or a new copy of Windows XP, Vista, or 7. Put the Windows CD or DVD in your CD or DVD drive and reboot. Follow the instructions to the spot where it asks whether you want to rewrite or destroy all information on your hard drive. To find this spot, you may need to select advanced options. Take a deep breath and answer Yes and then Yes again to all warnings indicating that all your files will be erased. They will — that's why we have you back them up — but they'll erase the worms, too.

When the reinstallation of Windows is complete, follow the onscreen instruction to reenter your Internet settings. Then immediately click the Start button and choose All Programs⇨Windows Update and download all suggested updates to Windows, which takes quite a while. Load your antivirus and anti-spyware software and apply their latest updates. Then reinstall all your applications. Yes, this process is a real pain.

Next, place your data backup CD in the CD drive and have your antivirus program scan it. We recommend that you do not reinstall all your data files at first; just the ones you need to use. If you made two copies as we told you to, keep them in two different places — preferably, in two different buildings.

Finally, create separate, password-protected accounts for everyone who will use the computer, and make them all Limited rather than Administrator accounts unless they have a good reason to be installing their own programs. Have a talk with everyone about the risks of free downloads and online game sites. Suggest that, in case you have to repeat this process, their use of your computer will be terminated. This isn't the kind of problem you want to keep dealing with, as you have no doubt concluded if you just had to rebuild your system.

The thermonuclear option

Because you can buy a reasonable computer for less than $400 these days and you can use the same printer and monitor (if your computer isn't a laptop) you have now, sometimes if you've had your old computer for a while, it's easier to buy a new computer and start over. The nice people at the computer store should be able to help you extract your files from your old, messed-up computer, perhaps for a modest extra charge, and install them on a new one. Even if the new computer is all configured and updated at the store, which it should be, you still should get a router to deter future hostile invasions.

The switcheroo

Plan B is to consider buying an Apple Macintosh computer or a netbook or tablet computer running the Google Android operating system, even if only for your e-mail and web surfing. As of this writing, no serious online threats exist for Apple's Mac OS X or Android. This situation could change, but at least Apple and Google have a head start over the hackers, rather than the other way around, which is the case for Microsoft. You should still keep your Mac's or Android's operating system up to date and rebuild your PC if you still plan to use it. If you need certain programs for the workplace, look for Mac or Android equivalents. If you have a Mac, you can also check out Boot Camp (`www.apple.com/support/bootcamp`), which lets you run your Windows system and programs on your Mac.

John also has nice things to say about Ubuntu, a free system based on the open source Linux system. You can download Ubuntu for free, burn a CD, and then load it on your former Windows computer. It runs Firefox, Chrome, and Thunderbird just like any other computer, and has free OpenOffice, which does pretty much everything that Microsoft Word, PowerPoint, and Excel do. (John used it to write his part of this book.) See `www.ubuntu.com`. Oh, did we mention that it's free?

1 Can't Send Large E-Mail Attachments

Some Internet service providers and some system administrators limit the size of files you can send or receive by using their mail servers. In the case of problems where you work, the solution may be as simple as talking to the person in charge of your Internet access and asking for the limit to be changed. Your ISP might not be as accommodating.

We have other ways to move giant files from point A to point B.

Our favorite method is to use a file transfer website, such as WeTransfer or Dropbox. Using your web browser, go to `http://wetransfer.com`, upload the file, and enter at least one e-mail address to notify about the file. WeTransfer sends messages to those addresses with instructions to click a link to download the file. After about two weeks, it deletes the file from its server.

Another method is to open an account on a webmail provider that handles large attachments. Google Gmail allows attachments of as much as 25MB, Yahoo! Mail allows 10MB for the free version and 25MB for its paid Plus version, and Windows Live Hotmail allows 25MB. The process of attaching a file to a message increases its size by about 20 percent, so the maximum file size is smaller than the maximum attachment size.

For local file transfers, *sneakernet* (a system of transferring files by walking them from one computer to another) has made a comeback in the form of USB flash drives. Flash drives, which work with recent versions of all major operating systems, operate like removable disk drives but are about the size of your thumb (or smaller, especially if you have big thumbs) and have a shiny, rectangular plug at one end. Some geeks carry them on lanyards around their necks or on their keychains. To use one, just plug it into a USB port on your computer. For very large files (many gigabytes), you can use an iPod as a portable USB hard drive. After you copy whatever files you want, you need to tell your operating system that you're done with the drive before you unplug it. Windows uses a tiny icon in the system tray for this task. On Macs, drag the Disk icon to the trash.

If your computer has a CD or DVD writer, you can also burn your files on a CD or DVD to give to your friend. It isn't as cute and compact as a USB drive, but it's more durable. Your camera's memory card can also hold files.

I'm Worried about ID Theft

The U.S. Federal Trade Commission (www.ftc.gov/idtheft) offers this advice to prevent identity theft: First, look out for *phishing,* or e-mail that claims to come from a bank or another online account, such as eBay, and claims that your account has a problem that you can clean up by clicking a link in the message. These messages are never real, but they're extremely dangerous. If your bank thinks that a security problem exists, it doesn't tell you by e-mail. If you aren't sure, contact the company by phone or type its web address (for example, www.yourbank.com) into your browser by hand and look for the customer service section. See Chapter 2 for more about phishing.

The Internet isn't the only source of information about you. Keep bills and other documents that bear your account and Social Security numbers in a safe place, and tear up or shred old bank statements and credit card bills. Get a shredder that cross-cuts the paper into short strips rather than the cheaper shredders that make strips the length of the page; patient thieves can paste them together. Those offers for preapproved credit cards are also dangerous if they fall into the wrong hands, not to mention dangerous to your financial health if you accept them. Shred them or stop them altogether by calling 1-888-5OPTOUT or visiting `www.optoutprescreen.com`. If your driver's license still has your Social Security number on it, apply for a new license.

Get in the habit of looking over your bank and credit card statements when they arrive (or even earlier, online). Don't worry about the bank's arithmetic, but look for charges that you don't remember incurring. If you find any, contact your bank or credit card company immediately. After you verify any fraudulent charges, tell the bank that you want new accounts with new credit card numbers. You may need to file a police report, although in our experience, if you have fraudulent charges, the bank will issue new cards without even being asked.

I Can't Remember All My Website Passwords

The standard advice is to construct passwords from a mixture of letters, numbers, and special symbols; to have a different password for every account; to never write down passwords; and to change them every few months. Most Internet users who have dozens of accounts ignore this advice because only a truly unusual person can remember dozens of different random passwords and which account goes with each one.

We suggest a compromise. Make up one good password to use on all your low-risk accounts — accounts in which letting someone else gain access has little consequence, such as online newspaper subscriptions. Use different passwords for the accounts that truly matter, such as online banking. If you feel that it's necessary, writing down these passwords and keeping them in a safe place is better than picking a password that's easy for someone to guess. Don't list your passwords in your desktop Rolodex or on a sticky note stuck to your computer's monitor. *Never, ever* choose a password that is a regular English word (a word that appears in a dictionary) or a common name. Do add punctuation and numbers to your passwords.

Another option is to store your passwords in a password-protected file. The free, open source KeePass program (available for download from `www.keepass.info`) enables you to create an entry for every website or other password you need to remember. You can enter a username, a password, a web address (a *URL*), and notes about the account, and you can organize accounts into categories (for example, Home Banking, Email and Chat, and Shopping). KeePass can also suggest extremely strong passwords for you (made of random strings of characters) and can copy a username and password into your computer's Clipboard for pasting into your browser. Of course, you need to remember the password to your KeePass file — don't write it anywhere!

Some decent programs are available for safely storing passwords on smartphones and the iPod touch, too. We like the free, open source Keyring for Palm smartphones, available at `http://gnukeyring.sourceforge.net`. Be sure to pick an extremely strong master password and have a backup plan for when your phone falls into the bathtub and dies. (Waterproof ink on paper has stood the test of time.)

I'm Worried That Facebook, Google Docs, and Google Calendar Will Lose My Data

Okay, most people don't keep anything all that earth-shattering on Facebook, but we keep our family calendar on Google Calendar, and many home and business users keep all kinds of important documents and spreadsheets on Google Docs. We'd like to be able to report that Google has never lost anyone's calendars or data, but we can't.

We know of one backup service that can back up these and other kinds of information. Backupify (`www.backupify.com`) can back up Google Docs and calendars, the address book (contacts) in your Gmail account, your Twitter tweets, Facebook postings, Blogger blogs, and other information. Backing up a few accounts is free, and it's reasonably priced for more accounts.

Also see Google Takeout at `http://google.com/takeout`, a project at Google whose goal is to let you download all of your Google data.

I Get Messages Telling Me That E-Mail I Never Sent Is Undeliverable

You can't do much about this problem after it has happened. Most spammers use computers that have been taken over by worms or viruses to send spam, using fake return addresses taken from the list of spam addresses. Make sure that your computer isn't the source of this type of unwanted message by keeping its operating system and antivirus software up to date, using a router as your firewall (see Chapter 5), and turning off the computer (or at least its connection to the Internet) when it isn't in use.

People Seem to Know a Lot about Me

The rate at which we're all losing our privacy scares us, too. Here are a few tips.

Get rid of spyware that may be lurking on your machine

Spyware does just what it sounds like — it spies on you and your activities. You think your Internet activities are private, but unless you keep your PC spyware free, they aren't. Browse one mortgage lender site and you'll hear from the universe of mortgage lenders. Buy from one pharmacy and you'll receive solicitations from other companies for drugs you didn't even know existed. Your inbox is full of names that closely resemble — but aren't quite — people you actually know. If all this sounds familiar, chances are good that software is recording your every keystroke. Get rid of it! (The software, not the keyboard.) When we use Internet Explorer (some websites still work only with Internet Explorer), we often have to clean our machines because worms and viruses often sneak through security holes in it. Because it's so widely used, it's targeted by hackers all over the world, which is why we use Firefox, Google Chrome, or Safari instead (see Chapter 6).

Don't be dumb

Don't put information on your web page that you don't want everyone in the world to know. In particular, don't include your home address and phone number unless you want calls and visits. We know at least one person who received an unexpected phone call from someone she met on the Net and wasn't too pleased about it. Why would Net users need this information, anyway? They can send you e-mail!

Don't order stuff while using a public PC

Normally, ordering products over the web or by e-mail is safe — at least as safe as handing your credit card to a *waiter!* However, some shopping sites store information about you (including a link to your mailing address and payment information) on your computer in a file known as a *cookie.* This system works perfectly when you're ordering from your own computer — you don't have to retype all the info when you visit the site the next time you order. But when you order stuff at the library or at a cybercafé, this personal information may be stored on that computer. The next person who uses the computer and goes to the site then has all your personal data available and may be able to use it to place an order. Better not chance it.

I Can't Get My Kids, Spouse, or Significant Other Off the Computer

Games and instant messaging are highly addictive and seem to be becoming more so. Microsoft CEO Steve Ballmer brags about the addictive nature of the games his company sells and smiles as he says he wouldn't let *his* kid play them. That ought to give you a hint.

Set clear limits on computer usage and stick to them. Have a talk with your spouse or significant other about which kinds of online chatting are okay and which aren't. Also think about how much time *you* spend in front of a computer screen. Use some of your Internet time to make a list of outside activities you enjoy and stick it next to your computer screen. Promise yourself you'll do at least one fun off-computer activity every day. Internet addiction is serious — you may need professional help to quit the habit.

On the other hand, if it's your spouse, sometimes it makes more sense to squander $400 on a second computer (see Chapter 5 for hints on connecting them both to the Net using a single account) than to squander your marriage.

When I Click a Link, My Browser Says "404 Page Not Found"

Web pages move about or disappear on the Internet. If you type a URL from a printed source, make sure that you type the URL exactly as it was printed, including capitalization. If you read a URL that's part of a sentence, watch out for the comma, period, or hyphen at the end. The comma, period, or hyphen may or may not be part of the URL — or it may be punctuation for the sentence.

If you clicked a hypertext link or you're sure that you typed the URL correctly and you still see this error message, the data on the site may have been reorganized. Try "walking up" the URL by deleting the portion back to the last slash character and trying again, and then delete the portion back to the next-to-last slash character, and so on.

If you see a File Not Found message when you try entering this line, for example:

```
epicurious.com/cooking/menus/cooknow/omelettes.html
```

try entering these lines, in order:

```
epicurious.com/cooking/menus/cooknow
epicurious.com/cooking/menus
epicurious.com/cooking
```

At one of these levels, you may find a hint about where the file you seek can be found. Alternatively, go to your favorite search engine and search for it.

A page long gone may still be found on the Wayback Machine at `www.archive.org`, a free site that has attempted the daunting task of periodically saving snapshots of the whole World Wide Web.

I Want to Include My E-Mail Address on My Web Page

Including your e-mail address in a web page is a sure way to attract spam. Spammers have programs that crawl the web looking for e-mail addresses to spam. You can thwart them by *describing* your e-mail address rather than just typing it out — "It's `al` at `blahblah.com`" — or use obscure HTML coding on the web page. At the least, we suggest that you set up a separate e-mail address for your website at a free webmail site, such as `www.gmail.com`, `www.hotmail.com`, or `http://mail.yahoo.com`. If the flood of unwanted mail becomes too great, you can abandon that account and set up a new one.

One useful trick is to ask website visitors to include a special word in the subject line of their messages. For example, if your web page is about belt buckle collecting, you can ask correspondents to include *buckles* in the subject line. You can send the rest of the messages to the trash.

Chapter 20

Ten Fun Things to Do Online

*Y*ou can use the Internet in hundreds of ways for work and profit. In this chapter, we focus on fun. When you find new and fun things to do on the Net, let us know by sending us an e-mail at internet13@gurus.org. If you want to spend your time online doing something more worthwhile — we're sure you do! — take a look at Chapter 21, too.

Share Pictures and Videos with Your Friends and Family

E-mail attachments (see Chapter 9) are an excellent way to ship snapshots anywhere in the world for free. You don't even need a digital camera; your phone can probably take stills and maybe even video.

If you have more than one or two pictures or videos and you want to share them with more than one or two people, making an online photo album is the convenient way to go. Create an account at Flickr (at www.flickr.com), Picasa Web Albums (at picasaweb.google.com), or Photobucket (at www.photobucket.com), upload your photo and video files, and tell the site who else can see them. You can point your friends to your album by giving them the URL, and they can view the pictures online.

Watch Movies, TV, and Ads

The Internet has created a new way for makers of short and experimental movies to find an audience. Many sites feature miniflicks that you can watch for free. The most popular is Google's YouTube at youtube.com, whose users upload vast amounts of video, from the profound to the inane. Try looking for *airplane landings.* You can upload your own videos, too, as long as you made them yourself, they're no more than ten minutes long, and they follow other YouTube guidelines.

Hulu, at www.hulu.com, puts television on the Web, so you can watch early episodes of shows that you tuned in partway through. The site is supported by ABC, Fox, NBC, and others, so you see the real shows, not chopped-up pirated recordings of shows, although shows are prefaced with advertisements because something or someone has to pay the bills. Blip.tv (at blip.tv — no *.com* at the end) hosts shows you may never have heard of because they're made by independent creators. If you belong to Netflix (www.netflix.com), you can stream videos from its website, too.

If for some reason you don't see as many ads on TV as you want, visit www.advertisementave.com, where you can catch up on all the ads you've missed. The excellent AdCritic (creativity-online.com/adcritic) also features the best current ads and classics. Either way, now you can catch those humorous Super Bowl ads without having to watch the tedious football.

These film sites mainly use Flash, which plays videos directly in your web browser. See Chapter 14 to find out how to watch videos on the web.

Listen to Current and Classic Radio Programs

Have you ever turned on your radio, found yourself in the middle of a fascinating story, and wished you could have heard the beginning? National Public Radio and Public Radio International in the United States keep many of their past programs available online. If you want to hear the whole program, visit www.npr.org and www.pri.org. You can also use the sites' search features to browse for stories you missed completely. Some radio shows have their own websites, such as *Car Talk,* shown in Figure 20-1, and *This American Life.*

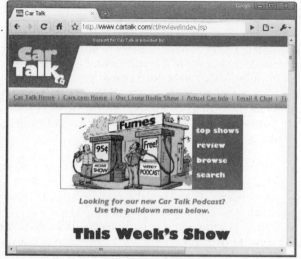

Figure 20-1:
The "Car Talk" podcast can provide advice about cars whenever you need it.

Many NPR affiliates and other radio stations have live streaming audio of their programs, so you can listen, live, to stations all over the country — go to Google or your favorite search engine and search for the station's call letters or the program name. (John recommends his local station at `wrvo.fm`, especially the old shows from the 1930s through 1950s, which they play in the evening.) Many other radio stations now let you listen to their live programs over the Internet, which is particularly handy in large office buildings with poor radio reception. You can listen to stations from around the world and get a taste of world music firsthand or hear the news from different perspectives.

If you have an iPod or another type of MP3 player, you can download audio files and listen to many radio shows at any time. See Chapter 14 to find out how to subscribe to podcasts.

Play Checkers or Bridge

Or play chess, poker, hearts, backgammon, cribbage, go, or any other board game or card game. The classic games hold up well against the ever-more-bloody electronic games. If you used to play *Diplomacy,* our favorite board game, back in the 1970s, try `www.playdiplomacy.com`.

True bridge aficionados like to think of bridge not as a card game but, rather, as a way of life. You can round up a bridge foursome at `www.bridge base.com` (for free) and `www.okbridge.com` ($99 per year after a free trial period). Many free and fee sites are listed at `www.greatbridgelinks.com`.

Play Lots More Online Games

Now you don't need to round up live friends to play with you — you can find willing partners at any time of the day or night at sites such as `games.yahoo.com`, AOL's `www.games.com`, and Microsoft's `zone.msn.com`.

Other good sites for both single-person and multiplayer games are `www.addictinggames.com` and `www.virtualnes.com` for re-created classic Nintendo games.

Find Out What Your Stuff Is Worth

You may already know about eBay, the online auction site where you can buy and sell almost anything. (If not, flip to Chapter 15 to read about it.) But you may not know that you can use eBay to find out the value of almost anything — at least, anything that has sold on eBay in the past 90 days — by searching completed eBay auctions.

You need an eBay account in order to search completed auctions, so start at `www.ebay.com` and register for a free account if you don't already have one. Then click the Advanced Search link (we can't tell you exactly where it is, because website designs change often, but it's probably next to the Search bar or the Search button). Type key words about your priceless treasure into the Search bar and select the Completed Listings check box. When you click the Search button, you see all auctions with those keywords and the item's final selling price. If any of the merchandise is similar to your fabulous object, you can see what people are paying for it.

(We're warning all you Beanie Babies speculators: You may be depressed to find out the current price of your vintage, rare, one-of-a-kind, limited-edition, collectible, new-in-box Beanie Babies.)

Build Your Own Jumbo Jet

Even staid corporate sites have the occasional goodies tucked away. Airbus builds airplanes, including the very, very, *very* large A380 superjumbo. Normally, an A380 lists for $300 million, but if that number is a little out of your price range, Airbus Goodies has some paper versions you can print, cut out, fold, and fly, at `www.airbus.com/galleries/goodies/index-cut-outs`. It also has some nice screen wallpaper pictures.

Visit Art Museums around the World

Art museums are interesting places to spend rainy afternoons. Now you can visit museums and galleries all over the world by using your browser. Not all museum websites have online artwork, but many do. Our favorites include the Louvre in Paris (at `www.louvre.fr`; click English in the upper-right corner if you don't read French), Boston's Museum of Fine Arts (`www.mfa.org`), Metropolitan Museum of Art in New York (`www.metmuseum.org`), Rijksmuseum in Amsterdam (`www.rijksmuseum.nl`), and State Hermitage Museum in Russia (`www.hermitagemuseum.org`). Check out the spectacular color photographs from Tsarist Russia by Sergei Prokudin-Gorskii, digitally reconstructed by the Library of Congress, at `www.loc.gov/exhibits/empire`, and the amazing American Memory collection of historical photos at `memory.loc.gov` (shown in Figure 20-2).

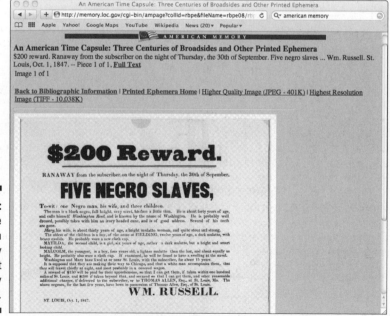

Figure 20-2:
The American Memory collection at the Library of Congress.

Tour the Earth

The modestly named Google Earth downloadable program (at `earth.google.com`) lets you fly around the earth and zoom in and out. After you get fairly close to the ground, you find links to pictures contributed by users (including some impressively remote places — try looking for South Georgia), Wikipedia links, and enough to keep you busy for hours, days, or even months, if you aren't careful.

Or, check out Google Maps Street View: Start at `maps.google.com`, visit an urban area (try *1 5th Avenue, New York, NY 10011*), and click Street View. You can make a 360-degree pan of the spot to see what it looked like the last time a Google employee was there with a camera.

Lots of other interesting maps are on the web. Watch the "walmartization" of the United States at `projects.flowingdata.com/walmart`. A wonderful analysis of the red-state-versus-blue-state political landscape is at `www-personal.umich.edu/~mejn/election`.

Tour the Solar System

The last half of the 20th century will go down in history as the time when humans began to explore outer space. Probes visited several comets and asteroids and every planet except Pluto. The probes sent back amazing pictures: storms on Jupiter, oceans on Europa, mudslides on Mars, and the Earth at night.

Which generation will get to play tourist in the solar system remains to be seen; here are some fascinating space sites:

- `marsrovers.jpl.nasa.gov`: Follow the adventures of the Mars rover or take a virtual tour at sites such as `sse.jpl.nasa.gov`.

- `apod.nasa.gov/apod`: Be sure to bookmark the astronomy picture of the day.

- `antwrp.gsfc.nasa.gov/apod/image/0011/earthlights_dmsp_big.jpg`: Above all, don't miss the incredible NASA montage of human civilization.

Build Your Own World

Virtual worlds are electronic places you can visit on the Web — kind of like 3D chat rooms. Rather than create a screen name, you create a personal action figure, or *avatar,* that walks, talks, and emotes (but doesn't make a mess on your floor). When you're in one of these worlds, your avatar interacts with the avatars of other people who are logged on in surroundings that range from quite realistic to truly fantastic. In some virtual worlds, you can even build your own places: a room, a house, a park, a city — whatever you can imagine. Other worlds let you make money, gain status, and battle complete strangers. People who enjoy role-playing games can disappear into online games for hours, days, or months at a time. The biggest, most successful online worlds are *World of Warcraft,* which costs money, at `us.battle.net`, and *RuneScape,* which is free, at `www.runescape.com`.

Most virtual worlds require you to download a plug-in or special software. Some are free, whereas others require monthly or annual subscriptions. For example, *Second Life,* at `secondlife.com`, lets you create your own part of a shared online world, including spending real-world money.

Web-based online worlds are an outgrowth of MUDs (which stands for Multi-User Dimensions or Multi-User Dungeons or various other names, depending on whom you ask), which were text-based virtual online worlds long before there was a web.

Read the Comics

Why get newsprint ink on your hands just to read your favorite comic strip? Ours are

- ✔ *Dilbert,* at `dilbert.com` (Okay, you knew we were geeks!)
- ✔ *Doonesbury,* at `doonesbury.com`
- ✔ *Foxtrot,* at `foxtrot.com`

GoComics (at `www.gocomicscom` has lots of other comic strips, including vintage *Peanuts* strips.

We also like web-only comics, such as `xkcd.com` (three comics a week, occasionally PG-13). You can find thousands more; the best way to find good ones is to follow links from comics you like and check out the comics they like.

Share Your Screen with a Friend

If you're doing something interesting on your computer, or if you need a friend's help to make your computer cooperate, you can allow your friend to see your screen. Go to Join.me (at join.me — no *www*), click Share, and download and install a tiny program. When the Join.me program is running, you see the little control panel shown in Figure 20-3. It displays a nine-digit number that identifies you.

Figure 20-3:
Let your
friends see
what you're
doing.

When you want to enable someone to see your screen, tell the person to go to join.me in a web browser and type your nine-digit number in the Join box. Poof! That person can see your screen. When you're done, close the Join.me control panel by clicking its X icon.

Chapter 21

Ten Worthwhile Things to Do Online

*T*he Internet lets you make the world a better place, by working directly on projects or making it possible for other people to do so. Whenever you find other ways to improve the world, send an e-mail to us at `internet13@ gurus.org`.

Feed the Hungry

On the web, you can donate money to fight world hunger while improving your vocabulary — what more could you ask of one website? Free Rice (`www. freerice.com`) asks you to match words with their meanings. For every correct answer you give, the site donates ten grains of rice to an international food relief organization. You start with easy words at Level 1 and work your way up; the challenge can become addictive. If you know a teenager who is studying for a standardized college entrance test, this site is a helpful way for them to learn some new, fancy words.

Support a Charity While You Shop

If you buy on the eBay online auction site (described in Chapter 14), look for charities selling things or people selling things and donating part or all of their proceeds to charity. A little blue-and-yellow ribbon icon indicates charitable listings. If you want to see only charitable listings, visit eBay Giving Works, at `givingworks.ebay.com`, where you can search, buy, or sell on behalf of charities.

Find Charities That Don't Waste Money

When you choose to give money to a charitable organization, you likely want the money to go to the organization's mission, not to its management, marketing, or overhead. Charity Navigator at `www.charitynavigator.org` helps you evaluate how efficiently your favorite charities spend their (or your) money.

Become a Microfinancier or a Philanthropist

Microfinance pioneer Muhammad Yunus won a Nobel Peace Prize for starting the Grameen Bank, which makes tiny loans to people in Bangladesh and other developing countries to start small rural businesses. Kiva (`www.kiva.org`) lets you become your own microfinance lender to groups of people in Latin America, Africa, and Asia for projects such as starting a sewing business, delivery service, or fish market. Loans start at $25.

Heifer International (`www.heifer.org`) provides livestock and other resources to poor farmers for both food security and income. A *heifer* (that's a young cow, for you city folk) costs $500, and a share of a goat or pig starts at $10.

Educate Yourself

Thomas Jefferson said, "If a nation expects to be ignorant and free, in a state of civilization, it expects what never was and never will be." Keeping up with national, international, political, and economic news is your responsibility as a citizen. Try searching the web for newspapers; almost all have websites.

Some prominent newspapers charge if you want to read more than a few articles a month, such as the *New York Times* (www.nytimes.com), but most online newspapers are free. At election time, go to Project Vote Smart (www.votesmart.org) to find unbiased information about issues and candidates.

If you need background information, you can take a course at the Ivy League level on almost any subject at MIT OpenCourseWare (ocw.mit.edu). Videos of lectures, lecture notes, and exams are all posted online. You receive no credit, but you can get educated for free!

Edit an Encyclopedia

Wikis were designed to enable groups of people to work together to make and maintain websites. A wiki (named for the interterminal bus at Honolulu International Airport, which is in turn named for the Hawaiian word *wiki-wiki,* which literally means "in a hurry" — no, really) can have an unlimited number of authors, all of whom can add and change pages within the wiki website. Unlike a blog, it doesn't have to be a sequence of journal entries. Instead, you can organize your text any way you like, including making as many new, interlinked pages as you like.

If this process sounds potentially chaotic when you have more than one author, it is, but most wikis have ground rules that keep the group moving in more or less the same direction. A wiki can work well if it has a single author or if it has a group of people who trust each other to edit each other's writing. For example, a group of co-workers can make a wiki that contains information about a project they're working on. A church or club can make a wiki with committee meeting minutes, mission statements, plans, and schedules.

The biggest wiki of them all is *Wikipedia,* at en.wikipedia.org, a collaborative encyclopedia that is, with more than 3 million entries (in English, plus millions in other languages), well on its way to including all human knowledge.

Not only is Wikipedia a free encyclopedia, but it also lets you edit its articles. If you feel knowledgeable about a topic, look it up in Wikipedia. Most pages have an Edit link so that you can add what you know. If you find mistakes or have more to say, just set up a free account and then click the Edit tab. If no article exists, Wikipedia offers to let you create one. Read en.wikipedia.org/wiki/Help:Contents/Editing_Wikipedia for more information on how to edit existing articles and write new ones, following the rules of Neutral Point of View. A page might have a sidebar with complaints about the article from the Wikipedia editors, begging you to help improve it.

Digitize Old Books

Many websites require that you decode some blurry text known as a *CAPTCHA* (which allegedly stands for Completely Automated Public Turing test to tell Computers and Humans Apart) before it will let you set up an account or post a message. The reCAPTCHA project at Carnegie-Mellon University uses CAPTCHAs to help digitize old books and newspapers. The scanning process first makes a photographic image of a page and then tries to identify the words in the text. It can recognize most words, but some are just too blurry or obscure for automatic identification. That's where you come in. Every reCAPTCHA challenge shows you two words: one that's already been decoded and one that hasn't, as shown in Figure 21-1. When you type the two words, reCAPTCHA checks the one it knows, and if you get that one right, it assumes that you probably got the other one right, too. Just to make sure, the unknown words are shown to several different people, and if they all agree, the word is considered decoded. ReCAPTCHA is used by thousands of websites all over the world, showing about 30 million CAPTCHAs per day. Not all of them are solved, of course, but that's still a lot of decoded words.

Figure 21-1:
Are you a person or a program?

You're helping the reCAPTCHA project every time you solve a two-word reCAPTCHA challenge. For more information, see its website at www. google.com/recaptcha.

Search for Extraterrestrial Life or Cure Cancer

The SETI@home (http://setiathome.berkeley.edu) scientific experiment uses Internet-connected home and office computers to search for *extra-terrestrial intelligence* (SETI). The idea is to have thousands of otherwise idle PCs and Macs perform the massive calculations needed to extract the radio signals of other civilizations from intergalactic noise. You can participate by running a free program that downloads and analyzes data collected at the Arecibo radio telescope in Puerto Rico.

If eavesdropping on space aliens seems a bit far out, you may enjoy lending your computer's idle time to solving problems in cryptography and mathematics. Distributed.net (`www.distributed.net`) manages several projects. (Feel free to join the Internet Gurus team there.) When you sign up to help a project, you can set up its program on your computer to run when the computer isn't otherwise occupied, and your donation of computer time helps achieve the goal of the project.

If math and cryptography don't ring your chimes, consider joining the Folding at Home project at `folding.stanford.edu`. This project studies how proteins acquire their three-dimensional shapes, an important question in medical research. By signing up to run its program, you're helping with basic research that may help find a cure for "Alzheimer's, Mad Cow (BSE), CJD, ALS, Huntington's, Parkinson's disease, and many cancers and cancer-related syndromes."

Mentor a Teenager or Young Adult Online

An adult mentor can make all the difference to a young person struggling with life. Several online mentoring websites match adults with youth. `Icouldbe.org` serves 2,300 underprivileged junior high, high school, and college students every year. Sign up to share your career expertise — or your life experience — with the next generation. iMentor (`www.imentor.org`) concentrates on the New York City area.

Adopt a Kid

Do you surf the Web for hours each day? Maybe your life needs more meaning. Adopting a child is more of a commitment than upgrading to the latest Microsoft operating system, but at least kids grow up eventually and you don't have to reinstall them to get rid of viruses. These two excellent websites list special children in need of homes: `www.rainbowkids.com` and `www.capbook.org`. It can't hurt to look.

Index

Notes

Notes

Notes

Notes

Apple & Macs

iPad For Dummies
978-0-470-58027-1

iPhone For Dummies,
4th Edition
978-0-470-87870-5

MacBook For Dummies, 3rd
Edition
978-0-470-76918-8

Mac OS X Snow Leopard For
Dummies
978-0-470-43543-4

Business

Bookkeeping For Dummies
978-0-7645-9848-7

Job Interviews
For Dummies,
3rd Edition
978-0-470-17748-8

Resumes For Dummies,
5th Edition
978-0-470-08037-5

Starting an
Online Business
For Dummies,
6th Edition
978-0-470-60210-2

Stock Investing
For Dummies,
3rd Edition
978-0-470-40114-9

Successful
Time Management
For Dummies
978-0-470-29034-7

Computer Hardware

BlackBerry
For Dummies,
4th Edition
978-0-470-60700-8

Computers For Seniors
For Dummies,
2nd Edition
978-0-470-53483-0

PCs For Dummies,
Windows
7 Edition
978-0-470-46542-4

Laptops For Dummies,
4th Edition
978-0-470-57829-2

Cooking & Entertaining

Cooking Basics
For Dummies,
3rd Edition
978-0-7645-7206-7

Wine For Dummies,
4th Edition
978-0-470-04579-4

Diet & Nutrition

Dieting For Dummies,
2nd Edition
978-0-7645-4149-0

Nutrition For Dummies,
4th Edition
978-0-471-79868-2

Weight Training
For Dummies,
3rd Edition
978-0-471-76845-6

Digital Photography

Digital SLR Cameras &
Photography For Dummies,
3rd Edition
978-0-470-46606-3

Photoshop Elements 8
For Dummies
978-0-470-52967-6

Gardening

Gardening Basics
For Dummies
978-0-470-03749-2

Organic Gardening
For Dummies,
2nd Edition
978-0-470-43067-5

Green/Sustainable

Raising Chickens
For Dummies
978-0-470-46544-8

Green Cleaning
For Dummies
978-0-470-39106-8

Health

Diabetes For Dummies,
3rd Edition
978-0-470-27086-8

Food Allergies
For Dummies
978-0-470-09584-3

Living Gluten-Free
For Dummies,
2nd Edition
978-0-470-58589-4

Hobbies/General

Chess For Dummies,
2nd Edition
978-0-7645-8404-6

Drawing
Cartoons & Comics
For Dummies
978-0-470-42683-8

Knitting For Dummies,
2nd Edition
978-0-470-28747-7

Organizing
For Dummies
978-0-7645-5300-4

Su Doku For Dummies
978-0-470-01892-7

Home Improvement

Home Maintenance
For Dummies,
2nd Edition
978-0-470-43063-7

Home Theater
For Dummies,
3rd Edition
978-0-470-41189-6

Living the
Country Lifestyle
All-in-One
For Dummies
978-0-470-43061-3

Solar Power Your Home
For Dummies,
2nd Edition
978-0-470-59678-4

Internet

Blogging For Dummies,
3rd Edition
978-0-470-61996-4

eBay For Dummies,
6th Edition
978-0-470-49741-8

Facebook For Dummies,
3rd Edition
978-0-470-87804-0

Web Marketing
For Dummies,
2nd Edition
978-0-470-37181-7

WordPress
For Dummies,
3rd Edition
978-0-470-59274-8

Language & Foreign Language

French For Dummies
978-0-7645-5193-2

Italian Phrases
For Dummies
978-0-7645-7203-6

Spanish For Dummies,
2nd Edition
978-0-470-87855-2

Spanish
For Dummies,
Audio Set
978-0-470-09585-0

Math & Science

Algebra I
For Dummies,
2nd Edition
978-0-470-55964-2

Biology For Dummies,
2nd Edition
978-0-470-59875-7

Calculus For Dummies
978-0-7645-2498-1

Chemistry For Dummies
978-0-7645-5430-8

Microsoft Office

Excel 2010 For Dummies
978-0-470-48953-6

Office 2010 All-in-One
For Dummies
978-0-470-49748-7

Office 2010 For Dummies,
Book + DVD Bundle
978-0-470-62698-6

Word 2010 For Dummies
978-0-470-48772-3

Music

Guitar For Dummies,
2nd Edition
978-0-7645-9904-0

iPod & iTunes For
Dummies, 8th Edition
978-0-470-87871-2

Piano Exercises
For Dummies
978-0-470-38765-8

Parenting & Education

Parenting For Dummies,
2nd Edition
978-0-7645-5418-6

Type 1 Diabetes
For Dummies
978-0-470-17811-9

Pets

Cats For Dummies,
2nd Edition
978-0-7645-5275-5

Dog Training For Dummies,
3rd Edition
978-0-470-60029-0

Puppies For Dummies,
2nd Edition
978-0-470-03717-1

Religion & Inspiration

The Bible For Dummies
978-0-7645-5296-0

Catholicism For Dummies
978-0-7645-5391-2

Women in the Bible
For Dummies
978-0-7645-8475-6

Self-Help & Relationship

Anger Management
For Dummies
978-0-470-03715-7

Overcoming Anxiety
For Dummies,
2nd Edition
978-0-470-57441-6

Sports

Baseball
For Dummies,
3rd Edition
978-0-7645-7537-2

Basketball
For Dummies,
2nd Edition
978-0-7645-5248-9

Golf For Dummies,
3rd Edition
978-0-471-76871-5

Web Development

Web Design
All-in-One
For Dummies
978-0-470-41796-6

Web Sites
Do-It-Yourself
For Dummies,
2nd Edition
978-0-470-56520-9

Windows 7

Windows 7
For Dummies
978-0-470-49743-2

Windows 7
For Dummies,
Book + DVD Bundle
978-0-470-52398-8

Windows 7 All-in-One
For Dummies
978-0-470-48763-1